All great truths begin as blasphemy.

The time to challenge your most sacred beliefs is at hand.

If you don't challenge your beliefs soon, your beliefs are going to challenge you.

TOMORROW'S GOD

This book is meant to be challenging.
This book is meant to save the world.

The *New York Times* bestselling author of the *Conversations with God* series offers one of the most extraordinary spiritual statements for our time.

NEALE DONALD WALSCH

"Walsch writes candidly . . . about great questions of purpose, peace and happiness that haunt humanity."

—*Publishers Weekly*

BOOKS BY NEALE DONALD WALSCH

The New Revelations

Conversations with God, Book 1

Conversations with God, Book 2

Conversations with God, Book 3

Friendship with God

Communion with God

Conversations with God for Teens

Questions and Answers on Conversations with God

The Little Soul and the Sun: A Children's Parable Adapted from Conversations with God (with Frank Riccio, illustrator)

Meditations from Conversations with God

Conversations with God: Guidebook

Moments of Grace

Bringers of the Light

Recreating Yourself

Neale Donald Walsch on Abundance and Right Livelihood

Neale Donald Walsch on Holistic Living

Neale Donald Walsch on Relationships

The Wedding Vows from Conversations with God

Honest to God: A Change of Heart That Can Change the World

Meditations from Conversations with God, Book 2: A Personal Journal

Conversations with God: Re-Minder Cards

Tomorrow's God

Our Greatest Spiritual Challenge

Neale Donald Walsch

ATRIA BOOKS
New York London Toronto Sydney

ATRIA BOOKS
1230 Avenue of the Americas
New York, NY 10020

ISBN: 0-7434-5695-5
0-7434-6304-8 (Pbk)

First Atria Books trade paperback edition January 2005

10 9 8 7 6 5 4 3 2 1

ATRIA BOOKS is a trademark of Simon & Schuster, Inc.

Manufactured in the United States of America

For information regarding special discounts for bulk purchases, please contact Simon & Schuster Special Sales at 1-800-456-6798 or business@simonandschuster.com.

AUTHOR'S NOTE

While the conversation transcribed here took place as one continuous progression, this book is offered in two parts.

Part One deals with humanity's current conception of God and the new ideas about Deity that will characterize God in our not-too-distant future.

Part Two examines how these new ideas will be put into place, how they will impact our lives, and how they will help us create a newer world.

If they do not help us in this way, they will, of course, mean nothing.

NDW

INTRODUCTION

This book contains the most exciting news of the past 100 years: Humanity is about to create a new form of spirituality on the earth.

Our civilization stands at the brink of its greatest adventure and its most extraordinary achievement. I want you to commit now to finding your place in that creation.

This book is a look at Tomorrow's God. It is about humanity's future—but not some far-off distant vision. Rather, it includes a startling prediction for the next thirty years. It is about our *near* future, and the role that humans will play in creating it. It is about the role that *you* can play in creating it. It is about what will happen and how it will happen.

Like the other *With God* books, this text takes the form of a conversation with God, but it is not necessary to believe that I actually had such a conversation in order to benefit from it. All that is necessary is that you have an open mind—and this book even tells you how to achieve that.

But now, fair warning. You will find information in this book that is not new to you. Very little here cannot be found, cumulatively, in the sacred writings of all the world's wisdom traditions. Very little has not already been spoken by all of humanity's master teachers. Very little, for that matter, has not appeared in my own previous writing.

What, then, would be the reason to read this book? I suggest that it is not that it contains wisdom that we have not been given, *but that it repeats wisdom to which we have not been listening.*

And the problem is, if we do not listen to this wisdom now, we may not have many more chances to have it repeated.

We are at the edge, you see. We have gone as far as we can go in the direction we have been taking. We need now to change course if we wish to preserve life as we know it on this planet.

Humanity cannot afford any more temper tantrums. We have found a way to pack the end of the world into a briefcase. We can seal the death of civilized society in a spore-filled envelope and simply mail it off. Talk about our fate being sealed . . .

We have trained ourselves to be able to fly airplanes into buildings, killing thousands of people, without flinching. We have talked ourselves into believing that preemptive strike—shooting first and asking questions later—is a perfectly acceptable means of conducting foreign policy.

We have decided that to have dominion over the earth means to destroy it—and to pretend that we don't know we are doing it. We have concluded that altering the basic genetic structure of our food is the way to improve it. We have chosen to allow 20 percent of the world's people to receive 80 percent of the world's income, and to call this the good life.

We are, in short, confused. Yet there is a way out of this confusion, *and you can play a role in taking us there.* This book talks about your role. It says that the next thirty years will see a paradigm shift within humanity so positive, so upheaving, so reshaping, so utterly inside-outing, that it will alter the course of human history. And it invites you—yes, you, the person now holding this book—to join in this reinventing of humanity.

That is why this book has been written. It is an invitation directly from God to you.

Think about this.

Now think about how this book came into your hands. How did you come to hear about it? Or, if you never knew about it until just this minute, how did it attract your attention? What made you pick this up and start reading it? For that matter, what makes you *keep* reading it?

Do you think this is all happening by chance?

It is not. There is no such thing as "chance." The universe does nothing by accident. This book has come to you to tell you that you can change the course of human history.

You.

Not only the people who run governments or own corporations or lead movements or write books or are influential for some other reason. Not only those people.

You.

You can change the course of human history.

This is not an exaggeration. Please believe me. This is not an exaggeration.

This book calls you to that singular undertaking. It invites you now to internalize the wisdom of both ancient and contemporary masters found here; not merely to hear it again, but now to *receive* it, to *take it in,* to absorb it at the deepest level of your being, until it becomes the essence of who you are at the cellular level.

Life will be inviting you in the years immediately ahead to act and respond from this level of Deep Knowing. What you place there now in terms of the things you profoundly believe, and how far you spread the messages found here through the living of your life in a new way, will make all the difference *in* the world *to* the world.

Yet do not feel that you have to do all this by yourself. Perhaps the most uplifting and exciting part of the message that is brought to us in this book is that now, none of us have to "go it alone." We have teammates, and we can join them and call them to us, to rally around humanity's greatest cause: changing ourselves and changing our world.

I said earlier that you might not find much that is new in this book. I was wrong.

You might find . . . a New You.

And a way to create a New World.

PART ONE

REDESIGNING GOD

I

THE GREATEST BLASPHEMY

We need a new God.

I know.

No. I'm serious. *We need a new God.* The old God isn't working anymore.

The old one never worked.

Some people think it did.

They were not looking at the world around them.

They weren't?

Not honestly. Not comprehensively. They were seeing only what they wanted to see.

They were not seeing the cruelty and the fighting and the killing that was going on in God's name. They were not seeing the separation and the oppression and

the fear and the utter dysfunction. Or, worse yet, they *were* seeing it and they *played into it.* They *used it* as a means of controlling the people.

In truth the old God, Yesterday's God, might have made individual lives work here and there—perhaps even many of them—but that God was never able to create a just society or a joyful, harmonious civilization, to say nothing of a peaceful world. *And that God can't do that even today.*

Even today, with all your powers of instant communication and total connection and advanced comprehension and increased awareness and sophisticated technology and marvelous miracles, you can't produce the simple, humble experience for which humanity has yearned from the beginning of time.

You can't produce peace.

I know.

You can't produce lasting joy.

I know.

And the God in whom you believe can't, either.

Why? *Why?* Why can't all the best efforts of humanity and all the help we've begged for, and *received,* from God, produce this result?

Because the God in whom you believe *isn't real.* The God in whom you believe is *made up.* It is a God you *created* out of *thin air,* having *nothing to do with Ultimate Reality.*

Well, there's a challenging thought. That's just about the greatest blasphemy.

All great truth begins as blasphemy.

The time to challenge your most sacred beliefs is at hand. If you don't challenge your beliefs soon, your beliefs are going to challenge you.

This book is meant to be challenging.

This book is meant to save the world.

Will it?

That's up to the world.

Why? Why isn't it up to you? If you're God, why isn't it up to you?

Because my function is not to save the world. My function is to create it.

And after you create it, you don't care what happens?

I care what happens as much as you do.

No, you don't. If you care what happens as much as we do, you won't let the world destroy itself.

You mean if I care what happens *more* than you do. If I care what happens as *much* as you do, I *will* let the world destroy itself, because that's exactly what *you* are doing.

Since I care only as much as you do, the world in which you live may very well be destroyed. At the very least, life as you now know it could be irrevocably altered. And if that's what happens, I will let it happen.

Why? *Why won't you do something to stop it?*

Because you won't.

We *can't.* You *can.* You're *God.* You can do what humans *cannot.*

Your statement is inaccurate. I can, *and YOU can.* But I will not, unless you do.

Why not? *What kind of a God are you?*

The best kind there is. The *only* kind there is. The kind who gives you free will, and who will never, ever interfere with that.

Not even to save us from ourselves?

If I saved you from yourselves, then you wouldn't BE "yourselves," but only a slave to me. You would not have free will. Your will would be free only until you did something that I did not want you to do. Then, I would stop the exercise of your free will and make you do what I want you to do.

Of course you would. If you were half the God that humans think you are, you would stop us from destroying ourselves. You would do what is *best* for us. You would make *us* do what is best for us.

By whose assessment, and by whose definition?

What?

"Best" by whose assessment, and "us" by whose definition?

By *yours.* By *your* assessment. By *your* definition. You would define what is meant by the term "us," you would decide what is "best" for us, and then you would make what is "best" happen for all of "us." We *depend* on you to do this. That's what God is *for.*

Really? Is that what you think?

2

GOOD-BYE TO YESTERDAY'S GOD

Most of humanity believes that God decides which humans are included in the word "us." We then form groups or clusters around what you have decided, and we call them religions or faiths. You, God, then assure "us" that you will be bringing "us" back to you, by telling "us" what is "best" for "us."

Those humans who are not included in your definition of "us" will not return to you under any circumstances, nor will those who *are* included if they do not do what is "best" for them. People in these two categories will be condemned. They will suffer in the eternal fires of Hell.

Is that what you believe? Truly? Is that how it is for you?

No. Not really. No, it is not. At least, not anymore. Not after experiencing and understanding all of my conversations with

God. But it is still the belief of most of humanity, and I come to this dialogue now to speak for most of humanity.

You do? Why? Why are you doing that?

I want to ask the questions that I think most of humanity asks, to say the things that I hear most of humanity saying.

Why?

So that humanity's question may be answered. So that humanity's voice may be heard. So that humanity's experience may be enlarged, enhanced, expanded, even as mine has been. So that joy may abound and peace may prevail upon the earth, even as joy abounds and peace prevails in my soul when I am in my highest place.

You want to give to humanity the gift that you have been given.

Yes.

Why?

Because I want to continue to *receive* the gift that I have been given, and the best way I know how to do that is to give it away.

Giving your gift away causes you to continue having it?

Yes. The gift that I give is the gift that I experience.

How so?

Because only through the *expression* of Who I Am can I have the *experience* of Who I Am. Withholding my expression withholds my experience. Because "that which flows *through* me sticks *to* me." Because there is really only One of us, and I am a part of that One, and so, what I cause another to experience, I experience, and what I cause myself to experience, another experiences.

Because what I cause another to know, I know, and what I cause myself to know, another knows. Because what I cause another to receive, I receive, and what I cause myself to receive, another receives.

Similarly, what I withhold from another is withheld from me, and what I withhold from myself is withheld from another, for I cannot give what I do not have, and I cannot have what I do not give. Only through the giving of something can I experience the having of it. Without the giving, the having is not experienceable.

Giving transforms Having into Being.

I can imagine myself as "having" creativity, but only through the giving of my creativity to others can I experience *being* creative.

I can imagine myself as "having" abundance, but only through the giving of my abundance to others can I experience *being* abundant.

I can imagine myself as "having" love, but only through the giving of my love to others can I experience myself as *being* love.

Giving transforms Having into Being, and the miracle of giving is that we are giving only to ourselves. This is always the case, and this is the great secret of Life. It is the unfolded mystery of every spiritual tradition.

This is the Universal Law, and it cannot be avoided, nor can it be bypassed, sidestepped, or ignored. It will play its effect in our lives sooner or later. Thus it has been taught: "As you sow, so shall you reap." And, "Do unto others as you would have it done unto you." And, "What goes around, comes around."

What I know is that the fastest way to experience myself as having answers to my questions is to cause others to experience themselves as having answers to theirs.

So now I speak for most of humanity, asking the questions of most of humanity, and making the statements of most of humanity, so that more of humanity may have and know God's responses to these questions and statements, even as I do, *so that I may continue to know that I know.*

> You have learned well. You have understood, and you have caused others to understand, and now you seek to cause even more to understand, so that *you may understand more.*
>
> And so a circle completes itself in you, and a prophecy is fulfilled through you. For I have said to all of humanity, unto you will I send my messengers, and among you will they walk. Not only one, but many, not only in ancient times, but through all the ages, bringing you the knowing of the truth of your being, even as that truth emerges in and through them, AS them.
>
> And they will say to you, *listen.* Listen to this invitation:
>
> There is another way. There is another way to experience God. There is another way to live life. Your differences do not have to create divisions. Your contrasts

do not have to produce conflicts. The variations in your beliefs do not have to bring violence to your lives. THERE IS ANOTHER WAY.

Yet you will not find that way by searching for it. You will only find it by creating it. And you will not create it by remaining stuck in old beliefs, but only by opening yourself to new ideas. New ideas about God and about Life that can truly light the world.

I want to help to bring those new ideas to humanity, even as they were given to me.

So continue, now, this dialogue, if that is what serves you, even as you serve humanity through this experience. For in this dialogue I will speak to you of Tomorrow's God, who will be different from the God of your yesterdays in many important ways.

I will also speak to you of a New Spirituality. A kind of spirituality that will allow humans to express their natural impulse to seek and to experience the Divine without making each other wrong for the way in which they are doing it, and without killing each other in the name of it.

I will describe how this New Spirituality will play its effect when overlaid upon the experiences and constructions of your human society, specifically in the areas of religion, politics, economics, business and commerce, education, relationships, and sexuality.

There is much to explore in our conversation, so yes, let us continue.

Yet as I do continue this dialogue, I want to repeat that I can no longer speak only for myself in every instance, with every comment, as the asker of every question. The truth is that I already have my answers to many of the questions I will be asking.

Yet many humans do not. Or they *do* have answers, but those answers do not work. They do not function to bring humanity the experience it says it seeks, or take humanity where it says it wants to go.

Still, these humans are trying to *make* the answers work. They are trying to be faithful to the answers they have been given, and they are miserable in the trying, they are tired and saddened in the effort, they are confused and angered by the process. And so you have a miserable and tired and saddened world. A world that is confused and angry.

This is evidenced all around you. Now, you have a choice. You can see this, announce it, and declare it, or you can deny it.

I choose to see it, announce it, and declare it. I think it is time to say what is "so." I think it is time to talk about it. In very real terms. Very openly and directly. To look at the issues and to look at the problems and to look, most important, at the solutions.

Good. Then we will proceed with the awareness that you are allowing yourself to ask rhetorical questions and to make rhetorical statements for the purpose of presenting the perceptions of many people, not just your own.

Thank you. And so, to get back to where we were . . .

. . . It is the perception of many people on this earth that your job—God's job—is to tell human beings what is best for them. You tell us what is best for us, and then it is up to us to do it, or else. This is a simplified restating of one of humanity's sacred beliefs.

That belief is a fallacy. That is not God's job and that is not God's purpose and that is not God's function.

It is the job and purpose of the God that many of you have created in your imaginations, but not of the God Who Really Is. It is the function of Yesterday's God, but not of Tomorrow's God.

That's the second time you've used that phrase. What do you mean by "Tomorrow's God"?

The God in whom you will believe on some future tomorrow. The God in whom you will have faith in your future.

So we *are* going to get a new God!

Not a "new God," but a new *understanding* of the present God. An expanded concept, a deeper awareness.

But you agreed with me when we started this conversation that we needed a new God.

I was going with the words you were using, not wanting to get into semantics in our first brief

exchange. I knew all along what I meant, and I knew all along that I would have a chance to explain it to you further.

So, what did you mean?

As I've just said, I meant not a "new" God, strictly speaking, but a new *version* of God. A *larger* version of God. This is the Same God Who Always Was, Is Now, and Always Will Be—it is simply not the God of your present understanding.

Your understanding has been incomplete. I am inviting you now to expand your awareness and come to a more complete understanding of who and what God is, and of what is true about Life. I am inviting you to create Tomorrow's God.

What if I don't want to let go of Yesterday's God? What if I'm really attached to those ideas and, by the way, happen to think they are the Right and True ideas about God?

Then you will continue to create your life as you now know it on your planet.

So? What's so bad about that?

Look around you. You like what you see? Then go ahead, continue to believe what you believe. But don't think things aren't going to change. It's not a question of "if," but "how." Everything is going to change. And, sooner or later, so will humanity's beliefs about God.

That is when you will say good-bye to Yesterday's God.

When is this going to happen?

Actually, it's beginning to happen right now.

Really? Well, so much for that being what saves the world, because it's not changing anything.

Yes, it is. You're just not seeing the change. You're not aware of it. But as the changes increase, as they spread, you'll become more and more aware of them. Indeed, you'll become part of them.

When will this process be complete?

Never. The process of seeing and experiencing more and more of God is never-ending. That's the joy of it.

Well, when will it be complete *enough* for things to start getting better around here?

Soon. Very soon. If humanity is willing.

What does that mean?

It means that if humanity makes this choice, a movement, a radical shift, in humanity's understandings about God could occur rapidly. Easily within your lifetime. Within three decades. Perhaps even faster than that, once the first domino falls.

It is simply a question of reaching critical mass.

What will that take?

Not nearly what you might think. Some people assume that critical mass is one more than half, but it is not. Nor is it 25 percent of the whole, nor even 10 percent of the whole, nor even 5 percent of the whole. Critical mass is reached when 2 to 4 percent of the whole is affected.

Watch the surface of water as it's brought to a boil. The boiling point is not reached at the point when over half of the surface is bubbling, but long before. The effect of critical mass is exponential. That's what makes it so powerful. A few bubbles break the surface of the water . . . then, in a sudden rush, all of the water is boiling.

So a relatively small number of us must make the choice to create that shift in our understandings about God. What could make humanity willing to make that choice?

One of two things. More hatred or more hope. Another world-shaking disaster born of rage and wrapped in violence and killing, or a global awakening produced in another way.

In what other way? Other than disaster and calamity, there doesn't seem to be a way for human beings to wake up.

Oh, but there is. There could be a worldwide movement to spread, not terror, but peace, joy, and love. There could be a massive grassroots undertaking, with people all across the globe mobilized at the community level to *change the way things are*. Just as there are now terrorist cells, there could be spiritual activist teams all over the earth.

This would require leadership, of course. And it would require great commitment on the part of those who follow these leaders. But it is possible. It can be done.

And the first step lies at the level of thought. Humanity's future depends on what humanity thinks about itself. It depends on what humanity thinks about God, and about Life.

From your thought springs your reality. From your ideas your future emerges. Thus, your beliefs create your behaviors, and your behaviors create your experience.

What you believe, therefore, becomes a most important thing.

What creates beliefs? Can anything in the exterior world of physicality create beliefs?

Yes.

What?

People.

People can.

People in your exterior world can create interior spiritual events. First in themselves and then in others.

Many have done this. This is what you are doing now. That is what all of humanity can do.

But *how?* How can we do this? That is the golden question!

There are many ways in which one may begin.

Name one.

You are holding it in your hand.

3

INTRODUCING TOMORROW'S GOD

So we're right back where we started.

Yes. When I said, "This book is meant to save the world," I meant it.

What is it going to tell me that other books haven't?

Nothing.

Nothing?

Nothing.

And this is going to save the world?

It could. It was meant to, and it could.

So, if all that I'm going to read here has been in other books, why bother reading this book? The world is on the brink of disaster, and all the stuff in the other books hasn't helped.

Correct on the first count, incorrect on the second. "All the stuff in the other books" has helped humanity stave off disaster in the past. The world's esoteric wisdom has helped it correct its course before, and it can do so again. But that wisdom must now be expanded to take into account humanity's expanded possibilities for self-destruction.

Education is the key. It is the most powerful tool you have. Educate *everyone*. Tell *everyone* about God and about Life. Eliminate illiteracy, then eliminate functional illiteracy, then eliminate spiritual illiteracy.

What is required is nothing less than a new worldwide communications network—and a new worldwide message from humanity to humanity itself.

The more you know about how to destroy yourself, the more you need to know about how to save yourself. It is time now to expand your base of knowledge of God and of Life, to grow in your understandings, to increase your awareness, and to enlarge your consciousness.

It is time to move from the Old Spirituality to the New Spirituality, to let go of Yesterday's God and to embrace Tomorrow's God.

That is not going to be easy. People don't like letting go of the old for the new.

So let's make it clear one last time that what we are talking about here is not a new God, but a new *experience* of the "old" God.

Sometimes it takes a new saying of an old truth, a new sharing of old wisdom, for that truth to be heard and for that wisdom to be understood.

All the truths and all the wisdom that I will share with you here have been shared before.

Every so often in human history your ancient understandings have been restated for modern times. Thoughts previously expressed have been expressed again, in a new and expanded way. Abraham did this. Moses did this. The Buddha did this. Jesus did this. Muhammad did this. Bahá'u'lláh did this. Jalal al-Din Rumi did this. Joseph Smith did this. Many masters and many teachers, known and unknown, have done this. Many are doing it today.

Okay, but what if I say that my old ideas do not include *any belief in God at all?* What if all this talk about "God" just turns me off, makes me frustrated, or takes me to no place in my mind in which it has any meaning or reality at all?

Tomorrow's God will not require you to believe in God.

He won't?

No, she won't. And that's the First Important Difference between Yesterday's God and Tomorrow's God:

1. Tomorrow's God does not require anyone to believe in God.

Wait a minute. Tomorrow's God will be female?

Yes. Except when she's not. Then, he'll be male. Unless he's not. In which case God will be neither male nor female, but rather, without gender.

Without gender?

Without gender, size, shape, color, or any of the characteristics of an individual living being. And that's the Second Important Difference between Yesterday's God and Tomorrow's God:

2. Tomorrow's God is without gender, size, shape, color, or any of the characteristics of an individual living being.

You mean that Tomorrow's God is not a living being?

No. Not in the sense that you mean those words.

How can that be? If God is not a living being, then what is God?

Well, now, that's what this conversation is going to be all about. But, let me tell you a story.

A woman steps onto a balcony late one night to gaze at a diamond-filled sky, tears in her eyes, seeking answers to her questions, healing for her breaking heart, as she searches the heavens. She feels alone, desperate. "God," she says, "if you're here, show yourself to me. I can't go on like this anymore, all alone." Abruptly, a shooting star streaks across the velvet sky. The woman's heart stops. She can't believe her eyes.

Now, I have a question for you.

Was that God?

Yes, I believe it was God who made that happen.

No, I did not ask you if it was God who made that happen. I asked you if *that was God, happening.*

Well, I don't know how to answer that. It could have been a coincidence.

And what caused the coincidence?

Well, I would say that God caused it, but then we're back to a definition of God that states that God is the Cause of things, not the things that are caused.

Do you suppose that God could be both the Cause and That Which Is Caused? Do you think that God could be both the Creator and the Created?

I never thought about it that way. I know that others have, of course. The great thinkers of human history have explored this topic repeatedly. An entire system of thought—*pantheism*—has developed around these explorations. Pantheism holds that the Universe is one with God—that the Creator and the Created are the same.

More recently, physicist John Wheeler has proposed a conception of the universe that he has called "observer-participancy," or a closed-loop participatory universe in which—as quantum physics would have it—nothing that is observed is unaffected by the observer. In other words, the Creator and the Created are One, *each creating the other.* Or, you have often put it, we are "God,

Godding!" But no, on first glance, I would say that God is the Creator and we, and the world, are the Created. And if I didn't believe in God at all, I would say that what caused the shooting star to fall just then was random chance.

And random chance randomly selected that random moment for that random occurrence?

Yes. If I did not believe in God, I would say that, yes, the occurrence was caused by *randomness.* What do I know? What are you asking me? I am telling you that it could have been nothing more than *what happened.* The fact that it happened *just then* would have no meaning at all, except the meaning someone gives it.

Now you have hit upon something. *Nothing* has any meaning at all, save the meaning you give it.

Now, in the story above, what meaning do *you* give to the star shooting across the night sky at the exact moment the woman is asking God to give her a sign of God's existence?

I don't know what meaning to give it, really. I don't know what to make of it. I was not there, having the experience, so I don't know what to say about that.

What do you think the woman might say about it?

She might say that the shooting star was caused by God, or that the shooting star *was* God, answering her prayer right then and there. She might be moved to believe either of those things, given the synchronicity of the event.

Indeed. And if she believed the shooting star *was* God, do you think she would experience God as male or female?

Uh . . . I see what you mean.

And I tell you that Tomorrow's God will change form as each moment and each individual seeking to experience God dictates.

Hold it. You mean *we* get to decide who and what God is?

Why are you so surprised? You've been doing that since time began. You call this Religion.

Religions don't decide who and what God is, religions simply tell us what *God* said about that.

And who says what God said?

Religions.

So who is saying what?

Religions are telling us what God told religions. Or, rather, what God told those upon whose teachings religions are based.

In other words, what God told human beings.

Yes, what God told human beings, but in very special revelations to very special people at very special moments in human history.

Such as the revelations being made here, to you, at this time?

Well now, that's a pretty big stretch for most people. I don't think that most people are going to believe or accept that God would choose to reveal Himself to me, personally, in the form of this on-paper dialogue, if that is what you're asking.

I am very clear that they might not accept that *Yesterday's God* would, given what you believe about him. But they might allow as to how Tomorrow's God would, because Tomorrow's God will talk with everyone, all the time.

And that's the Third Important Difference between Yesterday's God and Tomorrow's God:

3. Tomorrow's God talks with everyone, all the time.

How? How will this occur? Will everyone be having conversations with God?

Everyone IS having conversations with God, all the time. That will be an important message of the New Spirituality. God is communicating with humanity in every moment.

I did not stop talking to human beings 2,000 years ago, nor have I ever selected only a few human beings to whom to reveal myself. I am revealing myself to all human beings all the time, yet only a few human beings have embraced these revelations, have seen them for what they are, and have held them as sacred—and so it seems as though only a few have received them.

God—the force, the energy, the design, the experience that some call Divinity—shows Itself in your life in the way that is exactly and perfectly suited to the time, place, and situation at hand. You either call that experience "God" or you call it something else—coincidence, synchronicity, "random event," whatever. Yet what you call it does not change what it is—it merely indicates your *belief system about that.*

If you believe that the way Life is showing itself to you now is God, you will see it as God. If you do not believe that the way Life is showing itself to you now is God, you will not see it as God. Some say that seeing is believing, but I tell you that *believing is seeing.*

"As you believe, so will it be done unto you."

That is correct. That truth has been taught by many masters. And in the future, many more human beings will experience God's communications as exactly what they are: revelations from the Divine. People will not require God to "show up" in one way and only in that way. People's beliefs about God will expand, and this expansion will increase their awareness of the God that has always been there.

This reminds me of the story of the blindfolded man who was led to an elephant, upon whose side his hand was placed. He was asked to describe what he felt. He did his best, but when he removed his blindfold he was astonished to find how little he had grasped of the totality of the experience.

That is a very instructive little story.

So, you're saying that Tomorrow's God will be larger than we guessed, and that when we remove our "blindfolds," we will discover that God actually changes form, appearing in a multiplicity of ways depending upon the time and the place and the events of the moment.

That is how humanity will allow itself to experience God on this most blessed future tomorrow. Yesterday's God—the God in whom most of humanity has believed thus far—is thought to be a Constant. That belief will not change, but it will expand.

So, God is not a Constant?

God IS a Constant. God is that which is Constantly Present and Constantly Changing, suiting Itself to each moment, so that God may be *understood* in that moment, *embraced* in that moment, *experienced* in that moment, and *expressed* in that moment.

You are never alone. God is always with you. Yet you may often be unable to see God or to experience God if you are expecting God to show up in a certain way—as do so many of those who believe in Yesterday's God.

There is *no limit* to the ways in which God may show up. Many humans have attempted to place limits on God but have, as a result, only placed limits on themselves and on their ability to see and to experience God.

On your yesterdays you have believed in a limited

God. On a blessed future tomorrow you will begin to believe in a limitless God, who can appear in any form, under any circumstances, to any person, and, indeed, to all people in all places all the time.

In truth, *this is what is going on right now,* but you do not believe it. On that blessed future tomorrow you *will* believe it, and then you will see it.

On what "future tomorrow"? *When will this day come for me?*

On the day that you select.

I don't know what that means! *C'mon, help me out here.* I've been praying for peace, searching for truth, seeking enlightenment for decades. My species has been doing so for centuries and millennia! *When will I find it? What will cause me to do so?*

Whenever and whatever you choose.

What I choose to be the cause will be the cause?

That is correct. You may choose the cause to be some exterior calamity, or you may choose it to be a different kind of event. What you choose will be what you use.

You could even choose to use this dialogue, this book that you are holding right now in your hands, to be the cause of your awakening. Many people will.

Each of you will use something in this Life to wake yourself up. And each of you *will* wake up. You are in a sleep from which all of you will awaken.

Yes, but if we awaken too late, it will be bad for us. We'll be "left behind." We'll be deserted by God, because we didn't answer His call while we still had a chance.

That is not true. That is what someone has told you, but that is not true. That is the God in whom some people want you to believe, and those who want you to believe this have used Fear as their tool, and would have *you* use it, too. Yet, if your wish is to see the Source of All Love, shall you use Fear as your looking glass?

I tell you this: ALL of you will awaken. It is not my plan that some of you shall awaken and some of you shall not. What would be the good in that? What would be the point?

I assure you of this, my children: ALL OF YOU WILL AWAKEN.

It is part of the process of evolution that you should awaken. It is part of the process of Life Itself.

Life IS the process of awakening. It is the process of Becoming. It is the process of knowing that one has become what one always was. It is the process of rejoining the inseparable. And that is not a process of actual rejoining, but of simply knowing again that separation never occurred.

Let me repeat that, because it is extraordinarily important, and it is the theological lynchpin of the New Spirituality.

Life is the process of awakening. It is the process of

Becoming. It is the process of knowing that one has become what one always was. It is the process of rejoining the inseparable—and that is not a process of actual rejoining, but of simply knowing again that separation never occurred.

So this "knowing again" is the awakening.

Yes. Each of you will awaken, since no part of God will ever be deserted by God—*nor could it ever be.* For God cannot separate Godself from any part of God.

Desertion of God by God is impossible. Separation of God from God is impossible. Such a thing would only be possible if there were something that is not a part of God. Yet there is nothing that is not a part of God, for God is separate from nothing, but is the All In All, the Alpha and the Omega, the Beginning and the End, the Sum Total of Everything that ever was, is now, and ever shall be, world without end.

And that's the Fourth Important Difference between Yesterday's God and Tomorrow's God:

4. Tomorrow's God is separate from nothing, but is Everywhere Present, the All in All, the Alpha and the Omega, the Beginning and the End, the Sum Total of Everything that ever was, is now, and ever shall be.

This is the nature and the truth of God, and on the future tomorrow of your choosing, you will know it and acknowledge it.

We've heard that for years. How can we get a real understanding of what that means?

> You will understand what it means *when you become what it means.*
>
> What it means cannot be revealed TO you until it is revealed THROUGH you. You must decide that *you* are separate from nothing, and then begin to act that way. At first, it may not be easy. After all, you have been trained to think another way all your life. Yet the transformation can occur. Keep at it. Keep at it. And then one day, you will be "there." You will have crossed the dividing line, and nothing will divide you ever again.
>
> On that day you will embrace Tomorrow's God, and on that day shall you rejoice, for your world will change.

Why don't we know this now? Why don't we embrace it?

> Because this notion of God violates virtually everything you have been told and taught about God.

Yet what many of us have been taught has come from the world's major religions. Are you are saying that what we have been told about the God of the Jewish, Islamic, and Christian faiths is inaccurate?

> It is incomplete. These religions—and many others—teach of a Creator who is separate from His creation. So the message here that Tomorrow's God will be separate from nothing *is* a radical message. It is also a very

important one. Perhaps the single most important message of the New Spirituality. And it is the one element that is missing from most of the world's theologies.

It is the *Missing Message.*

Because this message has been missing, humanity has been *missing the mark* in its attempts to create a world of peace and harmony and happiness, and religions have been *missing the point* of Life itself, causing millions of people to be *missing the experience* of Oneness with the Creator—and with each other.

If humanity adopted this Missing Message as its next new truth in religion—just as it regularly adopts new truths in medicine, science, and technology—the world could change overnight. For the idea that you and all humans are one with God and one with each other is psychologically and spiritually revolutionary.

Could this be the missing piece of the puzzle? Could this be the reason why religion, for all its efforts and for all its sincerity and for all its many truly great insights, has not been effective through all the centuries in altering the self-destructive and violent behaviors of humanity?

You are asking a very good question.

What will it take for us to explore this Missing Message, and to embrace it?

Many of you are.

Yet not enough of us to make a difference in the world.

The number is rising. In this the human race is moving to critical mass. The day of atonement—that is, of *at-ONE-ment*—is near at hand.

What can bring it closer?

You.

You can.

Do you mean me, specifically, or any of us?

Any of you. All of you.

How?

Live this message of the nonseparation, of the Unity of Life and the Oneness of All Things. Live it in a practical way, not merely in a conceptual way. Allow it to seep into your being at the deepest level, and become a part of your subconscious and immediate response to every life encounter.

Living this message is the best way to share this message. Then share it in other ways as well. Carry it to the world. Make it available to all people. Tell them of Tomorrow's God, and of the New Spirituality. But do not try to do this individually. The job is too big, the task is too great, for one person to undertake. And if one person tries, that person may be called a false prophet, a charlatan, or worse.

Form a collective to do this work. The day of the

individual teacher has passed, and the time of the single master is over. It is now time to work together in multiple numbers, remembering that wherever two or more are gathered, there am I.

We could form a team. We could call it *Humanity's Team.* Then we could ask people everywhere to work together to create the space of possibility for a New Spirituality to emerge upon the earth.

That is an excellent idea. I invite you to do exactly that.

The only problem is that when ordinary people speak of these things to others, they are often at a loss for words. Many people wouldn't know how to articulate this message, to say it the way it is said here, to convey it the way you convey it.

Everyone has the ability to convey this wonderful message of at-one-ment. You have all the gifts of communication that you will ever require. *Your message is your life, lived. Your gift is your Divine Self, expressed.* Simply allow your Self to be expressed in your own unique way.

Hold nothing back. Do not fear failure, and save nothing for later. Do not hide your light under a bushel, but let it so shine that all may see the wonder of you, thus to know the wonder of themselves. For others see *their* possibility in the reality of *you.*

Remember that always.

Others see their possibility in the reality of you. Be, therefore, a model to all the world.

> *Be the hope of humanity.*

That is such an inspiring call! "Be the hope of humanity." Are we up to such an invitation? I wonder.

> Trust the love that flows through you. Trust the truth that lives within you. Trust the process of Life Itself that IS you. It will bring to you the exact way, the perfect conditions, and just the right moments to allow you to *become* the message you wish to send. Trust in this process, and you will have this experience.

We will! We will open to that trust, and open to that possibility. And, as you suggest, in addition to trying our best to live this message, we will do what we can to cause it to be circulated far and wide.

> Who is this "we" you are talking about?

Well, I guess I was assuming that I could speak in the plural here. I'm sure others will be inspired to be the hope of humanity, too.

> Yes, but it is important to be responsible only for the Self. You do *your* part, and do not worry about the person next to you. Otherwise, if you are not careful, you will be waiting for the person next to you. And they'll be waiting for the person next to them. And so on. And nothing ever happens, nothing ever gets started.

Okay, I will be the one. I'll do all that I can. What you've given us here, in this dialogue, can form a basis for beginning explorations of a new way to understand God. And I think that the Nine New Revelations presented in *The New Revelations: A Conversation with God* are also extremely important. They are breathtaking in their clarity. All of this, plus the Five Steps to Peace found in that earlier dialogue, may be all that is needed to create the space of possibility for a New Spirituality to emerge on the earth.

> Yes, all the tools have been given you. Not only in these books, but in all the esoteric writings and sacred teachings of your global civilization. And now, here, in this present book, I will speak to you in new ways about this "new God," so that you may come to understand more deeply the true nature of the Divine.
>
> In truth, God cannot be "explained," but can only be experienced in a place beyond understanding. Yet words can open a path to that place, and other people can help on the journey.
>
> Use this book, then, as one introduction to Tomorrow's God. Not the only one, and not the best one—a point we will discuss in detail later—but a helpful one, for it combines the perennial wisdom of the ancients with the fresh articulations of today's contemporary teachers to bring you the insights of all ages.
>
> This dialogue will allow you to see that your many teachers say the same thing in different ways, speak the same truth in different tongues, see the same

vision from different perspectives, and announce the same reality through different experiences OF that reality.

Taken together with *The New Revelations,* this book can lead you to foundational change, both individually and collectively. And *foundational change is what is required right now to save the world.*

4

SAVING THE WORLD

Okay, I've got to tell you now that I'm having difficulty every time I hear you use the phrase "save the world." You have taught me before that "everything is perfect" and "there is nothing you have to do." Now you keep coming up with this "save the world" scenario, and that sounds like just as much of a "scare tactic" as those being used by some religions to bring us to *their* understanding of God. It seems as though Tomorrow's God is simply using a different kind of Fear Tool, but a Fear Tool just the same.

That is a very fair observation. I can see how you could come to that. So let me clarify here that everything *is* perfect in the universe right now. Nothing is going "wrong," because "wrong" is a relative judgment, based on what it is you declare that you are trying to do.

The universe is not trying to *do anything*. The uni-

> verse simply *is*, and it is *perfect* as it is, since it has no agenda. If you, however, *do* have an agenda, then there could be some things occurring in your world, in your part of the universe, which you may wish to alter. The universe will allow you to do that. In fact, it will empower you to do that. But it will never require you to do that. Everything depends on what you choose, on what you desire.
>
> If you are enjoying life on your planet's surface right now, more or less the way it is, then you may wish to preserve it in that form. That is what I mean by "saving the world." By "save it" I mean "preserve it." That is, to *serve it first.*

To "serve it first"? Where did that come from? What does *that* mean?

> I spoke earlier about allowing the "Missing Message" of God's unity with all of Life to seep into your being at the deepest level, and to become a part of your subconscious and immediate response to every life encounter.
>
> If you wish to keep things the way they are on earth, or to make them even better for those who follow, then you must set as your first priority the serving of all that is life-sustaining. In a sense, you must place it even *before* your first priority. This is called PRE-serving.
>
> "Pre-serving" is when you serve something even before you make a conscious decision to do so.

Uh . . . you're losing me here.

"Pre-serving" is what you choose to be and what you choose to do *before consciously choosing anything.* You serve this choice first, before anything that you *consciously* choose in life. This is *pre*-serving.

That which you pre-serve, you preserve.

You save it.

I'm still not sure I understand. How do you choose to be or do something before you consciously choose anything?

You do so at a level *other than the conscious level.* You come from a *different level of creation.*

There are four levels of creation. These are:

1. The subconscious
2. The conscious
3. The superconscious
4. The supraconscious

Oh, yes. You have brought us this information before, in the book *Friendship with God.*

That is correct.

Everyone knows what the subconscious is. Could you explain about the superconscious and the supraconscious levels of awareness?

Human consciousness operates at four levels at all times.

The subconscious mind is assigned to handle all of the automatic tasks of the body, and, as well, to store every event, experience, impression, feeling, and data that has been brought to the Being through the body via the conscious mind.

The conscious mind is assigned to handle the task of total data collection in each moment of Now. It also performs past-data analysis, comprehension and limited awareness understanding, present-moment decision making, future projection, and all sensory feedback functions. By this means it produces your present moment experience. You can change this experience instantly by simply moving to a higher level of consciousness.

The superconscious mind is assigned the tasks of total awareness understanding, body-mind-spirit connectivity, spontaneous creation, visionary insight, and the manifesting impulse, or Now Purpose, of the soul.

The supraconscious mind is assigned all of the above tasks *combined,* as well the most important function of the Being: integration of the Individuation with the Nondifferentiation—that is, of the Single Soul with the Only Soul.

It is at the supraconscious level of the mind that you are connected with me and with All That Is in a nonlinear, total-infusion pattern that eliminates delineations even as it maintains specific energy-form integrity.

Uh . . . one more time?

It melts you into God, without forgetting who you are, individually.

Ah!

This is the exact reverse of the process of your subconscious mind, which melts you into you, individually, while *forgetting* Who You Are.

Put simply, the subconscious, or lowest level of mind, pushes you away from God, while the supraconscious, or highest level of mind, pulls you toward God.

This "push-pull" process is a micro version of the macro tension holding together the entirety of physical creation that you know as the Universe.

I am aware of the work of an obscure Russian meteorologist, Alexander Friedmann, who argued for years with Albert Einstein about the logical outfall of Einstein's theory of relativity.

Friedmann said that Einstein's equations could be used to prove the existence of an ever-expanding universe, a contracting universe, and even "oscillating universes that grow and shrink as if following the exhalations and inhalations of a cosmic Creator," as Corey S. Powell put it in his fascinating book, *God in the Equation.*

Your scientists have been trying to explain this "push-pull" process for years. Whether at the level of universal cosmology or at the level of individual human experience, this process exhibits as an inherent part of Life itself.

The subconscious performs its function by storing

every bit of data it has ever received from the conscious mind that would allow it to differentiate itself from the All.

The supraconscious performs its function by storing All Data Everywhere, allowing it to nondifferentiate from the All, even as it individuates. It can thus produce, in all humans at any moment, the experience of Nonseparated Separation, or what could be termed the Singular Duality.

It is doing that right now, as you, Neale, write these words, which are coming from Me but are coming through You, even as if the two were One—which is precisely the case.

This was not explained in *Friendship with God* at that level of detail or sophistication.

You were not ready to hear it at that level then.

First you had to *form* a "friendship with God" before you could begin to hear about the True Nature of Ultimate Reality. Until your most recent years you have *not* had a friendship with God, but a *fearship with God.* This relationship of Fear kept you from accessing, knowing, or understanding who and what God really is.

Once you formed a real friendship with God, however, following the seven steps given in the dialogue found in that book, you were much more able to know, and to trust what you knew, about me. The doors were flung open. Your fear of me was released. The mind was cleared and the soul was set free.

> The entire *Conversations with God* series of dialogues has been designed as a step-by-step process of freeing humans from their limited perceptions. That is, of pulling them from their subconscious to their supraconscious. This process is known as *consciousness raising*. It is the means by which human beings are moved to a larger awareness of Life, a grander experience of the Self, and a greater connectivity to the universal.

My wonderful friend Jean Houston described this in her astonishing book *Jump Time*. Said Jean:

> When individuals come into resonance with universal purpose, they know it in their hearts, they feel it in their bones. There is a great assent, a cosmic yes, an arc of energy across the void. What stands revealed in such moments is the entelechy, the *creative seed of greatness each of us contains.* [Italics mine.]
>
> Some people are given very young to an innate sense of their essential reason for being—the oak their acorn is destined to become. For others, even adults living full and successful lives, *the issue is activating an awareness of what more is possible.* [Again, my emphasis.]
>
> Many people I know, despite manifold professional accomplishments, are still wondering what they will be when they grow up. Few realize the answer completely. But when they do, their names become scriptural, for entelechy is the matrix of forms, the resonance of the divine in the human. It is ourselves writ large, the cosmic persona tuned to human purpose and possibility.

Isn't that just an elegant, *elegant* observation?

It comes from an elegant mind.

Yes, Jean Houston has such a mind.

No, you *all* have such a mind. Every *one* of you. That is the *whole point* of Jean's book, and of what is being said here.

When you form a "friendship with God," you allow me to become so much a part of your life that this point becomes obvious to you. It becomes experiential, not simply intellectual. An expanded awareness becomes part of your subconscious, is made manifest in your superconscious, and is expressed as all of Life Itself in your supraconscious.

When this process of reintegration occurs, your *conscious* choices and everyday decisions reflect more and more of the wholeness that you are, more and more of the ultimate reality of unified intelligence and unified understanding and unified expression that is often called, in the languages of your world, "God" or "Life."

As your knowledge and your awareness of this unified reality grows—that is, as you begin to remember more and more of Who You Really Are—you begin to *come from that place* even before you make conscious decisions about the various choices before you. You begin thinking in terms of serving Life Itself before you think in terms of serving the Little Self that you experience as your present human identity.

This idea of serving Life Itself before you serve the Little Self is what I mean by "pre-serving." It is not something that you consciously decide. It is a combination of the subconscious choice, the superconscious choice, and the choice of the supraconscious you—that is, the "Big Self."

You begin to act a certain way "intuitively."

You have picked up the signal from the Totality of Your Being and translated it into action even before your conscious mind has had a chance to review all of its data and come to a thought-out decision.

Can you give me an example of what we are talking about here?

Yes.

"Pre-serving" is the action of a woman who jumps into a swimming pool to save a drowning toddler, even though she, herself, cannot swim. It is the action of a man who runs into a burning, collapsing building to save others, with no thought of what it could mean to his own life.

This level of being and doing manifests itself in other ways as well; in smaller ways, ways not nearly so dramatic, but every bit as reflective of the Divine Impulse which lies at the heart of Life Itself, expressing through you.

Give me an example. I can understand what you're talking about when you use some dramatic illustrations, but give me an example of one of those "smaller ways."

A man puts a cigarette to his mouth and is prepared to light it. He has done this before, a thousand times. The action is rote. It is automatic. Yet on this day, at this moment, something happens. Perhaps he has read this book. Perhaps he has heard this dialogue. It doesn't matter. Right now, he is beyond thought. He is moving on impulse. The divine impulse within him has decided to serve Life Itself before it serves the Little Self. Without thinking, the man puts the unlit cigarette down. He drops the matches. He is suddenly clear that he will not smoke again. This clarity has come to him without thought. It is simply a knowing. His long struggle with tobacco is over.

A woman gets up in the middle of the night. She has heard her baby crying. She is exhausted. It has been a long day, and it is about to get longer. But she is not thinking about that now. She is not thinking about anything. She moves swiftly, lovingly, her heart wide open. This is a mother, and there is nothing like it in the universe. Here is a being acting on divine impulse. She IS the divine, impulsively expressing Itself. She smiles at the baby in her arms, and her smile is not created in her mind. It comes directly from heaven.

This is the serving OF Life BY Life through everything IN Life—before and *in advance of* any thought about it. This is serving before you even *think* of serving. It is the kind of thing that you do when you are out of your mind. You are not stuck in your mind about it. You are coming from a different place altogether.

This is PRE-serving, and it is only through this level of serving that Life Itself will be preserved in its present form on the earth.

And this is what the New Spirituality is all about.

Whoa.

Yes, "whoa," indeed. This is a new form of spirituality that emphasizes Life Itself as the prime value. And this is a form of spirituality that emphasizes opening to the highest levels of consciousness within you, expanding and raising your consciousness to include what you deeply know to be true at the subconscious, superconscious, and the *supra*conscious levels.

When you expand your consciousness in this way, you open to all the Knowledge Centers within you.

But how does one do that? How can I "open to the highest level of consciousness within me"?

This is what the New Spirituality teaches. It is explained and contained in many books, in many programs offered by many teachers. It is a multifaceted process that goes on for a lifetime—and can be completed in one minute. It is a process that never ends, because the higher the level of consciousness you reach, the higher the levels go. Even if you reached the Highest Level, that level of Consciousness would create *another* level, instantly. Aware that you can never reach the "end of the line," you may then choose to *start over at the beginning,* just for the sheer fun and the unbridled joy of it!

"Starting over" is fun? Boy, you have a different idea of fun than I do.

> **LIFE is fun! Life ITSELF is fun! Creating is fun. Creation is the stuff of Life. It is the Prime Act, the First Purpose. Yet you cannot create anything if you know that everything has already been created! Therefore, "starting over" IS fun, because in starting over you *forget* that everything is already created, and you *begin creating it all over again, as if it wasn't already there.***

Okay, if you say this will all be fun, I'm going to believe you. But right now I'm in the middle of this cycle, and I want to expand my consciousness and "open to all the Knowledge Centers" within me. How do I do this? You still haven't told me yet how to *expand my consciousness.*

> **As I began to say, the complete answer would fill—has filled—many books. Toward the end of this dialogue you will list some of them.**

I will?

> **Yes. These will be just a few of the many, many sources from which humanity may obtain this information. But I don't want to make you have to go to another source, other than this one, right now, because I know that it would be frustrating to you to have to leave this dialogue and go somewhere else for an answer that you seek right now.**

Thank you. That *would* be frustrating.

So I will give you the short answer here, with the stipulation that there is much more to it, much more that can be said, much more to understand at a much deeper level, and with your promise that if you are interested in pursuing this further, you will refer to some of the many other teachers and sources in your world from which this information may be obtained in greater depth and detail.

Fair enough.

The most immediate way for most human beings to expand their consciousness is to become conscious of the fact that they *have* a "consciousness."

Having a Consciousness is something of which you must become consciously aware. This is called *self-awareness,* and developing this can be a fairly easy thing.

The next 100 times you look at yourself in a mirror or reflection, do the Who Meditation.

The Who Meditation?

Say the word "Who?" to yourself three times, for ten seconds each time, stretching the *oo* sound of "who." You may do this aloud, or silently. Either way, stare directly at your own eyes in the reflection, take a deep breath, and ask, on a single breath, three times . . .

Whoooooooooo?

The question you are posing to yourself is, "Who is

this? Who is this standing before me? Who is this being that I think I am? Who? *Who?"*

If you do this 100 times in the next 30 days, you will become aware of your Self. You may not have come to a full understanding of Who You Are, but you will come to an awareness that you ARE. That is, you will become Self Conscious.

Once you know you have a Consciousness—that is, a part of you that is larger than you, that can separate Itself from the Little You and talk back to you—you are well on your way to discovering the truth of your being and stepping into enlightenment.

You will soon understand that enlightenment is experienced by not seeking to experience it. One does not become enlightened because one wishes to. One becomes enlightened because one is. That is, you are already enlightened, and simply now become aware of it.

It is *awareness* that we are talking about here. And now I will tell you a great secret. You cannot become aware of anything within yourself without seeing it outside of yourself, and you cannot become aware of anything outside of yourself without seeing it inside of yourself.

Oh, great, catch-22.

Not so. Both things can be done at once, and always are.

When you are open to the Outside World, when

you are moving in it and through it, keep keen your awareness of everything around you. Look at things as you have never looked at them before. Make every moment a meditation. See the cracks in the sidewalk, the leaves on the tree, the petals on the flowers, the faces in the crowd. Practice seeing them *all as You.*

Just see yourself there. Don't ask yourself what you are doing there or how you got there or how it's possible for you to be there, just see your Self there. Call yourself that. Do not say, "There, but for the grace of God, go I." Rather, say, "There, *because* of the grace of God, I go."

"There I go again, being a street person without money. There I go again, being a flower in that field. There I go again, being a domineering spouse. There I go again, being a dictator in a foreign land oppressing my people. There I go again, being that blade of grass."

Just see yourself *everywhere*. And smile when you see yourself there, knowing that you *are* there, and that what is there is in you.

Now then, set aside time each day to go to the world within. As you move through this Inside World, lose all thoughts and images of the Outside World. Allow your mind to go blank. Breathe deeply and simply concentrate on the sound of your breath. Make your breath your mantra—the sound that takes you within.

Now focus your awareness on a spot in the center of your forehead, just above your eyes. Keep "looking" there with your inner eyes. Stare into the dark space of that nothingness until you "see" something. Keep focusing on your breath and look at what you see. Look deeply. Do not "put" something there, but wait until what is *already* there is opened to your consciousness.

Something will suddenly appear to you. To many, it will look like a dancing blue flame. You will not only see this flame, you will feel it. The feeling of it will wash over you. You will call this feeling Love. It may bring you to soft and gentle tears. Let that happen. And . . .

. . . say hello to your Soul.

Wow. It is really that simple?

It is. Every one of you can do this. Very few of you have tried. You have said that you haven't known how. I have now given you a simple process. Use it, and you will become aware that you are aware. You will become conscious of your Consciousness.

Now, take this vision and this feeling of the Self that you have experienced in your Inside World and place it in your Outside World, overlaying it on everyone and everything. You will soon fall in love with everyone and everything. You will have literally turned your world Inside Out.

I can't believe this. I have never had anything like this explained to me so simply. What happens to me after I experience something like this?

You gain access to all that you know, and also to All That You Are. This, in turn, expands your choices of action. It increases your options. You find yourself thinking things you never thought before, saying things you never said before, doing things you never did before. You experience being "in this world, but not of it."

Everything changes in your reality, and everything changes in the reality that you create. Thus, you wind up changing your world. The part of the world you touch is never the same, *nor is the World Entire,* for your impact reaches beyond your imagining.

As the flapping of a butterfly's wings in San Francisco affects the climate in Singapore.

Exactly like that. Precisely that way.

This is happening right now. You are affecting the world *right now,* with everything you think, say, and do. The only difference is that, right now, most of you are doing this *unconsciously.*

The New Spirituality is about doing it consciously. It is a call to expanded consciousness. It is an invitation to conscious creation. It is the next step in the process of evolution.

This will create a revolution on your planet. It will be a nonviolent revolution, which is always the most revolutionary revolution of all. It will be the Evolution Revolution.

So it's not necessarily a "revolting" against something, but simply a changing, a growth.

> A revolution is a "revolving." It is a coming full circle. And this is what Life as expressed through Humanity is doing right now. You are on a circle, from the fullness of knowing to the emptiness of forgetfulness to the fullness of knowing again. From Oneness to Separation to Oneness again. From Total Consciousness to Unconsciousness to Total Consciousness again. This movement, this process, is part of the endless Cycle of Life. It is the coming and the going, the appearing and the disappearing, the being and the nonbeing, and what you have called the living and the dying.
>
> It is spoken of in your philosophies and revealed in your religions and expressed in all of your cultural stories. It is found in your poems and songs, in your dances and rituals of every kind. It is held in your minds and embraced in your hearts and known in your souls.
>
> It is the Truth of Truths, the Wisdom of Wisdoms, the Nature of All Things, the Wonder of Life.
>
> It IS Life, expressing AS Life, THROUGH Life, which process is circular and cyclical and circumferential. It encompasses All and it encloses All and it includes All, because it IS All.
>
> This revolving, this *revolution,* will come to pass with humanity's physical participation or without it. It does not need humanity for it to occur, and yet its occurrence will mean nothing without humanity. For the

activity of Consciousness without the activity of Physicality is akin to an action of the yin without the yang. It is empty and devoid of experience and meaning.

This is why God created Humanity, and that is why Humanity created God—and when you understand this, you understand everything.

That is . . . quite a mouthful. That is . . . more than I think I can take in all at once. I may have to read that again, to see what I can pull out of that. This conversation is moving faster than I ever thought it would move, and taking me to places I never thought I'd go.

You have asked to know about Tomorrow's God, and Tomorrow's God will have little to do with Yesterday's reality. Yet there will be nothing here that you cannot understand, nothing here that you are unable to comprehend. All that will be asked of you is that you open your mind.

How do I do this? That is a psychological trick that I don't know how to "do" on command.

It is not a psychological trick, it is a physiological process. It is something you can do with your body.

I can acquire an open mind through something I do with my body?

Yes. The body and the mind are interlinked and interconnected. They are not separate from one another.

Your brain is a part of your body. Your mind is not your brain, but you can *open* your mind *using your brain.*

Every mystical training and spiritual teaching tells you this, each in its own way. Avatars and masters of every tradition have declared it.

What do I have to do?

Simply breathe in the Life that is all around you. Breathe deeply, with the natural rhythm of Life, for an extended period. Sit or lie quietly while you do this.

Oh, yes, I have heard of this. In some trainings this is called "breath work."

Yes. Now, as you inhale, feel yourself taking in the energy of Life. After breathing deeply for a while, imagine this energy of Life entering through a portal at the top of your head. Watch with your internal eye as it courses through your body. As you exhale, let it exit through your feet. Do this a number of times. Scan your body with your mind.

Now, imagine filling your brain with this energy. Feel the oxygen fill your brain, feeding and nourishing the cells there. Feel the cells of your brain expand. Do this intentionally for seven minutes.

You may feel a little light-headed after this. Do not worry about that. You may feel light-headed because you will *be* light-headed. You have sent the golden-white light of the energy of life to your brain. You have directed it there, intentionally. This lightens your brain cells. You may feel a sense of *enlightenment.* With that physical feeling may come an increased awareness of Life, of everything around you. Do not be surprised if this occurs. You have opened your mind, exposing it to the gentle breeze of expanded consciousness.

Now you may go back and reread what you have just read.

I'm going to try that. I'm going to put the book down, and I'm going to try that.

Please do. And while you're at it, make a commitment to do this "breath work" every day. You may find that the simple act of breathing deeply in a meditative state may not only expand your consciousness, but enhance your physical well-being as well.

Try doing this breath work before doing anything else as you begin your day. Soon, it may become automatic with you. If that happens, you will be pre-serving Life. For breathing is the process by which the Life Force enters you, flows through you, and is sent *by* you back to Life Itself.

I know that you already understand how the cycling of this Life Energy through all Life Forms supports all Life Forms on your planet.

Yes. I understand that the oxygen I breathe in is created by the plants and trees all around me, which "breathe in" the carbon dioxide I breathe out, turning it into oxygen again and sending it into the environment for me to inhale. It is a circular system of mutual interdependence.

That is a very basic understanding, but it is correct. And breathing is not something that you have to be told to do. You do it automatically because it is Life-serving. It is the *first* thing you do in every moment. Before you serve the agenda of your Little Self you serve this larger agenda of the Big Self that is Life Itself, expressed through you as you. Life serves Life in this way, through its never-ending cycle, and you are part of that cycle. By serving that cycle *before serving anything else*, you *"pre-serve"* it—which, of course, preserves it.

Oh, my gosh, I just *got it.* I just *got* what you've been trying to tell me here. I just *got* the whole meaning, the whole picture! The cycle IS part of the overall and larger process that we call evolution, isn't it? *I see it now.* Even breathing—something as simple and as automatic and as seemingly nonimpacting upon the world as *breathing*—actually serves the whole cycle of Life by which Life Itself is allowed to sustain itself.

Yes, you are seeing more of the whole picture now. As you see more of this whole picture, and your place in it, you peer into the largest secrets of the universe, and grasp at the edges of supraconsciousness.

First, you became aware of your Little Self. Now you are becoming aware of your Big Self. This is the next step for you, and for all of humankind—part of which can be led through this evolutionary process *through you,* and through everyone who sees this as a *team effort,* the most crucial and exciting undertaking of Humanity's Team.

I see the process now. And now I remember that in his sweeping book *Awakening Earth,* social scientist Duane Elgin said that roughly 2.5 million years were required for our earliest ancestors to move from the first glimmerings of "self-recognition" to decisive awakening in the initial stage of "reflective consciousness." That is, consciousness that is able to reflect back upon itself.

It then took about 30,000 years for physically modern humans to move through the stage of awakening hunter-gatherers, approximately 5,000 years to move through the stage of agrarian-based civilizations, and only about 300 years for a number of nations to move through the stage of industrial civilization.

Elgin calls the present moment "a unique pivot point in human history," when we are moving from self-consciousness to what he terms "unitive consciousness," and what physician Richard M. Bucke called "cosmic consciousness" in his classic book of the same name.

> **Many authors, thinkers, and teachers, both old and new, understand and understood the nature of things, and long before 1901 your mystics, saints, and sages have been sending humanity signals about its oneness with all of Life, or what I have called here the "unified reality."**

Yes. Contemporary physicist John Hagelin is one of many scientists and advanced thinkers now once again proposing a Theory of Everything (TOE) that includes the idea that all of Life is a unified whole—a whole system, interconnected and interdependent and impossible to completely separate into its individual parts. The so-called superstring theory and other advances in particle physics are fueling such renewed speculations.

(Dr. Hagelin himself hardly considers it a speculation or conjecture. He announces confidently in speeches and presentations around the world that science has now proven that Life is a unified whole, that we are One with Everything, co-joined in a "unified field" of incomprehensible complexity.)

As Paul Davies writes in *The Mind of God: Science and the Search for Ultimate Meaning:* "Even the process of thinking involves the disturbance of electrons on our brains. These disturbances, though minute, nevertheless affect the fate of other electrons and atoms in the universe."

> That is the Unified Field, or the Unified Reality, that I am talking about. This is the original form, the natural form, in which Life is expressed.
>
> The opportunity now placed before humanity is to preserve life in its present form by pre-serving life in its pre-sent form. That is, in the form in which it was sent to you *before you began changing it.* That was its *pre-sent form.*
>
> You have changed the form in which Life is expressed on your planet. It is no longer expressed in the form in which it was originally created. Yet you can still preserve its form, and even improve upon it, if you can commit to pre-serving Life in its pre-sent form.
>
> To do this, you must know Who You Really Are, and pre-serve THAT.

This is what the New Spirituality teaches. This is what it says.

We have to serve, first, our highest *idea* about Who We Are, which is Life Itself, uniquely expressed. Then life as we know it can be preserved.

Exactly! You've got it. And that is what is meant by saving the world.

I see the challenge now, and the opportunity.

It is a great opportunity. You might say, a once-in-a-lifetime opportunity. You have an opportunity to pre-serve your world and the life you have created by pre-serving Life Itself.

Everything you do you must do with the purpose of pre-serving Life. That is, your first thought—nay, the thought *before* your first thought—must be of Life Itself, and how to preserve it.

This Thought before First Thought is what some of you have called "instinct." I have built it into the cellular memory of every living thing. It is *built in.* But here is something most people do not understand about "instinct." *How you act it out is something you can change.*

Many people think that one's "instinctual response" is something over which one has no control. In fact, "instinctual response" does not mean "automatic response," in beings of higher consciousness. It means the response that those beings believe serves their *best instincts.* That response can be created and controlled.

Beings of higher consciousness do exactly that, and that is what *defines* them as beings of higher consciousness.

The New Spirituality will bring you a new awareness and a fuller understanding of "best instincts," which are gifts from Life to Life Itself.

Your experience of Tomorrow's God will be based in this gift, and will be an expression of it.

5

CHANGING GOD'S NAME

You seem to be using the word "Life" a lot here. And you have said before, in previous dialogues, that this word is interchangeable for the word "God." Is this what you want humanity to understand at last? Will Tomorrow's God not require us to "believe in God" in the conventional sense, but merely to believe in "Life"?

When you believe in Life, you *do* believe in God, whether you say it in so many words or not. You can be an atheist or an agnostic or anything in between, and it will not matter to Tomorrow's God.

It does not matter today, but tomorrow all of you will know this. Tomorrow, every human will understand. And that understanding will be good, because it will eliminate much of the conflict that has resulted from each of you believing in your particular God in your particular way.

You have not been able to agree with each other on this topic when you have used the word "God," or "Allah," or "Jehovah," "Brahman," or the many other names you have given to the Essence and the Being, the All and the Only. Now I suggest that there is another word for God, the meaning of which you may all agree upon. When this word is exchanged for the word "God," everything suddenly becomes simple and clear.

And that word is "Life"?

Yes. "Life" is the one word in your many languages that comes closest to carrying the meaning that some of you are seeking to express when you use the word "Allah" or "God" or "Brahman," "Vishnu," or "Shiva," and that you hope describes or can be a container for the "stuff that God is."

In one word, LIFE is the "stuff that God is."

Life IS. Life is that which IS. It has no shape, no form, no gender. It has no color, no fragrance, no size. It is ALL shapes, all forms, all colors, fragrances, and sizes. It is both genders, and that which is genderless as well.

It is the All, and the Everything, and it is the No Thing from which the Everything emerges.

There is nothing Life creates that is not Life Itself. All that you see everywhere around you is Life, expressing. Life *is* everything. It runs in, as, and *through* everything. YOU are Life, expressing. And Life is You, expressing itself *as* you.

Everybody else is Life, expressing. There is no one,

not a single living being, who is not an expression of Life. Even those you consider the worst among you are an expression of Life.

None of these statements seems controversial. Not many people would seriously argue with them. The truth of these statements seems obvious on the surface.

Now, play a little trick on yourself. Play a little game. Exchange the word "Life" for the word "God," and see what happens. Watch your mind go crazy. Make the same statement, the exact same statement, as above, but use the word "God" in place of the word "Life," and watch what your mind does with it.

Go ahead. Place the statement in quotes because it is going to be an exact duplicate of the statement above, with the exception being that the word "God" has replaced the word "Life."

Okay, here goes . . .

"God IS. God is that which IS. God has no shape, no form, no gender. God has no color, no fragrance, no size. God is ALL shapes, all forms, all colors, fragrances, and sizes. God is both genders, and that which is genderless as well.

"God is the All, and Everything. There is nothing God creates that is not God Itself. All that you see, everywhere around you, is God, expressing. God *is* everything. It runs in, as, and *through* everything. YOU are God, expressing. And God is You, expressing itself *as* you.

"Everybody else is God, expressing. There is no one, not a single living being, who is not an expression of God. Even those you consider the worst among you are an expression of God."

Now, was that easy to say and accept?

For me, yes, for some others, probably not.

Indeed, for some human beings those words would be almost impossible to agree with.

Yes. Some people would find the first statement perfectly reasonable and the second statement blasphemous.

That is because some of you have been imagining that God is NOT Life, but rather, that God stands *outside* of Life, *creating* Life, but not *being* it.

Yet I tell you this:

The words "Life" and "God" are interchangeable. When you understand this, you will understand the basis of the New Spirituality, you will have a one-word definition of Tomorrow's God, and you will have the makings of an almost automatic inner guidance system for living the New Spirituality that can change the collective experience on your planet.

It is just so hard to accept a God who says that we do not have to believe in God. I am so used to a demanding God who not only says that I have to believe in Him, but tells me exactly *how* I have to believe in Him, *what* I have to believe about Him, and *why* I have to believe in Him.

Do you think that Life cares whether you believe in Life? Life does not go away, and it does not treat you any differently, depending upon how you feel about it.

Life simply is, and your believing in it or not believing in it does nothing to change that or to affect that.

Life will not "punish" you if you do not believe in Life, nor will Life "reward" you if you do. Life does not objectively create rewards and punishments. Life is a *process*.

But if the words "God" and "Life" are interchangeable, this would mean that *God* is a process.

That is correct.

God is a *process?*

That is correct.

Well, that's certainly a different definition.

There is much about Tomorrow's God that will be different.

Do you think this is a God that people are going to be able to accept?

Not today, perhaps. But tomorrow, yes. On a near-future tomorrow, yes.

What is the process that God is?

Life.

Ah, full circle.

Yes.

And this is the Fifth Important Difference between Yesterday's God and Tomorrow's God:

5. Tomorrow's God is not a singular Super Being, but the extraordinary process called Life.

This is not a small thing here. This is not an insignificant change in our theological constructions. For some, this is a *major shift*. For some, this is blasphemy.

Yet this shift in the way you view and understand God can save the world. It can preserve your way of life.

On humanity's yesterdays most people who believed in God thought of God as a Super Being, which allowed them to create a God in their mind who is *like a person*. In other words, a Bigger Version of themselves.

In thinking this way and constructing God in this way, they created God in the image and likeness of humans—which is exactly the opposite of what they said that God did.

Many humans say that God has told the world that God created humans in the image and likeness of God. And, of course, if you imagine God to be simply a larger, more magnificent, more powerful version of humans, it makes sense to you that you are the way you are—albeit imperfect—and that God is a Super Being, or a Super Version of you.

But if I tell you now that God is not a Super Being at all, but the process called Life, your theological apple cart is turned upside down. Suddenly, not only is *humanity* the image and likeness of God, *everything else is as well.* This changes your relationship with all things. Now, everything is *one* thing, and that One Thing is called God.

This is not a new idea. This is not "New Thought" or "New Age." Many of your scientists and philosophers have been saying this for centuries. In fact, this is the crossroad where science, philosophy, and religion meet. Each may continue beyond this crossroad, taking once again their individual direction, but if they forget or ignore the fact that they have intersected here, they do so at their peril. Their disciplines become useless, for they are incomplete.

The New Spirituality does not ignore this crossroad, but stands squarely in the middle of it.

That this New Spirituality, widely adopted, would change the world, there is no doubt. It could save the world from self-destruction.

Because human beings would never do the things they are now doing to the earth, much less the things they are doing to each other, *if they thought they were doing all these things to themselves.*

Exactly. Self-preservation would kick in. Your built-in cellular encoding—survival—would immediately preclude such behavior. You would *instinctively repel* from it.

You would never do things to your own body that

you do without a second thought to the body of another. You could never treat your own feelings the way you treat, without giving it a second thought, the feelings of another. You could never do to your own family, or your own country, what you do to the families and the countries of another.

The only way you can justify treating other countries, other cultures, other people, the way that you do is to imagine—no, to *insist*—that they are separate from you. To make this separation more vivid, and to give yourselves justification for acting the way you do, you also insist that these others are separate from God. Only YOU are united with God, only YOU are God's people, only YOU are following God's plan for salvation.

The fact that your understanding of God's Plan for Salvation is killing half the human race is of no concern to you. The reason they are dying is either because they *deserve* to die ("Kill the infidels!") or because they have unwittingly brought about their own demise by not following the path to the One and True God—who is separate from them and connected only to YOU by means of some special covenant or revelation or understanding.

This is how your human theologies have created your Cultural Story around Yesterday's God—and it is why Yesterday's God has become one of humanity's greatest downfalls.

Oh, my God, don't *say that.* It is *Satan* who is the downfall of Man. Don't say that *God* is Man's downfall. That is apostasy!

> **By Yesterday's God I mean Yesterday's ideas about God, Yesterday's conceptualizations about God. These are what have been humanity's downfall. They have not led humanity to the place where it says it wishes to go. They have not brought peace, harmony, and happiness. They have not produced the Golden Age of Enlightenment. They have brought tears and anger and violence and bloodshed and untold anguish and terrible destruction across the globe and around the world.**
>
> **God herself has not done this, but your ideas about God have. God himself would never do such a thing, but human beings would, and have.**

And Tomorrow's God will change all this?

> **The ideas about God that humanity will embrace on that future tomorrow can and will affect all of this in a very positive way.**

So, as I said, this really isn't just a modest shift in our conceptualizations about God. This is a major change, and would, in turn, create a massive alteration of our Cultural Story. It would dramatically alter what we *tell each other* about life.

I'm not sure humanity is ready for a change on that order of magnitude. Human beings have a complicated relationship with change. They don't like it very much.

> **And that is why human beings have always had a complicated relationship with God.**

6

REDEFINING GOD'S CHARACTER

Our complicated relationship with "change" has created a complicated relationship with God?

Yes.

Why? Why is that so?

Because there is another word that is interchangeable with God, and that is "Change."

Here we go again. Does this ever end, this continual redefining of God?

We are not redefining God, we are actually fully defining God for the first time.

Ah.

We are expanding that definition to include ever more subtle nuances that will allow the human mind to

more deeply understand the nature of God—God's *character,* if you please—thus to see Divinity in more places, so to heal its sense of separation and estrangement, and to embrace its unity with Deity.

That is exactly what humanity needs right now! It is what we need to see more of.

"Need" does not exist. It is an illusion. Given where humanity says it wishes to go, however, and given what it claims it wishes to experience, this expansion of its definition of God would be useful and beneficial.

Now, I said earlier that God is that which is Constantly Present and Constantly Changing, suiting Itself to each moment, so that God may be *understood* in that moment, *embraced* in that moment, *experienced* in that moment, and *expressed* in that moment.

I also said that the words "God" and "Life" were interchangeable. And now what I want to tell you is that *Life is a process of Change*. This is why the words "God" and "Change" are synonymous.

Here, then, comes another shift in your understanding. Yesterday's God was said to be that which never changes. That God has even been called the Unmoved Mover. So here is the Sixth Important Difference between Yesterday's God and Tomorrow's God:

6. Tomorrow's God is ever changing.

You really want the whole paradigm—practically *everything* we have ever thought about God—to be thrown out, don't you?

Not "thrown out," *expanded.* You have had a limited awareness. It is time to expand your awareness.

In a sense, your old idea of God as that which never changes was correct. It was simply incomplete. It did not contemplate or consider that the one thing which *never* changed about God could be that God is always changing; that *this could be the Constant.*

In fact, it is.

God is always expanding and becoming. The process of expansion and becoming never ends. It is how Life functions, it is how Life adapts, and it is how Life sustains Itself. This process is what you have called Evolution.

I hate to tell you this, but some things in life never change.

Nothing in life "never changes."

Nothing?

Nothing.

Well, some things certainly *seem* to not change.

Name one thing.

Wait a minute, we've been here before. You've discussed this before, in previous conversations, using the Parable of the Rock.

Yes, but it is good to visit this understanding again. Clarity emerges from wisdom revisited. And not everyone has read the transcripts of those previous dialogues.

Okay, so we'll stick with the rock example. We'll talk about the rocks in my garden. They're there, they've been there for years, and they've not changed a bit. They are inert objects, and they do not change.

> Wrong. They move. They change. They are in constant motion. Under a high-intensity microscope you would see this. You would see particles constantly in motion, racing at incredible speed relative to their size, spinning their tale. It is their story. It is the Story of the Rock.
>
> All of life is energy in motion. Nothing stands still. Nothing. Not a single thing in the Universe is static. All is moving. And movement is change.

Can't some things move and still remain the same? The rock in my garden looks exactly the same today as it did ten years ago. Twenty years ago. Heck, a *hundred* years ago.

> Not all of the energy in the Universe is vibrating at the same speed or frequency—or what you might call the same level of consciousness.
>
> Energy that is totally aware of Itself moves in faster ways to produce *difference*. Energy that is not totally aware of itself moves very slowly, producing over and over again nearly the same pattern that existed before, until that pattern alters itself over a very long period of time.

So that's why the rock looks as if it's staying the same, while my appearance changes from year to year.

Year to year? Try month to month. Actually, day to day, although those day-to-day changes, like the changes in the rock, are not noticed.

Energy systems that vibrate at lower rates of speed are more dependable, more reliable, more stable. This is precisely *because* they "produce, over and over again, the same pattern that existed before, until that pattern alters itself over a very long period of time."

The universe, for instance, spins in such a pattern. Your Milky Way has been spinning in the same way for billions of years, and you can count on it to spin the same way for billions of years more.

It all has to do with levels of self-awareness.

Are you saying that rocks are *self-aware?*

Everything is self-aware, but levels of self-awareness differ. Highly self-aware energy always seeks to become more self-aware. Once an energy system becomes increasingly aware of itself, it seeks to become more and *more* self-aware.

"How're ya gonna keep 'em down on the farm, once they have seen Paris?"

Exactly.

The more you know, the more you want to know. The more you experience, the more you want to experience. This is the nature of Life.

Life seeks more Life through the Process of Life Itself.

That's poetic.

It's also true. So, what I am saying here is that the faster an energy vibrates, the faster it is *going* to vibrate.

In other words, *things speed up.* But what about the law of inertia, which says that "an object in motion tends to stay in motion, an object at rest tends to stay at rest"?

Strictly speaking, *nothing is ever at rest.* So the New Law of your New World emerging from the New Spirituality would say that an object in motion tends to stay in motion, and *all objects are in motion.*

And that motion is the process of evolution.

Yes. Exactly. Yes.

Okay, I see this, I understand it. But what does this have to do with God and me and my daily life?

I said that what we were going to do here is redefine God's character. So long as humanity sees God the way it currently sees God, you will assign to God all sorts of characteristics that are simply not part of the true nature of God and have nothing to do with who and what God is.

Remember when I said earlier that the God in whom you believe *isn't real,* that the God in whom you believe is *made up?*

Yes, I was pretty startled when you made that comment.

Yet it's true. Yesterday's God is a God you created out of thin air, having nothing to do with Ultimate Reality. What I am explaining now is Ultimate Reality—a little of it, anyway—so that you can begin to understand, begin to grasp, the complexity of it, the sophistication of it, the subtlety of the Whole System.

Hang in there through this little short course in the physiology of God and Life, because after you hear this, you will never be able to think of "God" in the same way again.

Okay, I'm with you. I'm right with you.

Good. Now, to pick up where I left off . . . all energy is self-aware, but not all energy is *aware* that it is self-aware.

I beg your pardon?

All of Life, down to the tiniest cell, molecule, or submolecular particle, contains intelligence. This basic intelligence is *built in.* It is a cellular encoding. Because that is true, these tiny particles move in ways that *make sense.* Their movement produces a specific and predictable outcome.

This outcome is called Life.

At the macro level, it is called the cosmology of the universe. At the micro level it is called particle physics, superstring theory, and so forth.

And somewhere in the middle, there's *us!*

Now you're with me. Yes!

Some of you call this built-in intelligence the "survival instinct." All of your laws of physics and its predictability have been based on the understanding at which you have just arrived.

Now comes an interesting twist: At a certain point in the Process of Evolution, Life Energy becomes *aware* that it is aware of itself.

That's a big event, yes?

You bet. It is Life becoming aware of what Life IS in its present form. It is supremely impacting, because it produces what I call the Separation Phenomenon. This is when an element of Life first has the "idea" that it is separate from God. It is the First Pivotal Moment.

Prior to this moment, energy particles expressed themselves as part of an overall System. Their intelligence was experienced as the intelligence of the System.

Kind of like the Borg in *Star Trek.*

Actually, *exactly* like that, only without any malevolent intent.

In the First Pivotal Moment of self-discovery, an energy unit becomes conscious of Itself as a *part* of the System, rather than as the System Itself. Its identity as part of the System soon expands into a thought that it is separate *from* the System.

Oh-oh.

Yes, this is the Great Oh-Oh of the Universe. It is the Mother of all Oh-Oh's. Actually, that's true *literally,* because it gives *birth* to the next emerging process of Life: chaos.

Chaos? As in "chaos theory"?

Exactly. The thought of being something "other" than the System is what brings chaos to life.

Wow, you are making physics relevant here. This is great. So, go on. How does the idea of separation from the All create chaos in the System?

While a unit of energy becomes self-aware, it is losing its awareness of the larger System of which it is a part. Its intelligence—which is really the intelligence of the System—is now experienced as *its own* intelligence.

An example of this is what's occurring right now.

It is?

Yes.

In what way?

You think this is YOU talking, and really, this is ME. Part of you thinks that this explanation right now is something that is coming from *your* intelligence, and it is not, and *could* not be, because *you don't know any of this*. Yet, because it came *through* you, you think it belongs *to you*. You think it is *yours*, and really it is *ours*.

(The intelligence, I am talking about. I am talking about the intelligence that is now bringing these words forth.)

You're right. Sometimes I do think that this is all coming from me. Even when I know better, I sometimes think that.

Don't feel bad. It's natural. I am explaining to you here just how natural it is. It's part of how Life works. And, of course, the intelligence IS coming from you. It's coming from the *part* of you that is *me*. That is, it's coming from the System, of which you are an intrinsic part.

But when an energy unit such as yourself sees itself as *not* part of the System at all, but as *a product OF the System*, the Life Form has created an illusion. It is one of the Ten Illusions of Humans. It is the Illusion of Disunity.

And then along comes chaos theory and quantum physics.

Yes. And quantum physics is simply the scientific explanation for how God—"the System," if you please—looks at Its individual parts and watches Itself impacting those Parts.

You would call this phenomenon, in spiritual terms, a "higher level of consciousness," or "increased self-awareness." It is when That Which Is Aware experiences the fact that It affects that of which It IS aware.

"Nothing which is observed is unaffected by the observer." The first law of quantum physics.

> Good. That's very good.
>
> Now the energy unit, or Life Form, experiences Itself as part of a System again. It becomes aware that the more rapid is the vibration of its energy, the higher is its frequency, and the more impact it has on the energy around it.

This is absolutely fascinating, and I can even see how this applies to *my own life.* The more I become self-aware, the more impact I see myself having upon the life that's going on around me. And the more I have a sense of that, the more conscious I imagine I would become of my *potential* impact, and I can take that into account as I make future decisions.

> That's the way it's supposed to work, but many earthly Life Forms—most, actually—cannot always determine their impact with precision ahead of time. So, unpredictability becomes part of the System. This is called Creation. It is the Creation and the Creator being the same thing.
>
> Everything is predictable in the energy unit you call a rock. Left to its own devices, it will continue to manifest itself in precisely the same way over an extended period.
>
> Of course, even the rock is the outcome of a larger process that produced it. It *evolved* out of something else. But that process took a very long time, because

the energy units that produce it vibrate at a very slow speed and a very low frequency.

Now along comes a human being—an energy unit or Life Form vibrating at a much *higher* frequency—having the capacity to see in the rock what the rock does not and cannot see in itself. The human does something totally unpredictable, from the rock's point of view. The human being picks up the rock, puts it in a tumbler, and polishes it until it reveals itself to be a shining and beautiful stone.

The much slower energy system of which the rock is normally a part can also produce the same result, with the earth itself becoming the tumbler and its elements rubbing against the rock until a precious stone appears. Yet that can take eons, whereas a human being—who knows how to move energy around consciously to produce a specific result—can produce the same outcome in a few hours. This is Conscious Creation.

I get it! Everything I do is part of the Creation Process inherent in all of Life. And after I evolve to a really high level, I can actually predict and even *control* the way in which I am impacting Life. I can become *the master of my own destiny.*

Now you are, indeed, "getting it." Now do you see what this all has to do with your daily life?

Once you understand all of this, once you start looking at Life and God and Creation in a new way, it begins to shift your whole ground of being. It changes the way you hold the experience of Life Itself—and yourself IN it.

And so we see that all of Life is creative, with the more evolved elements of Life able to be *consciously creative*. And, the more evolved a Life Form is, the more consciously it will create.

Finally, as Life Forms become even more self-aware, they begin to access differing levels of consciousness, *including the level of consciousness from which they, themselves, emerged.*

This produces a reversal of the Separation Phenomenon—the Second Pivotal Moment: a disappearing of individual consciousness, a melting of it into the All in an experience that some Eastern mystics have called bliss, or Nirvana.

I can achieve this, I can get to that place right now if I want to. That is what you are telling me, right?

That is exactly what I am saying, yes. Bliss is the natural state of being of all Life, and all Life Forms return to it. Highly evolved Life Forms move in and out of this State at will.

It is the cyclical movement in and out of bliss that propels Life Itself, and causes it to Be.

Bliss is the highest vibration of energy that is possible. This is heaven. This is nirvana. This is reunification with the One. This is the End of the Cycle.

The emergence out of Bliss, the birthing that it produces, is the lowest vibration of energy that is possible. This is the Beginning of the Cycle.

This Cycle of Life never ends. If it did, Life Itself would cease to be. Such a thing cannot occur, because Life will not allow it.

Life is ruled by three basic principles: functionality, adaptability, and sustainability. It functions, or, having atrophied to the point of near dysfunctionality, it adapts, and having adapted, it sustains itself.

Always, Life sustains itself.

Life is eternal. All things in Life support Life.

Then we have nothing to worry about on this planet.

Ah, but it is the second of the Three Basic Principles of Life that you must watch carefully. For, you see, Life is eternally adaptable. That is, it will change Itself, it will alter the form in which it is expressed, in order to ensure that it is sustained.

What does that mean to me? What does that mean to humans?

It means that your planet could become a living hell. It means that the energy system of which you are a part, will adapt itself in whatever way it has to, in order to make certain that Life Itself is sustained.

And so if you, as a part of Life, adapt the Life System of which you are a part in such a way that the System itself is threatened at the level of functionality, the System will counteradapt in order to sustain itself, and you, my friend, may not like the way in which it does this.

The System is bigger than your Little Self, and the mistake you are making is in imagining that your Little Self is bigger than the System—which, of course, is the Big Self.

You do not stand outside of the System, but are part of the System, and the System will adapt the part of it that *you are* before it will allow you to adapt IT beyond its functional limits.

This "system" is the "process" that you called "change," isn't it?

That's correct.

This "system" is, then, what you called "God," yes?

You could put it that way.

Oh, boy, *another* definition.

7

PERSONALIZING GOD

This all sounds so . . . well, so *impersonal*. I was hoping that Tomorrow's God would be a personal God, but none of this seems to have any personal aspect to it, or a level of personal caring.

Your description of Life is accurate.

I was talking about God. I was talking about Tomorrow's God. Or the System, or "change," or whatever the heck you're going to call God next.

Let's go back to calling God "Life," shall we? As I said earlier, that seems to be a word most everyone can agree with. Do you have any problem with the word "Life" as a synonym for the word "God"?

Well . . . I guess not.

You hesitate.

Because to some it seems that God is *bigger* than Life. God is that which *created* Life, and everything in it.

Can you think of anything in Life that is not God?

Oh, sure, plenty of things.

Name one.

Spinach. I'm not sure that God is spinach.

No, seriously, I'm not clear on how to answer that question. If God *made* everything in Life, then God would not BE Life, but, rather, the Creator of it.

Does that mean that God is not living?

No, God is living.

You're sure? God is alive?

Yes.

So then, God created Life, and God was alive when he created it, is that right?

Well . . . yes, I suppose so.

So God WAS what he CREATED.

In a sense, I guess so.

Well, that's exactly what I've been telling you.

Wait a minute. Maybe God was the first thing that was alive, and then God gave birth to more life. Couldn't that be how it is?

But who gave *God* life?

God always had life. God was always alive. God always was, is now, and ever shall be.

So God is That Which Is Alive.

Yes.

So when God created more Life, he created more of what he is—namely, That Which Is Alive.

Yes, I suppose you could say that.

Well, my friend, that is the New Spirituality to the letter.

Yes, well, you cornered me into that. I'm sure some theologian, some theology professor somewhere, or some cosmologist could go around in that circle with you and come out better than I did.

That depends on what you call "better." Sometimes the more you know, the less you know. But let's get back to your comment about God being impersonal. My point, the point I wanted to make here, is that when the quality of being "impersonal" is overlaid on your conceptualization of "God," you have a sadness around that.

Yes.

But when the quality that you call "impersonal" is overlaid on your conceptualization of "Life," you've no problem with that at all.

No, I don't.

That's why I've said that interchanging the words "God" and "Life" makes it much easier to understand and accept God as God really is.

Life is not concerned with you, individually. It has no preference in the matter of how you are experiencing Life.

Yes, I know.

Yet Life is an energy that you can use at any time, with consistent and predictable results. Used in this way, Life becomes your greatest friend, your most effective tool, your most astonishing power, in the creation of the experience of your desires. You *are* Life.

Now, substitute the word "God" for the word "Life" in the above paragraph, apply it to yourself, and see if it does anything to your feeling of sadness.

Okay.

"God is an energy that I can use at any time, with consistent and predictable results. Used in this way, God becomes my greatest friend, my most effective tool, my most astonishing power, in the creation of the experience of my desires. I *am* God."

Any change? Feel any differently about "God" now?

I feel empowered. I feel befriended, cared for, and really empowered.

I tell you this: On some future tomorrow all of humanity will understand that what has just been said about Life can also be said about God. It *will* also be said about God.

It will be said about Tomorrow's God.

Yet only a *person* can befriend you, care for you, empower you.

Well, then, what I've done is that I've personalized God. I've conceived of this energy called Life in a personal way. That may not be the way it is, but that is a way that feels good to me.

And that is the best way to think about God. Think about God in a way that feels good to you.

But what if what "feels good" to me is thinking about God in the way we thought about Yesterday's God—demanding, punishing, requiring us to do certain things in a certain way and to come to Him along a certain path, or *else.* What if *that* is what feels good to me?

Then by all means keep thinking of God in that way. Look to see if this is producing the outcomes you want to see produced in your world, look to see if this brings to your life what you wish to see in your life, and if it does, *don't change a thing.*

But the world is a mess!

Then change a thing.

Okay, but as I observed before, making this happen is not going to be easy. Most religions have not seriously considered a new idea about God—I mean, a really new idea, a radically new idea—in centuries, in millennia.

That's basically true.

And now, all of a sudden, they are going to?

The people of the world will, and that will require religions to expand their point of view and to go along, or lose their followers.

You're sure all this is going to happen, yes?

Yes. It is inevitable.

And it will change everything?

Yes. It is all part of the process of evolution.

Then why do we have to save the world? What is all *that* about?

Back to that, are we? You don't have to save the world. You will save the world as it is—for yourself, your children, your grandchildren, and theirs—only if you choose to.

Life is never going to end. That is what I am telling you here. The System is self-regulating, self-sustaining. The System is always functional, adaptable, and sustainable. So Life is never going to end. Let's make that clear right here.

And your world, your planet, is not going away for a very, very, *very* long time, on the scale of time you are using. So when I use the words "save the world," I use them to mean "keep the world in place as you know it." I have explained that you "save" the world when you preserve it. And you preserve the world when you pre-serve it. That is, when you serve it before you even think about serving it. When it is the natural, *instinctive* thing to do.

Right now, you are violating your own instincts. Your instincts are *telling* you that what you are doing to your world and to your very Self is destructive, yet you continue to do these things anyway.

And so you are Life, ignoring the message of Life Itself. But you will not be allowed to ignore that message for very long. As I have said, Life will *change its form* (that is, adapt Itself to become sustainable) before it will allow any Part of Life to render Life Itself dysfunctional. And so you will see individuals who ignore the most important and functional messages of Life changing their form. To put this in your own terms, *they will die.*

Some of them will die very young. Most of them will die before they would have died had they not ignored the simple messages about what makes their present life more sustainable.

Therefore, if you are enjoying life in your present form, you are urged to learn more about what makes life sustainable in that form, and to *pay more attention to that.*

Learn and learn and learn until it becomes *second nature* to live in sustainable ways. Keep bringing in the information that will help you in this. Look at it over and over again. Tell yourself the same things. Repeat yourself.

Repeat, repeat, repeat the wisdom of the ages, until it has melted into your subconscious.

So *that's* why this dialogue keeps repeating itself.

Yes. This conversation keeps going around in circles because Life is nothing more than a process of going around in a circle. But we will yet be covering new ground, because each time you go around the circle, you see more than you saw before, you understand more than you understood before, you experience more than you experienced before. And so the circle expands.

This is the expansion of consciousness of which we have spoken. So read on, for there is more to be said about how the New Spirituality and Tomorrow's God will manifest in the day-to-day world of your collective reality.

Good, because that's what I want to know about.

Yet first you must understand all that you can possibly understand about Tomorrow's God. Only then can you preserve Life as you know it, by pre-serving it. Only then can you *serve Life first,* automatically, without thinking about it, instead of serving your own limited, short-term desires.

"Yesterday's God," and the "Old Spirituality" have done nothing to stop us from doing that, have they?

No, because the Old Spirituality of your forefathers spoke of separation and disunity and a universe that is essentially dead.

What do you mean, "dead"?

8

BRINGING THE UNIVERSE TO LIFE

Most humans imagine that objects in the universe such as the earth, the sun, and the solar system are "dead." They conceive of them as inert objects—"rocks," essentially—moving through Time and Space according to a pattern set in motion by a Primal Explosion . . . the so-called Big Bang.

Yes, I suppose that is true, most people do believe that, if they think about it at all.

This is an illusion, and when you live within this illusion you have no reason to act in any way in relationship to those "dead" things except to exploit as many of them as you can, so that you can "live better."

Yet when you envision and experience the objects in the universe as part of a *living system,* which is the

reality, your idea about your Self in relation to that System changes.

Right now you know that you, *yourself,* are living, but once you perceive everything *else* as being alive also, you experience yourself as one part of a Larger Whole, one energy package within a larger energy package, one Life Form within a larger Life Form, a Little Self that is part of a Big Self.

The "Missing Message" not contained in today's theology.

Yes. As I said before, this is the crossroad between the Old Spirituality and the new, between Yesterday's God and tomorrow's. Here is the intersection of Experience and Wisdom. You have experienced yourself in one way, and now wisdom invites you to change direction and walk a different path.

For the Old Spirituality insists that Yesterday's God created the heavens and the earth, while the New Spirituality says that Tomorrow's God IS the heavens and the earth.

The Old Spirituality says that God stands separate and apart from His creations, and breathed Life into Man, that he may have dominion over as many of these things as he could touch and see and feel and gather unto himself. The New Spirituality says that God is unified and one with everything, and breathes Life not *into* humans, but AS humans, that humans may express and experience themselves as God-made-manifest, and may know that everything they touch and see and feel is likewise God in manifest Form.

The Old Spirituality asks you to serve God, and the New Spirituality asks you to serve Life—*which is the same thing.* Yet the Old Spirituality allowed you to imagine that you could serve God by *destroying* Life, whereas the New Spirituality cannot imagine such a thing.

So, September 11 could never have happened "in the name of Allah" if people were serving Tomorrow's God.

It shouldn't even have happened in the name of service to *Yesterday's God,* but that's the problem, right there. The teachings of the Old Spirituality, of Yesterday's God, are so ambiguous—in some cases so open to the wildest interpretation—that you can murder each other in cold blood, kill unsuspecting innocent people by flying airplanes into buildings or dropping "smart bombs" onto cities, and do so with impunity, claiming that God is on your side, and indeed, that God *demands it.*

Yet the message and the invitation from Tomorrow's God will be much less ambiguous. Gone will be any sacred scriptures in which God is said to have killed, outright, thousands of people as punishment for "disobeying" Him or not believing in Him. Gone will be any portions of holy books in which God is portrayed as commanding and demanding that the world do the same, "protecting" His "honor" by massacring others.

> **Serve Life First. That will be the motto of the New Spirituality. That will be its credo.**

But there are those who will still interpret *that* to justify killing others at random. In fact, that is the *classic rationale for war,* whether conducted by governments or terrorists. "We have to do it. We have no choice. Our lives, our own survival, depends on it. We are serving Life by ending Life."

Others say that the proof of this justification is the fact that Life Itself destroys Itself when it has to, and point to Nature as the prime example of this.

> **It is true that the Cycles of Life themselves sometimes produce changes in Life Forms in order to serve the larger agenda of a Life Energy System. The universe itself displays such changes.**

Indeed. Just days before the writing of these words astronomers announced a huge stellar explosion in a small companion galaxy to the Milky Way visible from the southern hemisphere. This event produced a supernova remnant, denoted LMC N 49, within the Large Magellanic Cloud. Scientists say the material from this explosion will eventually be recycled into building new generations of stars in the LMC, even as similar debris of supernovae that exploded in the Milky Way billions of years ago created our own sun and planets.

> **Yet these events reflect the truth that all of the universe is a Living System, every aspect and every element of it interdependent upon the other, a giant matrix of interconnected and interweaving waves of**

> energy, vibrations creating Matter and Form, and that which is neither.
>
> Rarely, however, is it necessary to interfere with the *normal cycles of Life, regulated by Life Itself.* It is a fact that Life Forms that have become more self-aware are able to impact the normal cycles of life of other Life Forms. This is what makes Higher Life Forms both the blessing and the bane of the universe. Their activities often require Life Itself to make an adjustment, to adapt, in order to continue remaining sustainable. Individuals, families, nations, cultures, and societies all do this. Their "adjustments" are often called "war."
>
> To render themselves sustainable—that is, to keep life going as it has been—these groups think they have to perpetuate the process of killing.

Nowhere is this more tragically and vividly illustrated than in the Middle East, where the conflict between Israelis and Palestinians has raged for generations. Here, people are ending Life in a misguided attempt to sustain Life. What is sad—and almost unfathomable—is that *no one seems to be willing to admit that this way of life is not working.*

The key actors in this drama seem to imagine that if they *keep this up just a little bit longer,* things will all work out. Yet things are *not* "working out." And they never *will* "work out," so long as the actors on both sides can't imagine or create any alternative to this cycle of violence.

And this is just one of the many places in the world where this sort of thinking prevails.

Yes. This is a cycle gone bad. Such self-destructive cycles, once ignited within an energy system, are often difficult to reverse, and entire civilizations have been known to disappear in a "stellar explosion" at the civilizational level. When massive forces build up within the energy system (in this case, human society) and reach critical mass, something has to give.

Yet when *Life* is held as the Prime Value, and when the largest portion of society is imbued with this value and holds it as sacred, such self-destructive cycles seldom have the opportunity to reach critical mass, because somebody, somewhere—a person, a group, a collective body—intervenes and changes course.

And that can be the work, now, of Humanity's Team. We can actually gather people from all over the world to help humanity change course and to create critical mass around a *new* idea—the concept of a New Spirituality.

Indeed, you can. And that will put into the global marketplace a new thought about God and new ideas about Life and how it works.

This team can begin educating people to the fact that the universe is a Living System, and what that can mean to humanity.

The earth is a tiny part, a minuscule speck, in this unfathomably massive System, and you are a tiny part, a minuscule speck, within IT. And there are other specks within YOU that, compared to the Whole of You, are tiny and minuscule. Yet no part and no speck of You is unimportant to the Whole of You, for each constitutes what that Whole IS. And so, too, is it with You and the Living System known as the All, which is Life Itself.

This is an understanding that can be given to little children in the earliest years of their development. Your present society has lost its respect for Life because its members did not receive this information when they were children. Indeed, your children are not receiving it today.

Very few of your planet's offspring are told that the universe is a Living System. Very few are told that the earth itself is living. And very few children are told in school today that they are a part of that System, One with God and One with each other.

Even religious schools do not teach this.

Are you kidding? *Especially* religious schools do not teach this.

Rupert Sheldrake, the groundbreaking biologist, talks of "morphic fields" that underlie the structure of systems such as our galaxy—and that exist within those systems as well, such as here, on the earth.

Sheldrake (in his book *The Physics of Angels,* written with theologian Matthew Fox) says that such fields actually *animate* those systems, giving them their habits and their capacity to organize themselves. "In this sense, molecules, stars, and galaxies are alive, not just microbes, plants, and animals."

In the future, on the day when you embrace Tomorrow's God, your learning communities will share such perspectives with the youngest among you, so that they may carry the values that those perspectives generate into their adult lives.

Such concepts, held deep within the subconscious, will allow you to eventually create a New Society, made up of New Humans, who will revere and hold Life as the Prime Value, seeing it everywhere, including in the stars.

But do we have to wait until we create learning communities that teach children this concept, and until those children grow up?

No. But you may wish to begin the work of establishing such learning communities, so that the offspring that emerge from them—tomorrow's adults—will not have to struggle to let go of old ideas when they are grown up.

Yet right now, in this day and time, you can begin the process of changing your own beliefs, releasing those that continue to produce dysfunction in your life and embracing new thoughts that could produce a new reality and a new kind of world in your lifetime.

This can be done within thirty years.

Yes, you have said that.

And I meant it. Thirty years or *less,* depending upon how committed and dedicated you are to ending this nightmare in which you are living and getting back to creating the true dreams of all humanity.

You *will* create this, do not doubt that. It's merely a

question of *which* of your tomorrows will see this development emerge. Will your ideas about Tomorrow's God emerge *before* life as you know it all but disappears, or *as a result of* that occurrence?

Again I tell you that the answer to that question lies with you. It all depends on how committed you are to experiencing your earth as the paradise, and your life as the virtually unlimited opportunity, that they can be. If you have no commitment to that, you could experience your planet as a far more unfriendly place, and your life as a far more limited expression, in the near future.

Indeed, that is happening now for more and more of the world's people. Duane Elgin, in his latest book *Promise Ahead,* says that if we consider an income of $3 a day to be the poverty line, roughly 3.6 billion people fall below it—some *60 percent of humanity.*

By comparison, the official poverty level in the United States is approximately $11 a day—almost four times more than most of the people in the world subsist on. "What this means," Elgin says, "is that grinding poverty and the absence of opportunity are the way of life for the majority of humans beings today."

And let's be clear what we are talking about here. We are not talking about the kind of poverty that makes it impossible to buy that latest car, or to afford a computer. Elgin reports that in Russia, more than 44 million people live on less than $1 a day. In China, that number is 350 million. In India it is 500 million.

It is startling to realize that in this first decade of the New Millennium, nearly 80 percent of Indians do not have access to electricity. And in Indonesia "the poverty is so extreme that doctors at two clinics said the number of patients had fallen by half because people could no longer afford to pay the consultation fee," which was *the equivalent of five cents in U.S. currency.*

Worldwide, almost 3 billion people—*50 percent of the world's population*—use wood as their primary source of energy.

> From these observations it becomes clear that even today, only the smallest number of humans enjoy the largest number of the benefits of humanity's evolution. You are facing a Systems Crisis of the first rank.

That is putting it gently. Elgin reports that over half the people on our planet are living on an impoverished diet, without access to health care, in shantytowns without power, clean water, or fire and police protection.

"Will we or will we not take collective responsibility for the health of the human family on our planet?" Duane asks. "How we respond to that wake-up call will be a direct measure of our maturity as an evolving species."

> If you want this situation to change, if you want to head off the collapse of the entire system that has produced such inequities, you will explore the possibility of bringing a New Spirituality to the planet sooner, rather than later. Because the problem here is *spiritual.* It is not economic and it is not political. And it certainly is not military.
>
> It has to do with what people *believe* about each other, about their relationship to each other, about God, and about Life.

But you will create critical mass around the idea of changing things if, and only if, you "get" that *not* to change things is creating critical mass in another direction—a direction that you may not wish to take.

In other words, we had *better* change things, or things are going to change for us, in ways that we do not prefer.

In fact, as you yourself just said, they are.

And when these changes that we do not prefer start to really mount up, we *will* change. We will change our ideas about Life, if only as a means of survival.

Not "if only." *Primarily.*

Primarily as a means of survival, you will change.

If your survival is directly threatened, you will do what you have to do. You will even change your most sacred and long-held beliefs about yourselves, about God, about Life, about *everything,* if you have to.

You will always choose survival, make no mistake about that. You are encoded to do so. This instinct is, as I said earlier, "built in." Life is functional, adaptable, and sustainable. Always.

And if you have to choose just exactly what it is that is going to survive—your species or the *beliefs* of your species—you will choose your species and *abandon* your beliefs.

You would abandon those beliefs that are killing you, that are impairing your ability to survive, right now, but the negative effect of most of your most damaging beliefs is so insidious, is so slow in showing itself, that you do not recognize them as being damaging.

I suppose if aliens were attacking the earth, as in some of those science-fiction films, we would change our ideas *fast.* We would change our ideas about being separate from each other, and we would change our ideas about competing with each other and about how important it is that we believe in God in different ways.

Very little of this would matter to us. We would see *Life* as the prime value, and *instinctively* Serve Life First. We would join together to do what we could do to ward off the invaders. We would share our most secret technologies in a heartbeat, so that we could continue to *have* a heartbeat, and we would forget our differences rather than let them get in the way of our Serving Life First.

If we were thrown into that kind of fire, we would get out fast. But we are not in that kind of fire. We are as lobsters in a cooking pot. The water is heating, but oh, so slowly, and the lobsters do not know enough to crawl out—they do not even attempt to—until it is too late.

Perhaps it would be better if unfriendly aliens attacked us.

You do not need unfriendly aliens to attack you. You are *acting* as unfriendly aliens with each other, and you are attacking yourselves. You have thrown yourselves into the flames of your own fire. It has been ignited by the basic misunderstandings of humans about God and about Life, fallacies that have placed fear in the mind and hatred in the heart of humanity.

And these fallacies are explained with such wonderful clarity in *The New Revelations,* so I don't want to go into enormous detail here. But can we just list them? What are the biggest fallacies about God and about Life that do the most to produce crisis, violence, killing, and war in our human societies?

Your biggest fallacies about God are:

1. God needs something.
2. God can fail to get what God needs.
3. God has separated you from God because you have not given God what God needs.
4. God still needs what God needs so badly that God now requires you, from your separated position, to provide it.
5. God will destroy you if you do not meet God's requirements.

These fallacies about God are destructive enough, but they completely overwhelm humanity when combined with the fallacies about Life to which they have given birth. Many human beings—most, actually—believe that . . .

1. Human beings are separate from each other.
2. There is not enough of what human beings need to be happy.
3. To get the stuff of which there is not enough, human beings must compete with each other.
4. Some human beings are better than other human beings.

5. It is appropriate for human beings to resolve severe differences created by all the other fallacies by killing each other.

Humanity's major fallacies about God and about Life make for a deadly litany of error that has created, and continues to create to this very moment, a world of deep anger, brutal violence, terrible loss, unrelenting sorrow, and unremitting terror.

You think you are being terrorized by other people, but in truth you are being terrorized by your beliefs.

These are what you must change if you are ever to realize your dream of a world living in peace, harmony, and happiness.

If you wish to sustain life as you know it—if you wish to have something to pass on to your children and to your children's children—you will have to pay serious attention to giving birth to a set of beliefs, a new human theology, a New Spirituality.

Not a replacement for the old, but an enhancement of it. Not an abandonment of your present religions, but a revitalization of them.

You are going to have to *revitalize religion* if you are going to revitalize Life and sustain it in its present form. For religion—which is just another word for *what you believe*—is the bedrock of your civilization. Your beliefs create your behaviors, and, I repeat, that is true whether you believe in what you call "God" or not.

For these reasons I have come to you now. For your

world waits in silent apprehension, its people living in fear of the next great devastation, the next outbreak of war, the next fast-spreading virus, the next ecological disaster, the next terrorist attack, the next upheaval—as if the struggles of day-to-day survival were not enough.

I have come to you at this critical juncture in your species' history to bring you news of Tomorrow's God, of the kind of faith that humanity will create, of the kind of beliefs that humanity will embrace, in its future—and to invite humanity to create that future in the Present Moment of Now.

9

HOW RELIGIOUS BELIEFS CREATE CIVIL LAW

You are talking about—over and over again you are talking about—a wholesale shift in our most fundamental understandings about God and about Life. Am I hearing you clearly?

You are. As I have said, this is a shift that humanity will make. It is not a question of whether, it is a question of when.

And you are saying, the sooner the better.

If what you want is what you say you want, yes. If what you truly desire is to live together in peace and harmony and happiness, in good health and with long lives, in an environment that is a paradise among planets, with conditions ideally suited to the joyful survival of your species, and with beauty and natural wonders such as would take your breath away—yes. The sooner the better, yes.

But how do we get humanity to change its most basic beliefs?

By *challenging them.* By holding them up to the light of logic and scrutiny, and challenging them. You must *challenge* your most sacred assumptions, and you must challenge the *source* from which they have come.

Yet before you can challenge that source, you must identify it.

So where have our most basic beliefs come from?

From your exclusivist organized religions. The majority of society's most important laws and virtually all of humanity's fundamental beliefs were first articulated by your earliest mystic teachers, and then by their interpreters and followers. Those followers then passed the teachings of those mystics on to others, and they to others, until—through no deliberate fault of anyone—they became misinterpreted and distorted. And those teachings, in turn, became the basis of your most influential religions.

Ultimately, they became your Cultural Story as well. The teachings seeped into everything, including the law of your land.

It's true, isn't it? Our whole culture has emerged from our religions, one way or another.

Of course, and it's only natural, because religions have to do with what people most fervently believe, and it is what you *believe* that determines how you behave. It determines what you want and what you don't want, what you seek and what you don't seek, what you choose and what you don't choose, what you save and what you destroy; it determines everything.

It will even determine *now* whether we save or destroy *ourselves.*

That is exactly correct, my friend. That is spot on.

And so of *course* your culture emerges from your beliefs. And those beliefs, once they become religious doctrine, purport to tell the religious among you not only what humans should want and desire, but what *God* wants and desires. And this shows up in many important ways as your society creates itself.

Can you give me an example?

I can give you an excellent one.

Same-sex marriage.

Oh, boy.

Yes, well, do you want to be noncontroversial, or do you want to clearly understand?

I want to clearly understand.

Then get ready to shake the apple cart.

Go ahead.

Many societies have laws against same-sex marriage, and very few have laws supporting it. Yet there is no sound reason in civil law why this should be true. No one is being hurt or damaged by such liaisons.

There are those who would disagree. They would say that it damages our moral fiber. As a society, they would say, we are damaged, and that plays its trickle-down effect in every area of our lives. Nothing good and natural has to be honored, every decent value we hold can be cast aside with impunity. This kills us, morally. That would be the argument they would make.

So same-gender life partnership should be prohibited by civil law based on the fact that it is "immoral"?

Yes, that is the argument.

And so society should pass laws prohibiting all "immoral" behavior?

Well, we'll never be able to do that. We couldn't write enough laws to do that.

Oh, yes, you could. You could pass laws against *whatever* you felt was "immoral."

You could pass laws against drawing or displaying pictures of people or animals ("graven images"), against playing music (other than sacred music) in a place of business, against being unshaven, against females leaving their home without being accompanied by a male blood relative, and even against females being seen in public without a head-to-toe covering over their body.

And you could build severe consequences into those laws, such as being flogged in public, right then and there, at the moment the infraction is discovered, by the Morals Police.

Well, now, wait a minute. That's going a bit too far.

Oh, yes? Says who? What if everyone in your society agreed?

Everyone in a society would *not* agree to such arbitrary and capricious laws.

But what if a minority of powerful fundamentalists simply took charge and *forced* the society to obey its laws based on "morality"?

I see your point.

Or what if the majority of people were convinced of the "rightness" or "wrongness" of something like, say, same-gender unions because people in highly influential places simply told them it was wrong?

You know, there was a time when I would have said, "But who would tell them that? Who would support 'morality by legislation' like that?" These days, however, I find the answer in my daily newspaper. . . .

> VATICAN CITY (July 31, 2003)—The Vatican launched a global campaign against gay marriages Thursday, warning Catholic politicians that support of same-sex unions was "gravely immoral," and urging non-Catholics to join the offensive.
>
> The Vatican's orthodoxy watchdog, the Congregation for the Doctrine of the Faith, issued a 12-page set of guidelines with the approval of Pope John

Paul II in a bid to stem the increase in laws granting legal rights to homosexual unions in Europe and North America.

"There are absolutely no grounds for considering homosexual unions to be in any way similar or even remotely analogous to God's plan for marriage and family," the document said. "Marriage is holy, while homosexual acts go against the natural moral law."

The issue is particularly charged in the United States, where some lawmakers in the House of Representatives have proposed a constitutional ban on gay marriages to counter state laws granting legal recognition to gay unions.

President Bush said Wednesday that marriage was defined strictly as a union between a man and a woman and said he wants to "codify that one way or the other."

The Vatican document . . . says Catholic politicians have a "moral duty" to publicly oppose laws granting recognition to homosexual unions and to vote against them if proposals are put to a vote in legislatures.

If the laws are already on the books, politicians must speak out against them, to repeal them and try to limit their impact on society, it said.

"To vote in favor of a law so harmful to the common good is gravely immoral," the document said.

The document . . . said homosexuals shouldn't be discriminated against, but said denying gay couples

> the rights afforded in traditional marriages doesn't constitute discrimination. . . .
>
> On Thursday, a small group of demonstrators from Italy's Radical Party held up banners at the edge of St. Peter's Square to protest the document. The banners read "No Vatican, No Taliban," and "Democracy Yes, Theocracy No."
>
> Other opposition to the document came from the Green Party in predominantly Catholic Austria. Ulrike Lunacek, a party spokeswoman, said . . . "This hierarchy, which also rules on other issues like forbidding the use of condoms to avoid AIDS, is far from reality." . . .

You see from this news story that your objections are not based in civil law. Your objections are based in a moral judgment that you have made—and that moral judgment comes from your understanding of what you think that *God wants with regard to all of this.*

Or, rather, what God *doesn't* want.

Yes. The taboo against same-sex marriage, to use the current example, is a spiritual restriction, based on the idea that God has a preference in the matter of how individuals behave sexually in the privacy of their own homes.

This is the same thinking that kept laws on the books for many years prohibiting certain specific sexual practices while not prohibiting others, and even prohibiting "mixed marriages" between races. If the pope told you that God had *nothing* against any of this, it would send shock waves through your legal system, destroying all moral justification for many of your laws, past and present. Of course, the present pope will never tell you this, so I am going to have to tell you this.

Are you saying, categorically, here and now, that God has nothing against homosexuality, or gay marriages?

I am saying what I have always said. God has no preference and makes no judgment with regard to human behavior. I know you think that God does, and I know that the idea that God doesn't really ruins everything, but that's the truth.

You have made a judgment about homosexuality, and this is an excellent example of how religions and their teachings become part of the nonreligious, civil-society culture and experience of human beings, be they believers in God or not.

I'll give you another example. In utero genetic manipulation.

I think you *love* controversy, don't you?

If you know of a way to talk about God and not be controversial, let me know, will you?

Gotcha.

Yet controversy does not have to lead to conflict. People don't have to argue in order to discuss. They don't have to berate in order to explore. And they certainly don't have to divide and conquer and condemn and kill in order to fully express or defend their point of view.

Yes, well, tell that to the world's fanatics.

People become fanatics when they feel they aren't being heard. People become fanatical when they feel their point of view is not being honored.

For most, a point of view doesn't even have to be accepted, but it does have to be *honored.* Because, you see, if you dishonor another's point of view, it is as if you disappear it, discounting it as if it were not even there. And when you disappear another's point of view, you disappear *them.* Everything then becomes a question of survival.

Not many of you have learned to truly honor the point of view of others, especially when it is diametrically opposed to your own. That is why you have fanatics on your planet. You have created them. You have placed them there.

Whoa.

Now, are you able to hear a point of view with which you may disagree?

Yes. You were saying . . .

I was saying that another example of how religious views have become part of your civil discourse and civil law has to do with prebirth, in utero genetic manipulation.

In the very near future a doctor could be saying to expectant parents, "I have some bad news. Examination of the embryo reveals a genetic predisposition to Hodgkin's disease. Now we can make a genetic adjustment to reverse that, to eliminate that, and your child will probably never have to encounter that. But we need to do that now, at this early stage, while the fetus is in utero. May we have your permission?"

What should the parents say?

Well, they say NO, of course! Why, that's creating *designer babies.* It's up to *God* to decide what illnesses and diseases a human may be prone to. That's *God's* will, not the domain of humans! How can you even *ask* such a question?

You're getting the picture. And if enough humans agree, you'll actually pass a *law* against the practice of prebirth genetic medicine. *After* the birth, however, you will allow your medical doctors to do whatever they can to help your offspring in the struggle with Hodgkin's.

Of *course.*

So it's not a question of whether God wants the child to suffer from Hodgkin's or not, it's just a question of what God's preferences are with regard to *when you intervene.* Is that it?

Well, you put it so . . . so . . . I don't know, so simply, that it makes humans look almost silly.

I am not trying to make you look silly, I am merely asking a question.

After the birth of your child, if you find that the child has a predisposition to Hodgkin's disease, you will even *pray to God* for the child to be spared. Yet when the medical miracle of genetic intervention was offered to you *before* the birth, you said it was against the will of God.

So what is the issue here—God's *timing?* Is it that the miracle was not timed right? Or is it a matter of the specific procedure? You believe that working with genetic material before birth is against God's Law?

Some do, yes.

And *who said that?* Where is it written that God prohibits this? And what if it was written somewhere else that God does not? *Then* what? What source do you believe?

I get the problem.

And I tell you, entire *societies* create laws based on these kinds of judgments.

In some places there is not even an attempt to disguise religious law as civil law. An example of this is Pakistan's Ehtram-e-Ramazan (Respect for Ramadan) Ordinance, which during the fasting month of Ramadan (or Ramazan) prohibits eating and serving food or smoking in public places, and prescribes closure times of cinemas, theaters, and other such establishments. "Whoever contravenes the provisions . . . shall be punishable with simple imprisonment for a term which may extend to three months, or with fine which may extend to five hundred rupees, or with both," an official government decree says.

The ban on eating or drinking in public *applies to Pakistan's Muslim and non-Muslim residents as well as foreigners.* The ordinance is one of several penalties first enforced in 1981 by then military dictator General Mohammad Zia-ul-Haq as part of his controversial "Islamization" of Pakistani society, including possible stoning to death for adultery, amputation of hands for theft, and flogging for drinking.

These and other decrees are derived from the Shari'a, which is both the legal and moral code of Islam, and is the law of the land in many Muslim areas of the world. It is religious law, plain and simple.

So, too, in the first centuries of the Common Era, was the Halakhah, the body of oral or traditional Jewish law. The influence of these mandates is felt in Israeli civil law today.

In other places, such as the United States, civil law is declared to be separate from religious influence, but that separation is largely institutional, not functional. The law seeks to function as an absolute reflection of the religious views of society in any area in which moral issues are involved.

And this is how your cultures emerge from your beliefs.

Humanity's ideas about itself come from humanity's ideas about God and about Life—and those ideas

come from humanity's most powerful idea purveyors. Namely, religions.

Even today, at a time when society is bemoaning the influence of other idea purveyors—movies, television, video games among them—religion stands alone as the only idea purveyor able to add the weight of presumed *moral authority* to its messages.

For this reason, few dare to bemoan its influence, although it is precisely that influence which produced such atrocities as the 200 years of the Christian Crusades, or the flying of jetliners into buildings in New York City and Washington, D.C.

No one would ever seriously suggest that movies, television, video games, or comic books carry any moral authority, yet your religions do carry such authority.

Although some of their sacred texts have actually been turned *into* comic books . . .

Yes, well, that's another matter.

The point I am making here is that the weight of religion's moral authority carries tremendous impact. A government can tell you to go to war and you can claim to be a conscientious objector. Yet if God tells you to go to war in a holy jihad, *who is there to tell you to conscientiously object?*

No one. If you object to going to war, you have lost all moral ground if you are told that God *supports* war as a means of dealing with others.

When the United States in early 2003 declared a preemptive war on Iraq, claiming that Iraq was developing and storing weapons of mass destruction that threatened the security of the United States and the world, the Reverend Charles Stanley of the Charles Stanley Institute for Christian Living told his nationwide television and Internet audience that "God battles with people who oppose Him, who fight against Him and His followers. So, even though He hates war, God is not against it. Throughout the Old Testament, there are examples of God using warfare to carry out His plans."

Rev. Stanley also said that "God has divine reasons for choosing to use war as a vehicle to accomplish His will." And, just in case anyone would think of disagreeing with him, the good reverend went on to declare that "despite the many different opinions and philosophies about war, the most important consideration is God's viewpoint. Throughout Scripture there is evidence that God favors war for divine reasons and sometimes uses it to accomplish His will."

I was astonished when I first read these quotes myself. I thought they had been taken out of context, and so misrepresented the pastor's views. I was wrong. I ordered a videotape of the sermon in question, and a written transcript as well. The entire text of Rev. Stanley's remarks tells us all in scary ways and in no uncertain terms what millions of people believe about Yesterday's God.

It is instructive for all of us to hear what this Christian minister had to say on February 17, 2003, to his national congregation. I have urged everyone to order the complete—and frightening—transcript. If you would like a copy of this astonishing document, you may order one for free by sending an e-mail request to transcript@cwg.org.

And Christians are not the only ones being told that going to war has God's approval. This idea is, of course, what caused those Muslims who flew jet planes into buildings on September 11, 2001, to do so in the first place, shouting "Allah is great!" as they put themselves and thousands of others to death.

And it is religious scholar Karen Armstrong who notes, in *The Battle for God,* that "in 1980 Rabbi Israel Hess published an article entitled 'Genocide: A Commandment of the Torah' in the official magazine of Bar-Ilan University. He argued that the Palestinians were to Jews what darkness was to light, and that they deserved the same fate as the Amalekites."

And just what fate is that?

According to 1 Samuel 15:2–3: "Thus says the Lord of hosts, 'I will punish what Am'alek did to Israel in opposing them on the way, when they came up out of Egypt. Now go and smite Am'alek, and utterly destroy all that they have; do not spare them, but kill both man and woman, infant and suckling, ox and sheep, camel and ass.' "

So Saul summoned the people, "two hundred thousand men on foot, and ten thousand men of Judah," to go and do God's bidding.

> **Yes, this is an excellent example of what I mean when I say that the teaching of religion affects the religious and the nonreligious alike—even to the point of sending them off to war.**
>
> **So, to use the most recent example, you have a**

sacred belief that supporting your country's leadership during a time of war—even if it is a war that you did not support before your leadership declared it—is not optional. That is, you *must* support it. *God says so.*

What is sad about this is that only a *lack* of dissent makes it possible for human society to collectively undertake such self-destructive behaviors. And this is something that those who fail to dissent either do not understand . . .

. . . or understand full well and choose to ignore.

Yet if humanity is to alter its most sacred beliefs, and if, as you say, many of these most sacred beliefs have been placed into the mainstream of each human culture by its religion, then is humanity, in a sense, not being asked to challenge God himself?

That is what many religions hope that people will think. It is on this basis that they can call such behaviors inappropriate and label them "apostasy."

Which in some countries and cultures is punishable by death.

Indeed.

So, humans believe they are not *supposed* to challenge God. Humans believe they are not supposed to challenge what they believe. They believe in *this* belief perhaps most of all.

You know what? Humans believe that they must believe what they believe, *even if what they believe is unbelievable.*

That is very well put. And this is the credo of many:

> whatever you believe, do not challenge it—and persecute anyone who does.

Yet isn't it time now for us to declare that the emperor is wearing no clothes? When are we going to admit that we believe in a God of extraordinary contradictions, who we say loves and who we say kills, who we say creates and who we say destroys, who we say accepts and who we say rejects, who we say rewards and who we say punishes, who we say brings us good and who we say visits evil upon us, who we say is the All in All and who we say is separate from everything, who we say is Everywhere Present and who we say is not in us and that we are not?

> This is Yesterday's God, a deity bearing no resemblance or relationship to the God who actually is.
>
> These completely contradictory beliefs are called sacred, and are placed in the scriptures of the world's religions. The sum total of all the sacred scriptures of all the world's largest exclusivist organized religions, combined into one, could thus very well be entitled: *Benevolent God/Malevolent God.*

Or, a clever New York editor might suggest calling it, *Our Two-Faced God.* Now that would get attention.

> So long as you believe in a Two-Faced God, you will create ecstasy and terror side by side.
>
> You have imagined a God who is the epitome of both, and by telling yourself that you are created in the Image and Likeness of God, you have given yourself the moral authority to *demonstrate* both.

You love and hate in the name of God.

It would benefit you to see the contradiction and to stop that.

You create and destroy in the name of God.

It would benefit you to see the contradiction and to stop that.

You accept and reject, you reward and punish, in the name of God.

It would benefit you to see the contradiction and to stop that.

If you truly seek a world where peace prevails, it would benefit you to stop all that. For I tell you this: God destroys nothing, God rejects nothing, and God punishes nothing.

You refuse to believe this, because if you did, *you* would lose the moral authority to *do these things yourself.*

The stability of the social structure of your entire species depends upon your granting yourself this authority, *and upon your claiming that it was God who gave it to you.*

You can't imagine living any other way. Yet unless you begin imagining living another way, you may soon not be living at all.

I have said it to you before, and I will say it to you again: You are killing yourself with your beliefs.

Now I will say it to you in a new way, in a more dramatic way, in a more direct way, so that, perhaps, you may hear it at last:

Your God is killing you.

10

YOU'RE MAKING IT ALL UP

I need to discuss something with you before we go on.

Go ahead.

I touched on this before, when I said that now, in this dialogue, I wanted to speak not only my own words, but also the words that I hear being spoken by much of humanity.

Yes, go on.

There are some people who don't believe I'm having a conversation with God anymore.

Well, after that last chapter, they'll be sure of it.

Yeah. Well, of course, there are those who have *never* believed it, but now, even some of those who thought that I *was* having such a conversation at the beginning are saying that I'm no longer doing that, that I've lost my "connection."

Do you know why some people are saying that?

Yes. It's for two reasons. First, because of some of the things you are now saying.

Yes?

People claim that God would not have opinions or comments about "real world" stuff like politics, economics, education, and so forth. So when you comment like this, they say it is me, simply putting words into your mouth.

I see. No one else, of course, *has* put words into God's mouth, is that it? All the other writers heard directly from God. Is that how it goes?

Something like that, yes. All the other writers—meaning the writers of Sacred Scripture—were not talking about politics and medical questions and—

—whoa. Wait a minute. Have you actually *read* these holy books?

Well, yes.

And you don't see any commentary in there about politics or social conventions and issues?

Well, of course I do. The Bible is replete with them. So is the Qu'ran. So is the Bhagavad Gita, and virtually every other sacred text. They talked about everything from what we should eat to what we should wear to how we should run our societies at every level.

So?

Well, those comments were written long ago. That gives them more authority. If they were written today, and had never been heard of before, they'd probably be dismissed as heretical, or at best, their writers would be dismissed as being delusional.

Now I understand this. That's just how things are. When your comments of today have about 200 years of dust on them, perhaps they'll be accepted, too.

You don't have that kind of time anymore.

I know. That's the point being made here. I understand that.

So what is the second reason that some people do not believe you are having a conversation with God anymore?

Well, it's as I said before—because I still seem to have questions. People think that I have all the answers now, because I've had so many conversations with God. They think that when I continue to ask questions, I'm being disingenuous. They think I already know the answers and that I'm asking the questions gratuitously.

I'm not. As I said, I'm asking questions hypothetically. I'm asking the questions that I hear others asking, all over the world. But people say that I'm no longer being authentic, that this is no longer a real conversation with God, and that now it's just me who's making it all up.

Ah, now we're getting somewhere.

You *are* making it all up. You've been making it all up from the beginning. Do you tell them that?

Yes.

Well, yes and no.

It depends upon what state of consciousness I'm in when we talk about it. If I'm in a place of high consciousness, I can say that and explain that in a way that others can understand. If I'm in a low state of awareness, I'm not even sure that I can deal with that.

Why don't you explain what you mean by "high consciousness" and "low awareness"?

Well, there are times when I am really much more aware, when I seem to be more open to Life and the truth it is bringing me. I can't explain how I "get" there, I just know when I'm "there." Sometimes meditation will do it for me. Sometimes, just hearing a song on the radio, or listening to a rushing stream, or smelling a lilac. It can be anything. I just sort of "pop" into that space. I just find myself there.

Quite *literally.*

Yes! Literally, I *find my Self* there. Then there are times when I seem to be stuck in my emotions, in my "unreality." That's the only word I can find here. I know very well that what I'm feeling is just something I'm creating in my mind, but I can't seem to stop it, can't seem to pull out of it. This is what I mean when I say I'm in a low state of awareness. I'm usually pretty insensitive to others when I'm in this place. I'm not aware of much of anything except my own feelings, and those are usually pretty heavy. I mean, I'm not thinking about sunshine and lollipops here. I might be stressed about something, worried about something. Or maybe I'm just walking around in a daze, not enough sleep, that sort of thing.

Anyway, that's what I mean by being in a high consciousness state or in a low state of awareness.

And when you're in a low state of awareness you can't deal with the fact that you've been making this whole dialogue all up from the beginning?

No. Not when I'm in a place of low consciousness, or low awareness.

Yet that is the point of the entire dialogue. That is the point of *all* the *Conversations with God* books. The point is that *you're making it all up.*

With regard to your books, your outcomes, your whole life, you're making it all up. All of you are. Everyone on the planet is. *Every moment.*

People in low consciousness can't accept that.

Insulting them isn't going to help.

I didn't mean that the way it sounded. I'm in that group, too, plenty of the time.

I can't accept that, *I* can't see it, when I'm in a place of low consciousness. I'd like to say that these days I'm in a place of high consciousness all the time, but I'm not.

Do you feel you have to be?

Sometimes, yes. Sometimes I feel that way. I feel that others expect it of me.

Do you expect it of yourself?

Sometimes, yes.

Well, it would benefit you to stop that. Not expecting to be in a place of high consciousness all of the time is your only *chance* of being in a place of high consciousness all of the time.

Huh?

The moment you expect to be, you are not. The very act of expecting yourself to be something precludes you from experiencing it. You cannot "expect" to experience something that you are already experiencing. If you are expecting something of yourself, that means you are not now experiencing it. Either you are experiencing something, or you are expecting to experience it. You cannot do both. Expectation places what you wish to experience into the future.

Remember that. *Expecting something pushes it away from you.*

Not wishing or needing to be in a place of high consciousness all of the time may be the surest sign that you are there. So be careful not to create pictures of what "high consciousness" looks like. Sometimes "high consciousness" looks like simply not having to be in a state of "high consciousness." In other words, being "okay" with whatever state of consciousness you are now in can be a very high state of consciousness.

When you are "not okay" with the state of consciousness you are now in, you wish for more, and wishing for more—of *anything*—always lowers your state of consciousness, because it causes you to feel that you do not now have what it is you wish for, and therefore cannot now be totally happy. *And that is the lie about you.*

You can *always be totally happy* with *exactly the way things are right now.* It is the master who knows this.

Yet, if that is true, why bother trying to change things?

Being happy right now and choosing to change things right now are not mutually exclusive. The decision to change things does not have to spring from judgment, dissatisfaction, or unhappiness. It can spring from simple preference.

Pure Creation knows nothing of judgment, but only of desire.

Remember, Change is a process called Life. The decision to change things is the decision to *live.* It is the choice to live intentionally, to be at Cause in the matter of how things change, rather than to be at the Effect of it.

You can create the best apple pie in the world, and still seek to create an even better one. You can know much about the world, and still seek to know more. This is called growth, and the urge to grow is not a negative energy, but a positive one. It is not a judgment, but a desire. It comes not from dissatisfaction, but from passion. The passion OF Life for MORE Life.

This passion lies within you, and is the driving force behind all creation.

Therefore, it has been written: Judge not, and neither condemn. Yet nowhere has it been written: Create not, and neither change.

You cannot help but change, nor can the Life that is around you. Yet while you cannot stop change, you can control *how change occurs*. You can control how your life changes, and how the world changes.

The way you change your life and the way you change the world around you defines who you are, and who you now choose to be.

You can change the world in two ways. One way saves it, the other way destroys it. Your species is deciding which way it wants to change the world right now.

In this, and in all things, you are making it all up. That is, you are creating it on the spot. You are the Creator and the Created. The Alpha and the Omega. The Beginning and the End.

So tell yourself, and everyone else, the truth, which is that you are not in what others might define as a place of "high consciousness" all of the time, but that when you are, it is clear to you that you are creating your whole life, including this dialogue.

But most people still want to believe that God is separate from us, so if I say that I *am* making this all up, they'll lose their faith in you, in me, and in this whole process.

You could use a new idea about God, you know that? Right now you're describing yesterday's God, a God who lives outside of you, a God who is separate from you, a God to whom you speak.

Tomorrow's God will not be a God TO whom you speak, but a God WITH whom you speak. There's a tremendous difference. In fact, that is, if you remember, the Third Important Difference between Yesterday's God and Tomorrow's God. Shall we state it again?

3. Tomorrow's God talks with everyone, all the time.

Yet the turn of phrase "a God *with* whom you speak" can have a double meaning. It can mean that you are speaking "with" God—as in, "conversations with God"—and it can mean that God and you are speaking at the same time—as in, saying words "along with" me.

The first meaning is the meaning associated with yesterday's God; the second meaning will be associated with Tomorrow's God.

In the future, we will conceive of a God and envision a God and believe in a God who speaks TO you and THROUGH you—all of you, all the time—and not just a God to whom *you pray.*

When you make this shift, everything in your world will change, because seeing God in this new way will cause you to see *each other* in a new way. For if you agree that God speaks to you and *through* you, you cannot help but see each other in a different light.

And when you see each other in this new light, in this new way, you will see each other AS the light and the way, and you will no longer be able to treat each other as you have been. That will alter everything. That simple change, that simple shift in your perception, will alter everything.

That does not seem like a "simple shift."

Yet the movement is really very slight, theologically and philosophically. You already say and agree that God is the All in All. In the future you will simply include *yourself* in the "All in All."

Where, by the way, DO you think you stand in relationship to everything that is? Are you part of it?

Yes, of course.

You are part of all that is?

Certainly.

Well, then you will see that if God is the All in All, and if you are *part* of the All in All, then God is obviously in you, and you in God, and there can be no separation between the two.

Well, of course, this is the message of the entire *Conversations with God* trilogy, and of all the CwG books that have followed. And that idea is very exciting to me. Yet, how do I see God in the terrible people of the world? How do I see God as speaking to, and *through,* the world's despots and the world's killers and the world's oppressors and the world's madmen?

Until you see God in the face of your enemy, you cannot see God at all. For, in truth, there is no such thing as an "enemy." There is only that part of you which is in contrast to another part of you. God doesn't exist for you if He exists for you only in the things and the people you like. God isn't real for you if She is experienced by you only in those things with which you agree.

The real master is the one who knows and understands that God exists in, as, and through all things. That God is absent from no one and nothing.

If that is true, how can some people act the way they act?

People act in ways that are not beneficial to themselves or others when they have forgotten Who They Are.

Why have they forgotten?

Because they have been *taught to,* because they have been *told to.* Your ancient cultural stories tell you of your separation from the Divine, and most modern societies repeat some version of that story to their offspring to this very day.

It is all part of the cycle of forgetting and remembering that is Life Itself. Remember, I have told you that you are moving in a circle, from the fullness of knowing to the emptiness of forgetfulness to the fullness of knowing again. From Oneness to Separation to Oneness again. From Total Consciousness to Unconsciousness to Total Consciousness again. This movement, this process, is the coming and the going, the appearing and the disappearing, the being and the nonbeing, and what you have called the living and the dying.

But what can we do when people act in ways that hurt us?

Remind them of Who They Really Are. But first, you must remember who *you* really are—and act like it.

When people hurt you, it is very often an opportunity for reconciliation. Very few people hurt other people intentionally without having what they consider a good reason. When someone has hurt you, you can do one of several things. You can (a) defend yourself, (b) attack back, or (c) find out what they thought their good reason was. Learn why they attacked you and seek reconciliation, mutual forgiveness, and collaboration on the reconstruction of your relationship.

I have told you in this and other writings, all attack is a call for help. When you know this, you begin at once to look deeply into the question of what kind of help is being called for. You might even ask directly. Try saying, "Please tell me . . . what hurts you so much that you feel you have to hurt me to heal it?"

It is not always the case, but it is most often the case, that when nation attacks nation, religion attacks religion, culture attacks culture, group attacks group, or person attacks person, the attacker feels that the one being attacked did something or is doing something to which a defensive response is required.

When you find out what it is that your attacker was imagining he had to defend himself against, you have gone a long way toward healing both you *and* the attacker.

Healing opens the door to recognition—that is, to re-cognition, or "knowing again" Who You Really Are.

You are One with the Divine, and so is your attacker. Your opportunity is to remind the attacker of that.

How do you remind a madman that he is God? Most of the time the problem is that *he already thinks that.*

When people think they are God, but act insanely, then they have not only forgotten who they are, they have also forgotten who God is.

Your opportunity then is to remind them of who and what God is, and see if they want to step into that.

I am going to remind *others* of who and what God is?

You may if you choose. This is the invitation of the New Spirituality. This can become the assignment of Humanity's Team.

And just exactly what are we supposed to say?

Love. Say that, in a word, God is Love.

And freedom.

In a word, God is freedom.

And joy.

In a word, God is joy.

And peace.

In a word, God is peace.

And unity.

In a word, God is unity.

These are the grandest aspects of God and Life, and when people are being anything other than these things, they have forgotten Who They Are in their grandest version. Your opportunity is to remind them.

You are all messengers, and you have only one message.

"I see you."

That is the only message you will ever need.

"I see you. I see the real you. I know you. I know the real you. I love you. I love the real you.

"You cannot fool me. I know you and I know who you are. You can act in any way that you wish, but I will not change my mind about you. I know who you really are.

"I see you, and I will always see. You cannot disappear, you cannot hide, you cannot change or lose your identity. You cannot be something you are not. You can *act* as if you are something you are not, but you cannot *be* something you are not.

"I will always see what you are being. I do not care

what you are doing, because what you are doing is not who you are. I will always see you at the level of being.

"I see you. I see who you are. Nothing that you do can blind me to that."

That is the only message you ever need to send to anyone. It will heal everything.

11

THE ROAD TO MASTERY

I'm sorry, but I'm still having trouble here. How do you send a message of love to someone who is killing you? How do you send that message to someone who is oppressing you? How do you tell someone that you see them as who they really are when they are not seeing *you* as who *you* really are?

By seeing yourself as Who You Really Are even when others are not. *Especially* when others are not.

All great masters have done this, and in doing so they have changed the world.

Is this not what the Buddha did? Is this not what Abraham did? Is this not what Jesus did, and what Muhammad did? For that matter, is this not what Gandhi did, what Mother Teresa did, what Martin Luther King did, what Joan of Arc did, and exactly what Nelson Mandela did on the day he was released from jail?

Look at the people who have changed the world. Is this not what they all have done?

Yes, yes, but I am not one of them! I am not on that level, I am not in that group.

You are when you place yourself there. No one excludes you from magnificence except you.

I can't do this! This is too much to ask of me!

If you think you have to do it alone, I can see why it might seem like too much to ask. Yet if you thought you had ten thousand others, or one *hundred* thousand others, or one *million* others, to change the world with you, then would it be too much to ask?

I don't know. Maybe not. I don't think so.

Then *form that team* you talked about. Form Humanity's Team. Get together with many, many others. For now your world would benefit from having more than one master, or two, working wonders here and there. The time of the individual master is over. The time has come for many masters to appear. The question is, are you ready now to move into mastery collectively? Do you still need to pretend that you do not know what masters know, that you do not understand what masters understand, that you cannot do what masters do?

If you still need to reside in this world of your self-pretending, there is little you can do to change your world, even collectively. For the process must be this:

Change yourself, change your world.

This process cannot be sidestepped or leapfrogged or circumvented in any way. First you must change yourself. Then—and only then—can you change your world.

I guess I just don't see myself in the "master" role. I know too much about myself. I could never put myself in the category of Jesus or Abraham or Muhammad.

Was it not Jesus who said, "Why are you so amazed? These things, and more, shall you do also?"

Yes, but I don't think that was meant as a personal reference to me.

Yet that is *exactly* how it was meant, and until you hear the message of Jesus in this way, you have not heard it at all.

Jesus, and all the great masters, called upon *each member of the human race* to move into mastery. Each of those masters promised that such a thing is possible. Indeed, this is the promise of God.

But what would that take? I don't think I have what that takes! Based on my past performance in life, I don't think I have the makings of a "master" of anything, except, maybe, a Master Messerupper.

"Past performance" has nothing to do with it. Yesterday has nothing to do with Who You Are. It has only to do with who you *thought* you were.

Here is a central tenet of the New Spirituality: the purpose—and the greatest opportunity and gift—of life is to *re-create yourself anew* in the next grandest version of the greatest vision you ever held about Who You Are. And you can do this in every single golden moment of Now.

The time of your transformation is at hand.

It is always at hand.

It is not a question of whether you "have what it takes," but of whether you *take what you have*—and then *use it.*

Take the gifts you *have*—they are plenteous—and share them with all the world. Apply them to the challenge at hand. Use them and give them in your life as if there's no tomorrow.

Cultivate the desire to do this. If you have the desire, you will have what it takes—precisely because *desire is what it takes.*

This reminds me of a story I heard about the student who came to his guru pleading, "Master, tell me what I must do to achieve mastery!" And the guru took the student to a small pond. "Look into the pond," he told the student. "Now tell me what you see."

"I see myself, Master," the student reported.

"Dunce!" the master rebuked. "Idiot!"

"Master, what have I done wrong? Why do you call me names?" the student cried.

"When you look at your reflection but do *not* see yourself, that is when you may *begin* the walk to mastery," the guru replied. "Otherwise, don't even think about it."

"But, Master," the student asked, "how can I not see myself? My image is there, right in front of me, clear as day. So when will I be ready to embark on this path?"

"Where do you see yourself?" inquired the guru.

"There," said the student, pointing into the pond at his reflection. "Right there."

"Look more closely," the guru ordered, and the student did so. "No, more closely than that," the guru directed, and the student leaned in and looked even closer. "No, no, no. Look deeply *into* the reflection . . . like *this,*" the guru commanded, and he reached over and shoved the student's face into the water.

There the student was held, with one powerful hand that belied the age of the guru. The student wiggled and waggled and writhed with increasing panic as each second passed, but the guru did not let up. Finally, the student summoned strength from a place he did not know existed, jerking upright out of the water with one gigantic, convulsive heave.

"Why did you *do that?*" he demanded of the guru after he'd caught his breath.

And the guru answered softly, "When you want to embark on the path to mastery as desperately as you wanted to get your face out of that water, that is when you will be ready to undertake the journey."

Yes, this is a story of desperate desire. It is an illustration of commitment.

Commitment?

The guru's student was committed to *life*. He was committed to *living*. He wanted to *continue to live*. And so he found a strength that he did not know he had, power that he did not know he possessed, and he stood upright. He had no intention of drowning.

When you, too, have no intention of drowning, then you, too, will stand upright. You will get your head out of the water—or the sand, as the case may be—and you will be ready to embark on the journey to mastery.

Still, even if I embark, it could take me years—*lifetimes*—to get there. What good will that do the world right now?

Every soul embarked on the journey to mastery begins by leaving ignorance behind. This, alone, is an enormous first step, with far-reaching consequences not only for that individual soul, but for all those whose lives that soul will touch. And, at some level, for all the world.

So beginning the journey is important in and of itself.

Profoundly so, for it increases the speed and raises the frequency of the vibration of the Life Energy. That shift affects and impacts the vibration of all the energy around it.

Is it possible to raise my individual vibration to the level where I can affect the Whole, the All in All, the Everything That Is?

You *are* affecting the All in All, right now. You can never *not* affect the All in All. You are affecting It because you are a part of It. What you do, It does. Especially that part of It that is in close proximity to you.

You cannot do a thing without affecting the All, because you *are* It, and It *is* you. Therefore, what you do affects It, immediately and profoundly.

Okay, I get it. This is why the world now needs many masters, or at least, many people willing to *begin the journey* to mastery. Because such an up-shift in the vibration of Life Energy can change the direction in which humanity itself is now heading.

Correct. And this is where you come in. You and all others who choose now to be on Humanity's Team. The moment has arrived for all of you to step into your own mastery. For I have placed you all on the earth to be good stewards, and the time for stewardship is at hand.

And the first thing of which you must be stewards is the Truth. You must be the ultimate stewards of the Truth of Your Being.

What does that mean?

To be a steward of the Truth of Your Being means to protect that truth, and never let it be lost or forgotten. It means to speak that truth, and never let it go unsaid, about you or anything or anyone. It means to live that truth, and never let it die for lack of your having given it life in, as, and through you.

Then you must be stewards of each other. You must

choose to care for each other and guard each other and protect each other and help each other and guide each other and *recognize each other.*

I have said to you before that to recognize means to *re-cognize.* That is, to "know again." And so, you must *know each other again.* For once you know each other again as Who You Really Are, all self-injury will end and all self-healing will begin.

At what level of consciousness does this "recognizing" occur?

This is an act of the subconscious, the superconscious, and the supraconscious working together. *It is beyond the conscious will.* It is about reaching a new level of consciousness. It is something that occurs automatically when you are being Who You Really Are. You will preserve Life. You will put Life first.

Then you will be stewards of your home, of your place in the universe. You will care for your home and protect your home and help your home help itself.

If living together in peace and joy and health and happiness and harmony is what you say you want, then these are things you must do to have that.

I thought you have taught, "There's nothing you have to do." You told me that in our very first conversation.

You do not *have* to do these things. In that sense, there is nothing you "must" do. You only "must" do them if these are things you wish to experience. That is because there is no other way to experience them.

There is no other way to create them. There is no other way to get from where you are to where you want to be.

All of this reduces itself to one word. Love. That is the new level of consciousness to which you are called. You are called to experience a level of consciousness in which you ARE that. You ARE Love.

Remember that the words "Love" and "God" are interchangeable. So, too, the words "Life" and "God." So, saying that you are Love is saying that you are Life, and that is saying that you are God.

This is a daring thing to utter, yet you are being called now to experience and to express God Consciousness. Are you up to this call? Can you hear it? And how shall you respond?

I say again, the Invitation to Stewardship is the Invitation to Love. For to be a steward is to care for something, and to love is to care for something, too. Therefore, love the truth. Love each other. Love your home, the earth. And love me. For if you love me, you will love all the rest . . . for I AM THAT, and there is nothing that I am not.

And do not worry about whether people believe that you are having an actual conversation with God or a conversation with yourself. You and I know that they are one and the same.

There is no God separate from you.

12

THE JESUS FACTOR

I know that there is no separation between God and me. When I am in my place of higher consciousness, I can even experience moments and glimpses of that.

And yet, sometimes, as a matter of psychological convenience, it seems to serve me to place God outside of myself, to imagine me as being "over here" and God as being "over there." In this way, I can talk to God, pray to God, discuss things with God, explore things with God, and ask God for help.

> **That *can* be a good device, and if it is, *use it.* This is the way in which the Little Self communes with the Big Self.**

My wonderful friend Barbara Marx Hubbard, an extraordinary author and spiritual teacher, refers to these aspects of Divinity as the Local Self and the Non-Local, or Universal, Self.

> **Yes, I inspired her to do that. When I speak as her**

and when she speaks as me, we do use that terminology, because it increases understanding.

Wait a minute. I just thought of something. If we are all You, how can any part of You not understand You?

Do you thoroughly understand yourself? Do you always understand everything you do, all the things you say, each of your motivations and agendas and intentions?

No, I don't.

You've just answered your own question.

I have a sense there's more to it than that.

There is. The very fact that you are an individuated part of me means that, by definition, you cannot possess the Totality of Understanding, Recollection, and Knowing that the non-individuated Ultimate Reality you call God possesses.

Why?

For the same reason that a drop of the ocean does not contain the power of the ocean, even though it is made of the same *stuff*. It is identical in its composition and its characteristics and its qualities, but it is not the Collective, it is the Individuation, and the Individuation and the Collective are not equal.

So God and I are *not* One.

You most definitely are.

But we cannot do the same things.

You most definitely can, but not on the same scale. Except when you do.

What can cause that?

Elevating and expanding your consciousness. "Coming from" your subconscious, your superconscious, and your supraconscious Self. In other words, the Big Self, the Non-Local Self, the Universal Self.

As all enlightened and sanctified beings do.

Yes, exactly.

As Jesus did!

Now you understand perfectly the relationship between God and man, as well as the Man Who Called Himself the Son of God.

A few years ago, after the first *Conversations with God* book was published, I was asked about Jesus, and where he "fits into" all this. I said that he, too, taught that God and we are One, but that no one wanted to believe it, because it did not serve the human agenda.

Yet if that agenda does not change, life as you know it will. That is the point being made here.

I understand. I also said that the impact of Jesus' life was so extraordinary, it will never be forgotten. That is because Jesus was—and is—a savior to all humankind. As I can be, and as every human being is invited to be.

You were correct in teaching this.

Human beings are living in a world of their own creation; an Illusion, a nontruth; an experience that has nothing to do with Ultimate Reality or with Who They Really Are, and I believe that Jesus knew this. He also knew Who He Really Was. So he declared it for all to hear.

He declared something else as well. He said that what he did on the earth, we could do also. Yet a high level of faith is the key to experiencing those gifts. That is what Jesus taught. That was his central message.

A few years ago I wrote a small booklet, *Recreating Your Self,* which addresses much of this.

That booklet contained many wonderful insights. You may wish to share some of those here.

Okay, I will. Because many of those who read this booklet said they got so much out of it, I will quote from it directly here:

It was Jesus himself who said, "According to your faith be it unto you."

It was Jesus himself who said, "O woman, great is thy faith: be it unto thee even as thou wilt." And the woman's daughter was made whole from that very hour.

And it was Jesus himself who said, "If ye have faith as a grain of mustard seed, ye shall say unto this mountain, Remove hence to yonder place; and it shall remove; and *nothing shall be impossible unto you."* (Italics mine.)

Still, if we cannot believe in ourselves and in our own divine heritage (and because so many people cannot), Jesus, in an act of enormous love and compassion, invites us to believe in him.

"Verily, verily I say unto you, He that believeth on me, *the works that I do shall he do also;* and *greater works than these shall he do;* because I go unto my Father. And whatsoever ye shall ask in my name, that will I do, that the Father may be glorified in the Son. If ye shall ask any thing in my name, I will do it." (Italics mine.)

Isn't that an extraordinary promise? So great and so complete was Jesus' understanding of who he was, and of who we are ("I and my Father are one," he said, and later, "all ye are brethren"), that he knew deeply there was no limit to what we could do if we believed in ourselves, *or in him.*

Could there be a mistake about Jesus' declarations here? Could there be a misinterpretation? No. His words are very clear. He wanted you to consider yourself One with the Father, exactly as he is One with God.

So great was his love for all humankind, and so full was his compassion for their suffering, that he called upon himself to rise to the highest level, to move to the grandest expression of his being, in order to present a living example to all human beings everywhere.

And then he prayed that we would not only see the evidence of *his* Oneness with the Father, but our *own* Oneness with God as well.

("And for their sakes I sanctify myself, that *they also might be sanctified* through the truth. Neither pray I for these alone, but for them also which shall believe on me through their word; *that they all may be one;* as thou, Father, art in me, and I in thee, *that they also may be one in us:* that the world may believe that thou hast sent me. *And the glory which thou gavest me I have given them; that they may be one, even as we are one."*) (Again, italics mine.)

Now, you can't be much clearer than that.

Conversations with God tells us that all of us are members of the Body of God, though we imagine ourselves to be separate, and not part of God at all.

Christ understood our difficulty in believing that we were part of God, part of God's very body. Yet Christ did believe this of himself. It was therefore a simple matter (and a marvelous inspiration) for him to invite those who could not imagine themselves to be a part of God to imagine themselves to be a part of *him.*

He knew that it would be easier for us to see ourselves as Brothers in Christ than as One with God. And since he had already declared himself to be One with the Father, if we could simply believe that we were a brother of Christ, we would, by extension, necessarily be One with the Father, and part of God, also.

Jesus must have emphasized this point many times, because the record of his teachings and the commentaries upon them in the Bible contain countless references to this relationship.

String together just a few of these separate references, and you have an extraordinary revelation:

"I and my Father are one (John 10:30). And the glory which Thou gavest me, I have given them; that they may be one, even as we are one (John 17:22). I in them, and Thou in me, that they may be made perfect in one (John 17:23). That the love wherewith Thou hast loved me may be in them, and I in them (John 17:26).

"So we, being many, are one body in Christ; and every one members one of another (Romans 12:5).

"Now he that planteth and he that watereth are one (1 Cor. 3:8). For we being many are one bread, and one body: for we are all partakers of that one bread." (1 Cor. 10:17).

"For as the body is one, and hath many members, and all the members of that one body, being many, are one body: so also is Christ. For by one Spirit are we all baptized into one body, whether we be Jews or Gentiles, whether we be bound or free; and have been all made to drink into one Spirit. For the body is not one member, but many. If the foot shall say, Because I am not the hand, I am not of the body; is it therefore not of the body? And if the ear shall say, Because I am not the eye, I am not of the body; is it therefore not of the body? (1 Cor. 12–16).

"But now are they many members, yet but one body (1 Cor. 12:20)."

These repeated references, stating over and over and *over again* the truth of our oneness, make it very clear that no movement away from presently held beliefs is necessary for Christians to embrace Tomorrow's God, or to explore the New Spirituality.

All of us are members of the Body of Christ. And if Christ is one with God, so too are we. We simply do not know it. Refuse to believe it. Cannot imagine it.

Yet it is not true that going with Jesus on the way to God requires us to be going *through* Jesus on the way to God. That was not his message. If Jesus could put his message in contemporary terms, in the words that we use today, speaking to people with today's greater sophistication and larger understanding, I believe he would say:

"I observe that you do not believe in yourself. You do not believe that humans are divine. Clearly, you could use an example of that. I will be the example. I am that.

"I and the Father are One. I am the Son of God, and you and I are siblings. That means you are the sons and daughters of God as well.

"I am the Life and the Way. Live your life as I live mine, go the way that I have gone—that is, *follow me*—and you will experience God. Yet if you cannot even believe in me, if you do not even believe that I am who I say I am, even with all that I have done, then you will never believe in yourself, who has done less, or in who you are, and your own experience of God will be virtually unattainable, for you do not believe in the possibility of Humanity being Divinity—and that is the truth I came to reveal to you."

> Therefore, belief in the Divinity of Christ—in Jesus as God made human—is *required* if you wish to believe in yourself as divine. For if you believe in yourself as divine, you necessarily believe in Jesus as divine, yet if you do not believe in Jesus as divine, you cannot believe in yourself as divine, lest you think yourself greater than Jesus.

But what if I do not want to think of myself as divine? What if I only want to think of Jesus as divine, and myself as a poor, humble, very *non*divine being, not worthy to hold Jesus' shoes?

> Then you will have missed the whole message that Jesus sought to bring you. For he came to exalt you, not to humble you. To raise you up, not to put you down.

And what if, on the other hand, I do not want to think of Jesus as divine? What if I just don't buy into this idea that Jesus was the Son of God?

> Then you will again have missed the whole message that Jesus sought to bring you. Jesus' message was that he is greater than none, nor is any one greater than any other, for You All Are One, and a thing cannot be superior to Itself.
>
> So if was he was not divine, then you are not divine. And if you are not divine, then how could he have been divine?

This is the argument used by all of those who deny the divinity of Jesus, of course. We are all just human, and he was no less human than the rest of us. We are not divine, so how could he have been? Unless he was a being from Another Realm, *pretending* to be human.

> You are ALL beings from Another Realm, *pretending to be human.*

Oh, boy, here we go.

> Yes, that's right, here we go.
>
> *This is the core of the New Spirituality.* Herein lies the mystery and wonder and the glory of Tomorrow's God. Herein lies the mystery and the wonder and the glory of *you.* All that is needed now is for you to know that, and to accept it.
>
> Jesus yearns for you to do so even now. So, too, do

all the masters and all the messengers. For all live today, even as they did then, in the days of what you call your past. And all the masters and all the messengers—Buddha, Abraham, Bahá'u'lláh, Jesus, Krishna, Moses, Muhammad, and all the others—love you today as they did then, and invite you today as they did then to accept and embrace the wonder and the glory of Who You Are, that you might end forever your suffering, and your infliction of suffering upon others.

Jesus said what he said, did what he did—performed miracles, healed the sick, raised the dead, even raised *himself* from the dead—that you might know Who He Was . . . and thus know also Who You Are.

It is this second part of the Jesus Encounter that is most often left out of the traditional teaching about Christ. And it is this second part of the equation that forms the basis of the New Spirituality.

The New Spirituality does not abandon traditional teachings, but expands them.

So we need merely to accept who Jesus is—that he is the Son of God—and then we can accept and experience our own Sonship. Often, what is hard for us to believe about ourselves, we can believe about another—and Jesus knew this.

You are now understanding Jesus' mission exactly. That is precisely what he knew, and why he chose to do what he did.

I see now that we have *all* come to save the world. Not from the "snares of the devil," or from "everlasting damnation." There is no such thing as the devil, and damnation does not exist. We have come to save the world *from its own mistaken notion of itself.*

That is correct. You now understand your *own* mission exactly.

We are the hope of humanity.

Indeed, you are. And this is the message of the New Spirituality which will emerge on the earth. Soon, many more people will understand this, and it will be their urgent plea to all humans:

BE THE HOPE OF HUMANITY.

13

FOUNDATIONS OF THE NEW SPIRITUALITY

That is the invitation of the New Spirituality.

Yes.

That is the invitation, and Oneness is the message.

It is the Foundational Truth of the New Spirituality.

I am getting that, because we keep going back to that over and over again.

You have no idea how important this is. It is worth an entire book, not just half of one. Everything would change if this one idea was "gotten," if this one thought resided in your subconscious and became your natural instinct, if this one concept became your operating philosophy, and the operating philosophy of your species.

Everything would change. *Everything.* Politics would

change, economics would change, careers would change, your ideas about relationships and sexuality and conflict resolution and the purpose of all of Life—*everything*—would change.

So this is not a small thing, it is not a say-it-once-and-brush-it-aside thing, it is a *big* thing, worth repeating over and over again, worthy of coming back to time and time again.

Teach *this*. Teach *this*. All else will fall into place.

Here are four words to memorize:

We are all One.

Model *that* when you make your next choices and decisions. Model *that* when you make your next moves and plan your next strategies. Model *that* when you set your earnings goals, establish your employee salary scales, make up the sticker price for the product or service you sell.

Model *that* when you go into the War Room or the Boardroom or the Bedroom. Model *that* when you enter the mosque or synagogue or cathedral or temple.

Model *that* when you live your life, in every moment of your life, and you will teach everything there is to teach about the New Spirituality and Tomorrow's God.

I've got it. I truly do. Oneness and the unity of all Life is a foundational principle of the New Spirituality, and the application of that principle to everyday life is its guiding ethic. I've got it.

Are there any other really basic principles that I should know about?

Needlessness.

Needlessness?

In the days of the New Spirituality you will come to conceive of Tomorrow's God as needless.

In fact, that is the Seventh Important Difference between Yesterday's God and Tomorrow's God.

7. Tomorrow's God is needless.

Now be careful of that word, because I mean it two ways. Be sure that you see both.

First, I mean that you will experience God as being without any needs at all. Therefore, God will be needless.

Second, I mean that you will experience that you do not need God. In the times of the New Spirituality you will not conceive of yourself as needy beings, having to pray to an almighty Deity for succor and for favors. Therefore, God will be needless.

In *Communion with God* you said that the Illusion of Need was the first of the Ten Illusions of Humans.

That's right, and it is. It is the illusion upon which all other illusions are based. It is a very powerful illusion, and when you step back from it and see it as the illusion that it is, you begin to live a whole new way; you step into a new world.

Imagine a world in which God needed nothing, and you did not need God. Imagine a world in which you could truly say that you feel you need nothing.

This is a hard one for me. This is difficult to grasp, to make real. I can understand that God needs nothing, but I can't understand how it could be true that I need nothing. And I certainly feel that I need God. I am having this conversation with you right now because I need answers.

Okay, one thing at a time here. Let's go over this one step at a time. You can understand that God needs nothing?

Yes, of course. God is the Supreme Being, Creator of Heaven and Earth. What could God possibly need?

How about your allegiance? How about your loyalty? Or how about your obedience? If you don't give me that, I'll be sad. Maybe even angry, depending on how badly you disobey.

Well, there is that.

And how about suffering. Do I not need you to suffer?

Of course not.

Oh, then it is okay to end your own life if you have a terminal illness from which you are suffering unceasingly?

No, no, no, wait a minute, I didn't say that.

Then, it's not okay?

No.

Why not?

Because ending your life at your own hand is not part of God's plan. God decides when you are to die, not you. Life is God's greatest gift. He gives it and only He can take it away. It is not up to you to throw it back in His face!

I see. So God becomes angry if you throw His gift back in His face?

I don't know whether God gets angry, or what, but it's just not right, that's all.

Is it more "right" for an eighty-seven-year-old woman to suffer horribly and endlessly from a disease eating away at her body than for her to allow herself to slip out of the anguishing pain and declare her life gratefully and wonderfully over?

Yes! It is more "right" for her to suffer. That's God's Law. Suffer interminably until you die naturally. *You shall not take your own life.* That's not only God's Law, that's the Law of the Land in many places. I mean, doctor-assisted suicide is against the law.

More civil law based on God's needs, eh?

I didn't say that God *needed* it this way. This is just the way it *is.* It's God's *Law.*

Why would God have to have a Law like that? Or a law about anything, for that matter?

Because some things are Right and some things are Wrong. It's just that simple.

But what does God care, if God doesn't need anything? I thought you said you could understand that God needs nothing. But if God needs nothing, then why does He need you to obey His Law?

He doesn't. He doesn't *need* us to, He just *wants* us to.

And if He doesn't get what He wants, He gets angry and punishes you, right?

Right.

Sounds pretty much like "need" to me.

Say, are you making fun of me here?

No. Are you making fun of *me*?

No, I am not. There is nothing funny about this. We're talking about Heaven, Hell, and everlasting damnation here. You want to make a mockery of that, go right ahead.

You are doing a good job here, you know that? That is just the way many people think. You said earlier that you were going to speak rhetorically in this dialogue, voicing the questions and comments of the whole human race. Good job.

Thank you. So I guess what is true is that most people think of God in two ways—as having no needs, and as having many. We have kind of a Dichotomous God. He requires nothing, really, on the one hand, and on the other, He requires everything.

Yes, these are the two faces of Yesterday's God. Tomorrow's God will not be nearly so difficult to understand. Tomorrow's God will not have such a split personality.

Tomorrow's God will simply say, "I require nothing of you. You may do as you wish. I give you Free Will." And Tomorrow's God will mean it. She will not say, "You have Free Will, unless, of course, you do not do as I require, in which case I will punish you forever." What kind of Free Will is that? You're free to do *what I want you to do?*

Would *you* call that freedom?

No.

Your church does.

I know. But in a way, it could be argued that we *are* free. I mean, just as we're free to step out into traffic against a red light. We're free to do that, if we don't care about the consequences. If we're willing to pay the consequences, we're free to do anything.

Well, there's some good logic for you. You're free to vote, but if you don't vote for me, I'll have you shot. You're free to own your own business, but if you don't give me most of the profits, I'll have you fined and put

out of business. You're free to speak, but if you say anything I don't like, I'll have you thrown into prison. No problem here. You have Free Will, right?

You know, in the world in which you live, you call that kind of freedom a mockery. You call it a dictatorship.

Well, it is.

So the Kingdom of God is a dictatorship?

I didn't say that.

Why don't we just agree that most of the human race does think of God as a dictator? A benevolent dictator, perhaps, but a dictator nonetheless. People imagine that there is something God has to have in order to be happy, don't they? Now, be honest.

Yes, yes, okay, most people think that.

Good. Now you're being honest. And I'm glad, because if you hadn't been honest, I would have to have punished you.

That's funny. That's cute. Let's move on.

Now, you said that where you really had a hard time was imagining *yourself* as needing nothing.

That's right.

So what I want you to know is that the reason I have been making such a point about your idea about

God being needy is that this thought about God forms the basis of your thought about yourself.

The reason you cannot imagine *yourself* needing nothing is that you can't even imagine God needing nothing. And if even *God* has needs, how can you not?

Do you see the trap you've gotten yourself into?

I didn't before, but I do now.

Good. Because what I'm trying to show you here is that your *many* ideas about God form your many ideas about yourself. Or maybe it is the other way around. Maybe your ideas about *yourself* have formed your ideas about *God*.

Do you think this is possible?

Well, I guess so. I mean, I don't know. I hadn't thought about it that way.

Well, think about it. Don't you see God pretty much as a "big You"? I mean, a bigger version of humans?

I was struck by that when you said it earlier, and here we are circling back to it again.

Well, I want to make a point that I don't want you to forget, so I'm repeating it here. Don't you see God pretty much as a bigger version of you?

I suppose so, yes. Some people do, anyway.

Most people, actually. Most people think of God as a bigger, more powerful version of humans.

Well, the Bible does say that we were made in the Image and Likeness of God.

And the Bible is *right about that.*

Then you *are* just a bigger version of us.

No. *You* are just a smaller version of *me*.

Okay, same thing.

Decidedly not, my friend. Decidedly not.

14

LIFE'S SECRET FORMULA

If the Bible is right in saying that I am made in the image and likeness of God, then you would look like a human being, right?

Right.

So, okay. So that's that.

When I want to.

What?

When I want to look like a human being, I would look like a human being. When I want to look like a shooting star, I would look like a shooting star.

Here we go again.

Well, you just can't get away from it. The truth will follow you around and find you wherever you are. Especially if you're looking for it.

The point: the statement that you are made in the image and likeness of God does not mean that God is like *you,* but that *you* are like *God.*

Do you understand that?

Well, I thought I did.

Really? Do you understand the implications of that?

Why don't you tell me what they are?

If you are like *me,* that means that you are not a being, not a physical form, at all, but can *take the form* of a physical being whenever you wish. It also means that you can take whatever *other* form you wish, whenever you wish. (This, by the way, you have done.)

It means that you are Pure Energy, with the power of Creation, expressing as a source of Infinite Wisdom and Unconditional Love.

It means that you are not your body, but the Essence that surrounds your body and creates it. It means that you are Life Itself, manifesting in a particular way at a particular time because it pleases you to do so.

Well, I've got news. It is not always pleasing to be human.

Indeed, for many of you it is displeasing much of the time. That is because you have forgotten Who You Are. You imagine you are separate from me, separate from Life, and separate from each other. This imagining brings you the experience. And the experience of separation—an illusion—is the only thing that can bring you the experience of lack, or insufficiency—another illusion. One illusion produces another, and this is the source of your displeasure, this is the source of your unhappiness, this is the source of your despair.

What is the solution here? Assuming this all *is* an Illusion, how do we deal with it? How do we function within this illusory world and still find peace, harmony, and happiness? What is the "secret formula"?

Ah, now you are asking the fundamental question.

And the answer?

I can give it to you in one word.

Don't let me stop you.

Service.

Service?

Service to Life Itself.

When you serve Life, Life serves you. That is because you and Life are one, and service to Life *is* service to you.

This is why God's job is to serve you.

No, no, you don't understand. It's the other way around. *Our* job is to serve *God.*

It is you who do not understand. Your job is not to serve God, because God needs nothing from you. You thought that Yesterday's God did, but Tomorrow's God will not.

We will not have to serve Tomorrow's God?

No, you will not have to. It will not be a requirement. In fact, Tomorrow's God will serve you. It is the function of God to do so. In fact, that is the Eighth Important Difference between Yesterday's God and Tomorrow's God.

8. Tomorrow's God does not ask to be served, but is the Servant of all of Life.

Whoa, wait a minute. God is the *Master,* not the "servant." *We* are the servants, and it is ours to grovel at the Master's feet.

I tell you this: a true Master is not the one who creates the most servants, but the one who creates the most masters.

It is my joy to demonstrate to you that *you* are all masters. I do not need you to demonstrate to *me* that this is what *I* am. I already know what I am. It is you who have forgotten.

I, therefore, place my Self at your service, that you might remember. And when you place yourself at my service, you demonstrate your own mastery.

I thought you just said that we would not have to serve you.

I did, and you will not. Serving God will no longer be a requirement on the blessed day that you embrace

Tomorrow's God. Yet when you *do* serve God through your own free will, in that moment you demonstrate that you need nothing, that you have everything, and that it is your great joy to give to God all that you have—and *this is the definition of a Master.*

Now, substitute the word "Life" for the word "God" in the above sentence, and you will have uncovered a secret formula for finding (indeed, *creating)* peace, harmony, and happiness upon the earth.

Serve Life first, in everything you think and say and do. Ask yourself, "Is this thought life-enhancing or life-depleting? Is this word life-enriching or life-detracting? Is this action life-supporting or life-damaging?"

These questions, and the answers you give to them, become part of an automatic process, a process that you don't even have to think about, when your intention is to preserve Life as you know it on your planet. For when that is your intention, you will always preserve it.

Yet you cannot serve Life first if you think that you, individually, lack something. You will always be serving your needs, seeking to have them met, before you can do that which serves Life. On the other hand, if you know that you *are* Life, then you will see immediately that serving Life means serving your Self.

This is the beginning way of all masters.

Mahatma Gandhi, Mother Teresa . . .

Yes.

Martin Luther King . . .

Yes.

And you.

Me? No, I would not put myself in that category.

That's the problem, right there.

I know, I know. But I just can't imagine myself at their level. You are talking about great human beings here. These are people who changed the world.

Thank goodness their view of themselves was not as limited as yours.

Yes, thank goodness. Yet if I wanted to think of myself in a new way, how could I do that?

By *not* thinking of yourself at all, but by thinking only of your Self.

What is that supposed to mean?

It is supposed to mean that when you think of "yourself," you are thinking of the Little Self, but when you think of "your Self," you are thinking of the Big Self.

When you think of the Big Self—

—what Barbara Marx Hubbard calls the Non-Local You—

—you automatically play a bigger game, go for higher stakes, seek a grander goal than is held in the limited vision of the Little Self.

You begin seeing what is "best for others" as what is "best for you," because you know that you *are* those others; you are part of them, you are one with them.

You are now understanding.

There are many kinds of service, and your soul knows when it is doing what is best for you, and what is best for others. And when these two notions conflict, your soul knows how it feels to do what is best for others even though it is not your idea of what is best for you.

That feeling is the feeling of bigness. You suddenly feel bigger somehow, larger. It's a feeling of inner expansiveness. Some call it "selflessness."

It's when you've lost your sense of Self as the Little One and adopted a sense of Self as larger than that, bigger than that. You've become the Big Self. Sometimes for only a moment, sometimes for a longer period, sometimes for a lifetime. But the experience is something you never forget.

That's my biggest challenge in life. I always see my own personal agenda first. I always seem to serve the Little Self first. And I always want other people to serve it first, too. It seems to me that I do things for other people only when I see that it serves me. If it does not serve me at some level, I'm not there for them. I've lost a lot of important relationships because of that.

How does that feel?

Terrible. It feels terrible.

So you haven't been serving your own agenda after all, then, have you? You haven't served yourself at all.

No. Not if my agenda is to be happy, I haven't. How can I stop this? How can I let go of this behavior?

You've recognized it, that's the first step.

It doesn't seem like a very big first step.

It IS. Seeing one's own unwanted behaviors and claiming them, declaring them, owning them, is a *huge* first step. It is a step many, many people never take. It's too painful.

And now you're sharing your painful experience with the world, through this dialogue, and others will see themselves there as well. And they, too, will move closer to healing. *Don't you see how this all works?*

You're here to *wake each other up.*

I have already said to you . . . Others see their possibility in the reality of you. Be, therefore, a model to all the world.

You have stood as that for millions. You have laid your life open, you have been transparent. You have allowed your frailties and your foibles to be known by everyone. And your magnificence, too. Through your example, others are healed. Through the sharing of your pain, others are relieved of theirs. Through your experience, others have hope.

This is how *everyone* can help *everyone.* All you have to do is tell the truth to each other about yourselves.

That's what my friend Brad Blanton says. He wrote a wonderful book called *Radical Honesty.* He believes in what you're saying here, right down to the letter.

> Truth is a form of service, don't you see that? It is one of many forms of service one can enter into daily.
>
> And through blessed service you will discover that you never needed anything, and that lack was all an illusion.
>
> When you *give away* that which you thought you lacked—love, compassion, companionship, money, anything—you suddenly experience that you had it to give all along. This changes everything. This turns your thinking completely around, allowing you to see that you *have* what you thought you lacked.
>
> You *have it.* You *have it.* Now all you need to do is multiply it. *It's impossible to multiply something you do not have.* But now that you know you *have it,* you can expand that experience easily.
>
> But remember, the experience ultimately has nothing to do with quantity. If you have a dollar and you give a quarter, it is as much as if you give a quarter million when you have a million. You cannot quantify *beingness.* You are either being Giving, or you are not. You are either being Loving, or you are not. "Givingness" cannot be quantified. Neither can love.
>
> You cannot love one person "a lot" and another person "a little." You either love or you do not. *How you demonstrate your love* is another matter. Love

may be demonstrated in many ways, but if it is love, it knows no condition, least of all the condition of quantifiability.

So, if I enter even more fully into service, my life will work more of the time?

Your life is working all of the time right now. You simply *say* it is not working in the moments that it is not bringing you what you want.

Well, isn't that a pretty good definition of "life not working"?

No, it's a horrible definition. Your life is *always* working, whether you know it or not. Sometimes it works to bring you what you want, and sometimes it works to keep you from what you *think* you want, until you can mature and grow and see that it isn't what would have brought you the highest and best, that it wasn't your next most beneficial step.

This is hard to swallow, you know that? You're standing there now trying to tell me that a family starving to death in some far-flung place where nobody can seem to get any food, or a child being raped by her father in a moment of unspeakable cruelty, is life *working?*

I know. I know. When you try to apply what appear to be simplistic explanations to complex life situations, the explanations seem to fall apart.

Seem to? Uh, excuse me . . . they *do.*

You cannot know the agenda of the soul. You can only know the *apparent* agenda of the body. You cannot even be absolutely certain about *that,* but you can make some educated guesses.

Yeah, I would say so. For instance, it's a pretty solid bet that everybody wants to stay alive, and that nobody wants to be hurt, or injured or damaged in any way.

That is a safe assumption a lot of the time. It is the survival instinct at its most basic level. But there are other levels at which the Essence of Who You Are survives—and other reasons, too.

Remember that I've told you, you are not your body. You said that every *body* wants to stay alive, and that no *body* wants to be hurt and that is correct. Yet, your physical body is the most primitive, basic expression of the Life Form that is You. At another level of expression, the Life Form that is You may have a different agenda. You do not know. Unless you do.

Some human beings are very deeply in touch with the Totality of Who They Are all of the time. Some are in touch part of the time. Some are in touch once in a while, and some are in touch not at all.

When you are in touch with the Totality and the Essence of Who You Are, everything looks different. Suddenly, what seemed important is not important. What appeared to be crucial becomes trivial. What mattered, no longer matters at all.

Like being physically assaulted, or dying of starvation?

Or crucified on a cross?

No fair. None of us are gods here.

Correction. All of you are gods here. Has it not been written, "Ye are Gods"?

15

IS GOD NEEDLESS?

Of course, I have heard that before.

I tell you, needlessness is the State of Being in which God resides. God needs nothing. You, also, need nothing, but you do not know this. So you are constantly going around trying to have your needs met. Once you reach mastery, however, you realize that there was nothing you had to do. Your needs were always met.

In fact, you did not *have any* needs. You were making it all up.

People move in and out of mastery around this all the time. They understand it one moment, fail to understand it the next.

Needlessness is not a quality of personal being that you think about. It is something that you *know about yourself* at the deepest part of your being. When you come from that knowing, you can do extraordinary things.

A woman jumps into the pool to save a drowning toddler even though she, herself, cannot swim—not because she *thinks about it,* but precisely because she *does not.*

In that moment the woman knows. She *knows all about herself, and that she needs nothing.* She does not even need her own life. She does not even think about it. She simply jumps into the pool. She sees the toddler falling in, and she doesn't think. She jumps. She reaches the baby, pushes it above her head, someone takes the child, then the woman has to call for help to get herself out of the pool.

She makes it and she's all right, and when someone asks her how she thought she could possibly save the child when she can't even swim, she says, "I wasn't thinking. I just knew what I had to do and I did it."

This is Instinct, overlaid with Story. It is your Cultural Story, playing itself out as action in moment-to-moment life.

The Basic Instinct is survival—that is, Life—and your Cultural Story tells you what you have to do to preserve Life. Not even your own. It is Life outside you that you will seek to preserve. Something inside you, something at the cellular level, tells you that Life inside you is not the issue. So it is that the mother bear fights off the hungry tiger to save her cub. It is instinct. It is about the survival of your species.

This is the instinct you have been ignoring. The survival strategy of human beings is killing you. You are being destroyed by your own Cultural Story. What you hold in your subconscious is a series of messages that have been placed there when you were very young. The placers of the Story were the tellers of the Story—namely, the elders and the caretakers in your community of origin. And the first thing they told you was that you need something. You need something to be happy, you need something to be acceptable, you need something to be successful in the world.

You need something.

That is the message of your culture.

Your media reinforces it at every turn. Even your present religions, from which you hope to receive the highest wisdom, tell you this. They tell you that you need God. And God needs *you* to behave in certain ways.

What humanity would benefit from right now is a new Cultural Story. That is what the New Spirituality is all about. That is what Tomorrow's God has to share.

This sharing will occur in many ways, across many moments, in many lands, offered by many people. It will be part of the work of those people who have chosen to join together to work as one for the healing of humanity's collective consciousness.

Well, we've said a lot about this here now, but I have to tell you that the idea of a God who needs nothing, or a Deity who is not needed by *us* for anything, is going to be pretty hard for most people to embrace. Either meaning is deeply confrontational. "God will be needless?" Wow. Tough one.

I know. Your present theological construction of a God who has needs that must be met is the basis of your entire belief system. And your present conceptualization of yourselves as helpless, needy beings depending upon a needy God deeply reinforces it. This is a recipe for dysfunction in any relationship. It is no wonder that humanity's relationship with God is barely functional.

Humanity's relationship with God is becoming less functional every day as people try to apply the concept of a God who needs something to their lives and begin using jetliners turned into missiles, and smart bombs, as tools with which to do it.

Remember, Life is obedient to Three Basic Principles. Life is functional, adaptable, and sustainable. When it moves toward the edge of functionality—when it cannot function much longer the way it is going—it adapts. Life on earth is about to adapt. It cannot go on like it is. Something is going to have to change, and it will. Life will not let Life down. *It will adapt.*

Often it has been said here, now, and often it should be said everywhere around the world: This adaptation could take the form of Life changing dramatically from the way you have known it on your planet, with your civilization's best days behind it (things are already moving in that direction), or it could take the form of the *complete transformation* of your planet, with its people living together in a new way, retaining the best of yesterday and wrapping it in the highest hopes for tomorrow—in which case your civilization's best days will lie ahead.

So we have no choice but to accept this idea of a needless God? This is the theology of the future? This is the nature of Tomorrow's God?

You always have a choice. If you observe that your present theology works, that it is functional, that it is producing peace on earth, goodwill to humans, then change nothing. Do not even think about change. Why change when everything is going so well?

But if you observe that all the religious instruction from all the world's great religions through all the years has done little to move humanity from the brink of self-annihilation, then you may wish to, at the very least, entertain the *possibility* that there is more to know here about God and about Life.

There is no requirement that you "accept this idea" of a needless God, but can you at least look at it? Are you willing to explore it? Can you open your mind to the possibility that this might be, at minimum, worth examining more closely?

Because the problem with your world today is that too many human minds are closed. You imagine yourselves to know everything there is to know on the subject of God.

You are willing to continue exploring other things. You are willing to explore new developments in science, you are willing to explore new procedures in medicine, you are willing to explore new theories in economics, you are willing to explore new approaches in education, you are willing to explore new frontiers in outer space, you are willing to explore new avenues in psychiatry and psychology and physiology, but many of you—most of you—are unwilling to explore any new ideas at all in your theology.

That is blasphemy, you say. That is apostasy. That is unallowable. And, in some cases, that is punishable by death.

Yet now, here, I bring you an invitation to both explore and experience a New Spirituality—and then to work with others to create the space of possibility for that New Spirituality to emerge across the globe.

Okay, so let's keep exploring. What is another Foundational Truth of this New Spirituality?

Unconditionality.

Is that even a word?

It is now.

Right.

It is a state of being having no condition at all.

I don't understand.

Life IS. It simply IS. There are no conditions to that. There are no conditions under which Life "is not."

I don't know. There are some people who would say that when you are *dead,* life "is not."

They would be wrong.

The condition you call "death" is not death at all, but Life in another form.

Yes, I know. I understand this larger truth. You have shared it many times before. All of the world's great religions agree on this.

So, *Life exists,* without any conditions.

That means that God exists without any conditions.

That means that Love exists without any conditions.

Remember that the words "God," "Life," and "Love" are interchangeable. All three are one, and this is a Holy Trinity.

True love is unconditional. Love that places conditions is not love at all, but a counterfeit version of it. Real love, like the real God and like real life, knows no conditions.

Conditional Love is an oxymoron.

Because this is true, the idea of a God who places conditions on the receiving of his love is unworkable. It is a contradiction in terms. Yet this is the idea you have had about Yesterday's God, requiring you to try with all your might to get close to a God of whom you are deeply afraid.

Love and fear are mutually exclusive. Because they

cannot exist simultaneously in the same space, humans have had a massively conflicted relationship with Yesterday's God.

It is not insignificant that the single most oft-given instruction of virtually every spiritual teacher is "Fear not."

There is nothing to fear from God, because God wants nothing from you. Nothing.

Here we go again. This is so hard, so *very* hard, to accept.

Yes, I know, because you have been taught of Yesterday's God, who needs so much, and, worse yet, does not have the ability to meet His needs by Himself, and so must make demands on you. And you have been taught that if you do not meet these demands, God will judge you, condemn you, and punish you. I know, I know.

I know all about that.

And this brings us to the Ninth Important Difference between Yesterday's God and Tomorrow's God.

9. Tomorrow's God is unconditionally loving, nonjudgmental, noncondemning, and nonpunishing.

Don't I wish *that* were true.

It is true.

It seems too *good* to be true.

Let me see if I understand this. You think God is too good to be true?

The God you describe very well may be, yes. Tomorrow's God very well may be, yes. Many of us want to believe in a God who *does* judge, who *does* condemn, who *does* punish. We want to believe in Judgment Day. We want to know there is a Last Judgment.

Then you're in luck. Tomorrow's God says there IS a Judgment Day. There IS a Last Judgment.

Oh, good. That makes me feel better.

EVERY day is Judgment Day. Every moment is the Last Judgment.

Hold it. What are you talking about?

Everything you think, say, and do announces your judgment about yourself.

I have told you: *Every act is an act of self-definition.*

Okay, I get where you're going. Matthew Fox, an Episcopalian priest, in his book *The Physics of Angels* (with biologist Rupert Sheldrake), says it was Hildegard of Bingen, a twelfth-century German abbess and mystic, who observed that "every creative act is a last judgment because you don't get to redo it. It's a one and only choice."

In this, Hildegard "melts down the dualism between this life and the next, and between heaven and hell and earth," Fox asserts. "She is saying, in effect, that our choices bring about hell on earth or heaven on earth."

Hildegard was profoundly correct.

But there is no Judgment Day after death?

There is no DEATH, so how can there be a Judgment Day after it? *Life never ends.* Everything you think about yourself manifests in your reality, in this lifetime or in the next. Everything you say and everything you do creates Who You Are.

That was the point of producer Stephen Simon's wonderful, precedent-making movie, *What Dreams May Come.*

Yes, it was. He was very brave to make such a movie. It violated all the thoughts that most of your society holds about hell and damnation.

Those are thoughts that many more people can accept. Yesterday's God, humans can deal with. We know where we are with Him. We do good, we have good done to us. We mess up, we get messed up. Simple stuff. Easy to understand.

Yet what does it look like to "do good"?

Is it "doing good" or "messing up" to eat meat on Friday? Is it "doing good" or "messing up" to eat pork on any day? Is it "doing good" or "messing up" to eat anything at all from dawn to dusk during the holy month of Ramadan?

Is it "doing good" or "messing up" if you are a female and pray aloud at Judaism's most sacred spot, the Kotel, or Western Wall?

What says the Halakhah about this? What says the Bible? What says the Shari'a?

What says *God* about all this?

It depends on whose God you're listening to.

Or *when* you're listening. Yesterday's God says one thing about all of this, Tomorrow's God says another.

But the so-called New Spirituality or Tomorrow's God leaves so many questions unanswered. *Yesterday's God answered all our questions.* That was the beauty of Him. Now it's true, He answered them differently for different people, but at least He answered them. Tomorrow's God seems to leave us with more questions than answers.

That is good. Questions are better than answers.

I don't know, I guess I just wanted to believe in a God who knows everything. You know, the Source of All Wisdom, that sort of thing.

Wisdom is not having all the right answers, it is having all the right questions.

Even for God?

Even for God.

How can that be? I thought that God was "the Source." Yet, if God is the Source, how can He not have all the answers?

God is the Source of all that is creative. Answers are not creative. As soon as you think you have an answer, you stop creating. *Answers kill creation.*

The last thing you want is the final answer to

anything. A "possible answer," maybe. An "interim answer," perhaps. But a "final answer"? Never.

Ultimately, there is only one question in life. That question is, "Who am I?" It is a question to which you *never want a final answer.*

Stay within the question. Remain always with the inquiry. For within the inquiry is the power and the motivation and the passion to create. And creation is the glory of God, made manifest over and over again in ever new and never-final ways, through the process called Life Itself.

So you are saying that what the world would most benefit from right now is a spirituality that announces that *it does not have all the answers.* A spirituality that says, "Let us continue to ask Life's greatest questions, and to always honor that process of sincere inquiry, and the paths on which it takes each of us. Let us announce that there is no One Right Path, but that many paths can lead us to the mountaintop."

Yes! And let us declare that once we get to the mountaintop, *there will always be new mountains to climb.*

Let us happily observe that the top of one mountain is the bottom of the next—and that the mountains never end. Let us rejoice in the awareness that they reach to infinity.

This rejoicing in the infinite nature of your Being, without hesitation or condemnation of another, is what will transform religion, and your world, forever.

That is the kind of spirituality I have been talking

about here. That is the kind of spirituality I am proposing. And this change in humanity's spiritual expression *will occur.* It is not a question of whether, but of when. When will it occur, and who will bring it about?

You've asked this question about six times now.

Indulge me.

Will it occur after humanity moves closer still to the brink of self-annihilation, when there is precious little left of your present way of life to save and you have to spend generations to dig your way out of the pit into which you have thrown yourself? Or will it happen before you get to that place of sheer and utter desperation, while you still have a chance to keep in place so much of what is good and wonderful about life on earth?

Okay, so now you've asked it *seven* times.

And I am asking YOU to ask it seven *thousand* times. I am asking you to ask it seven *million* times. I am asking you to ask it over and over and over again *until someone hears you, until someone listens.*

Because now the question is urgent. Life cannot wait much longer for a response. Soon, it will be forced to provide a response of its own.

The "System" will correct itself if we do not.

You can bet your life on it. In fact, you are doing so.

16

THE END OF THE SINGLE SOURCE

All right, okay. We see that Oneness and Needlessness and Unconditionality are some of the Foundational Truths of the New Spirituality. I know there are more, so what are they?

I'm not going to tell you.

I beg your pardon?

I said, I'm not going to tell you. Not here.

Why not?

Because if I put all of them here, you would turn this book into your bible.

I would not.

Well, some people would turn it into theirs, believe me.

Yes, I understand the problem.

So we're going to avoid that by not putting everything into one book or setting you up as the only single source.

The truth is that the Single Source lies within each person. *That* is another Foundational Truth of the New Spirituality, and it is the last that we will discuss in detail here. Anyone who wishes to know more of the foundational truths may do so by going deeply within.

Search within, ask within, inquire within, seek within, *go* within—for if you do not go within, you go without. You go without answers that satisfy you, you go without peace that remains with you, you go without joy that emanates from you, you go without love that becomes you.

Love does become you—it makes you look very wonderful, indeed—and it *turns into* You while it turns You into *it*. That is what Love does. It is transformative. It turns everything inside out. Yet it, like wisdom, must come from within you—*each of you*—for the experience to be *personal* and *lasting*.

So now, if you wish to know more about the New Spirituality, it is time to go within. Meditate. Cogitate. Ruminate. Review what you have received here, and ponder these things in your heart.

But what if people genuinely wish to expand their awareness and uplift their consciousness using the tools of their exterior world? Can they not do that? Is it not a "legitimate" process or practice to reach outward to see what others are experiencing, and what they have to say of their experience?

Of course it is. As long as outward reaching does not turn into outward *placing*.

Help me with that.

If you reach outward to collect what your world has to offer as you search for your inner truth about God and about Life, you will receive the information that you seek. It will practically fall into your lap. As I suspect this very book did.

If, on the other hand, you place outside of yourself all authority in these matters, you will turn what you find outside of yourself into what can only be found inside of yourself—your Holy Source.

Remember this always. Your Holy Source lies in one place, and one place only: within You.

Yet there are some wonderful helpers in our outside world—"angels," you would call them—who, if I understand the cosmology of this New Spirituality correctly, have come to us to assist us in our inward seeking by sharing the fruits of their own search.

Yes, and *all of you* are these angels, each of you assigned the task of waking each other up, of reminding each other of Who You Really Are, and of sharing with each other your own experience and process as authentically and transparently as you can.

Because we never know when something we say or do will

turn on the Light inside of another, showing them to themselves, opening them to their next deepest wisdom, and giving them back to themselves.

Exactly! You've *got it* now!

So we're not going to put it all down in one book, or give it all to one person and have it all emanate from one source, but rather we're going to let Life source Life with the secrets of Life through the process of Life Itself.

We will tell everyone to simply look around and see what Life brings them as their next exterior experience leading to greater wisdom from within. And the willingness to engage in that process will be the test of anyone's real commitment to creating the space for a New Spirituality to emerge upon the earth.

Anyone who thought it was going to all be found—that anything and everything there is to say on this subject would all be contained—on the pages of one book is still caught up in old paradigm thinking.

It was *Yesterday's God* whose total message was said to be found in one book, in a single sacred text. Those who know of Tomorrow's God would never make such a claim.

Indeed, that is the claim that made Yesterday's God so dangerous. Because if you did not embrace one specific doctrine, brought forth by one individual source, recorded in one sacred book, you were not part of the "community of believers" and were disapproved of, derided, shunned, outcast, condemned, oppressed, attacked, and killed.

Tomorrow's God will make no such claim of singularity of source, and the concepts of the New Spirituality will contain no such doctrine of exclusivity.

The New Spirituality is an open system, not a closed one, ever growing, ever expanding, ever *becoming* what it is next going to be, sourcing itself from Life Itself, and the cumulative experience of those living it.

We are not talking here of a single doctrine, spelled out in a single document, but of an *experience*, shared by many in a multitude of books and records and personal accounts of that collective experience.

So the New Spirituality is not just a turning of the *Conversations with God* books into a "new religion."

It is anything and everything BUT that. If that's what it was, I would tell you to burn those books and forget them forever.

These books have great value—but only as the individual experience of one human being. Taken in that context, their value is inestimable. Turned into the "official text" or the "sacred source" of some new form of spiritual expression, they could be dangerous. And so could you.

I have no intention of becoming dangerous.

Then you will make it clear wherever you go that the experience you have had, everyone can have, and many *have* had. You will cause the world to understand that *everyone* is having "conversations with God" all the time, and that the question is not *To whom does God talk?* but *Who listens?*

You will resist every temptation to allow others to place you, or the material you have brought through, into some kind of special category, or to call you or it the "source" of their spiritual truth.

Believe me, I will resist that. I have been, and I will continue to.

Good. Because nothing will kill the New Spirituality faster than the idea or impression that it is coming from One Individual Human Source. It IS coming from One Source, but not from one INDIVIDUAL HUMAN source. It is coming from the Single Source that flows through all humans—and indeed, through all of Life—everywhere.

Because this is true, it will not look exactly the same from person to person. As it emanates through each individual Life Form and is expressed by that Form, it will contain the specific reflection of that Form. It may look and sound and feel very similar, but it will never look and sound and feel identical. If it does, beware. That is a sure sign that a dogma is being created.

I am always reminded that "dogma" spelled backward is "am god." When people get things backward, that's what can happen. They begin to make their dogma their god. Yet it is not dogma which is god, but every living thing.

Be on guard, then, lest others turn this writing or any other message into dogma—and then that dogma into their god.

Look not to one source, but to all sources, and even to all of Life, for your definition and experience of the Divine. Reject nothing, but also include everything.

Do not say that the truth is exclusively "here" or exclusively "there," but, rather, that the truth is "neither here nor there," but *every* where.

It is in the Qur'an, and it is in the Upanishads. It is in the Bhagavad Gita, and it is in the Bible. It is in the portions of the Bible called the Torah and called the Psalms and called the New Testament. It is in the Book of Mormon and the Book of Hidden Words. Yet know this: It is found in Whole *nowhere,* and in Part *everywhere.* All of those sources, taken singularly, contain incomplete understandings.

Therefore, entreat those who would live the New Spirituality to consider every book sacred and every messenger holy, even as they, themselves, are holy, and as the living of their own lives writes the book of their most sacred truth. Remember that always.

The living of your own life writes the book of your most sacred truth, and offers evidence of it.

PART TWO

THE FOURTH TRANSFORMATION

17

NEW WAYS FOR YOU TO EXPERIENCE GOD

In her landmark book *The Battle for God*, Karen Armstrong, who, I mentioned earlier, is one of the world's foremost commentators on religious affairs, argues that "the collapse of piety rooted in myth and cult during the Enlightenment forced people of faith to grasp for new ways of being religious." What I am hearing said here is that the same thing is about to happen again, in the very near future. Is that correct?

> Yes. And for the same reason. Humanity is very soon going to reach critical mass in its collective realization that Yesterday's God cannot serve tomorrow's world.
>
> Yes, there will soon be another "collapse of piety rooted in myth and cult," and the human race will once again "grasp for new ways of being religious."

I think that I will call this upcoming shift the Fourth Transformation.

Yes?

To place that into a context, let me return to the insights of my friend Duane Elgin, who wrote in *Promise Ahead:*

"Only three times before in human experience has our view of reality been so thoroughly transformed that it has created a revolution in our sense of ourselves, our relationship with others, and our view of the universe.

"The first transformation . . . occurred when humanity 'awakened' roughly 35,000 years ago. . . . The second time . . . was roughly 10,000 years ago when humanity shifted from a nomadic life to a more settled existence in villages and on farms."

As part of this second shift, and about 5,000 years ago, we saw the rise of city-states, and the beginnings of civilization as we know it. Duane says that "the third time that our perceptual paradigm was transformed was roughly 300 years ago, when the stability of agrarian society gave way to the radical dynamism and materialism of the scientific-industrial era.

"Each time that humanity's prevailing paradigm has changed, all aspects of life have changed with it, including the work that people do, the way they live together, how they relate to one another, and how they see their role in society and place in the universe."

That sounds like exactly what you are saying is going to happen as humanity embraces Tomorrow's God.

Yes, you have captured it exactly.

Well, actually, Duane did. All I am doing is extending his logic and calling this spiritual awakening the Fourth Transformation.

This is a revolution long in coming. As noted before, it seems there has been a revolution in everything in our society *except* spirituality. Science has seen advances that have taken humanity's breath away. Medicine has seen advances that have extended humanity's life span beyond our previous wildest imagining. Technology has seen advances that have catapulted our species to the edge of its own ability to comprehend and deal with what is being created. Politics and economics and industry and the arts—everything, virtually *everything*, has advanced except religion, except our spiritual understandings, which seem to have remained just about where they were several thousand years ago.

And the conclusion is this:

Humanity cannot continue to resolve twenty-first-century dilemmas with first-century guidelines—much less guidelines that came from *before* that time.

This is akin to going into a twenty-first-century operating room with first-century healing tools.

Tomorrow's moral, ethical, and social challenges cannot be met using eighteenth- or tenth- or sixth-century understandings and instructions. Those instructions and those understandings were not "wrong," they were not "bad," they were simply *incomplete*.

Yet unless you acknowledge this, unless humanity can admit that *it does not know all there is to know* about God and about Life, there can be no hope of continuing life as you have known it on your planet a great deal longer.

You have, in fact, *already* given up much of "how it used to be" on the earth. How much more are you willing to sacrifice before you see what is right in front of your eyes?

Yet there are those who say that the problem is exactly the opposite from the way it is being stated here. They would say that the real problem is that we have gotten *away* from the understandings and the instructions of our fathers and of theirs, and that humanity needs to *return* to the ancient guidelines of its wisdom traditions, not move further away from them.

Fundamentalist understandings of the holy scriptures of all your wisdom traditions are wise in many ways—and incomplete, and therefore dangerous, in many other ways. Honor the tradition, but expand the understanding. That's the trick now. That's what religions must do right now if they hope to be helpful to humans in the years ahead—or even to survive.

Honor your wisdom traditions, but expand their understanding. This is what will occur when humanity embraces Tomorrow's God.

So, *can* we get more specific as to when this will all occur?

Taken individually, the process of evolution itself will move much more quickly for those who are choosing to consciously create the way in which they are evolving. For those who see themselves as witnesses, rather than participants, in the process of evolution, it will move more slowly.

Considered collectively, the speed with which the process moves forward will depend upon the number of people who choose, individually, to create their evolution consciously, how rapidly they find each other and can agree to cocreate their tomorrows together, and how soon that number reaches critical mass.

This, too, is a condition that humanity can control. If large numbers of people get together, create a team, and choose to experience *conscious evolution,* humanity could reach critical mass within a very short period. Decades, not centuries. Perhaps not even decades, but years.

It is all up to you. It all depends on how you answer the call. It all depends on whether you even *hear* the call. For the soul of humanity calls out today, "Who will be on humanity's team?"

But this is not a team in a sense of "us against them," right? I mean, it is not a competition, or anything.

No. It is a team in the sense of a unified effort, a cocreation, a joint undertaking. You are not competing with anyone, because there is no other team to compete with. Think of Life as a game, but not as a competition.

In the past, you have thought of it as a competition. You were competing against nature, you were competing against each other, you were competing against Life itself, which you saw as your natural opponent. Yet Life is not your opponent and never has been. Nature is not your opponent, and never has been. Other human beings are not your opponents, and never have been.

And *God* is not your opponent, and never has been.

It feels as if this has been a big part of our challenge. Humanity has been placing God, and virtually everything God has created, in the role of *opponent.*

In many ways that is true, yes. You have been seeing many things as negative. You have imagined that God opposes you and that you have to fear God. You have imagined that nature opposes you and that you have had to conquer nature. You have imagined that Life itself is a struggle, *and was meant to be.*

You do not have to conquer nature, you merely have to cooperate with it. You do not have to struggle with Life, you merely have to flow with it. And you do not have to fear God, you merely have to be One with God.

And the same is true of religions. They, also, are not our opponents. We merely have to cooperate with them and assist them as they continue to seek higher truth and help us to find our own way to that.

That is correct. The New Spirituality will never condemn traditional religion, but seek always to *include it* in the process by which divine truth continues to be revealed.

There are far too many treasures in your religious traditions to abandon them. The future of humanity with regard to religion is not about desertion, but dissection, not about rejection, but rejuvenation.

What humans will do in the years just immediately ahead is begin to dissect their religions, looking at them closely, exploring them piece by piece, examining them doctrine by doctrine, to see what makes sense and what doesn't make sense, what is functional and what is dysfunctional, what works and what doesn't work in tomorrow's world.

Then they will rejuvenate those traditions, gently releasing what is no longer beneficial and adding new insights, new ideas, and new truths, born of the new awareness and the expanded consciousness that will be the basis of the New Spirituality.

So religion will not disappear from the face of the earth.

On the contrary, it will be more ubiquitous than ever. But gone will be the teachings of an angry, jealous, punishing Deity. Gone will be the moral justifications for vengeance and retribution. Gone will be the doctrines of exclusivity and "betterness" that have cast their shadow across the face of many religions in the past.

And alongside religion will stand a new form of human expression of the impulse toward the Divine, an expression that will not be rooted in codified texts and teachings, but in the moment-to-moment experience of each person sincerely seeking God.

And hopefully neither form of expression will claim superiority, nor will either diminish the other in any way.

> That is how it will be. Difficult as it is to now imagine, your established religions are going to stop making each other wrong. And the New Spirituality will throw the doors of acceptance open to all forms of the true and honest search for wisdom. This will be the new way that humanity will interact with God, and it will produce a new way of interacting with each other—a way that could change the world forever.

How will this happen? Who will bring all of this about? And how can I help if I want to?

> This will not occur through the leadership of one person, but through the leadership of many.
>
> It will begin through the process of waking up. That will be the first step. Many people will suddenly awaken.
>
> There are many things that will occur during this awakening. Some of them are occurring right now. All will add to the creation of critical mass around the idea that *there must be another way.*

Yes, I can see that as the one-line message of the "Wake Up Movement": *There must be another way.*

There must be *another way* to do religion. There must be *another way* to do politics and governance. There must be *another way* to do business with each other. There must be *another way* to educate our children. There must be *another way* to have relationships.

There must be another way to live our lives! A way that makes *sense.* A way that *works.* There *must* be another way.

There is. It will be called the New Spirituality, and it will extend into all areas of life, not just religion, because there is no area of your life that is not a demonstration of what you deeply believe about Life Itself.

Politics is your spirituality, *demonstrated.*

Economics is your spirituality, *demonstrated.*

Education is your spirituality, *demonstrated.*

Relationship is your spirituality, *demonstrated.*

Sexuality is your spirituality, *demonstrated.*

Your life is *your spirituality, demonstrated.*

As you begin to collectively wake up to this, more government decisions will be challenged. More major corporations will be asked to explain their accounting and other business practices. More violence and turmoil will be seen for what it is: attributable in far too many cases to religious teachings. Religious teachings that have never been seriously challenged. Instead of challenging the teachings, you challenge each other. Why not challenge the teachings? Why not challenge what sets you against each other?

It is the culture from which you emerge that is causing you to destroy the culture from which you emerge—and you cannot even see this, much less admit it. Why not retain what is best in your culture (that which is Life Enhancing, Life Supporting, and Life

Sustaining), and release at last that which is self-destructive?

As more and more of you embrace Tomorrow's God and practice the New Spirituality, more and more of you will be calling more of what you see all around you unacceptable. Not because it is "wrong," but because it simply is not who you are and who you now choose to be. Neither individually, nor as a society.

What you are saying is that humanity will begin losing patience with itself.

It is already doing so.

And this is why this movement for a New Spirituality will emerge, and will complete its work within the next twenty to thirty years.

Yes. Humanity is now growing impatient to *do something* about what it is seeing. In the very near future, humans will observe with greater clarity, objectivity, and honesty the role of religious teachings and doctrines in the creation of the many Cultural Stories that are producing continuing distrust, hatred, violence, and killing on your planet.

Each person will do what she or he is called to do, but few people will do nothing, for it will become increasingly and more widely apparent in the months and years just ahead that the time has come for ordinary, everyday people to take things into their own hands and stop relying on others—much less *authorizing* others—to create humanity's collective tomorrow.

Many people don't feel qualified to become involved in this kind of world-changing work. They'd like to help, but they don't feel they have the background, training, skills, or qualifications to play a role in this.

God does not call the qualified, God qualifies the called.

People everywhere who feel called to this work find they have the skills and abilities needed—as well as the time and the energy. Humanity will soon become aware that humanity has been betrayed. It has been betrayed by the very individuals, organizations, and agents that it had entrusted to safeguard its well-being.

Humanity will soon understand that humanity has been undermined. It has been undermined by the very doctrines, teachings, and beliefs that it had imagined would free it from its limitations and, more important, from its suffering.

Humanity will soon awaken from its long slumber to notice that a new day has begun, and to decide whether it will be the darkest day in human history, or the dawning of its brightest tomorrow.

In the years just ahead millions of individuals will be catapulted to the edge of their consciousness, to the limit of their understanding, perhaps even to the brink of despair—yet not beyond the point of no return, not beyond the time of deciding, not beyond the moment when magic can occur.

And those whose minds have not been closed,

those whose hearts still beat boldly, those whose soul can yet be heard, will declare their membership on humanity's team, and move with thunderous power and lightning speed to reclaim the future.

On that day will you thank, and embrace, Tomorrow's God. For Tomorrow's God will inspire all of this.

18

A CIVIL RIGHTS MOVEMENT FOR THE SOUL

I am inspired right *now*. I want to get started. What can I do? Specifically, *right now*, right here, *today and tomorrow*, what can I do?

The first assignment for anyone wishing to seriously explore Tomorrow's God and to personally live the New Spirituality will be to *go within*.

Begin a schedule of daily practice in meditation, deep prayer, silent listening, whatever you are comfortable with. You can begin this right now, this instant. Fifteen minutes in the morning and fifteen minutes at night can change your life. Some of you have gone your entire *lives* without spending that much time in quiet communion with your soul.

Second, exercise your body. Your mind does not fully and easily take in new data if your body is lumping through the day. If you are not on a regular exercise regimen, establish one now. This is something you can do within the next twenty-four hours. Twenty minutes a day used in this way can change your life. Some of you have gone your entire *lives* without spending that much time in purposeful physical exercise.

Third, eat well. You are dulling your mind and killing your body with what you are ingesting. This effect is slow, and it is insidious. You do not know it is happening until it has happened, and then to reverse it becomes extremely difficult.

Two-thirds of the people in Western society are overweight. You take in sugar, you take in starches, you take in animal fats, you take in all manner of things that even the most sophisticated digestive system evolved on your planet cannot handle, and you end physical life in your present form years and *years* before your body was designed to. You won't stop it no matter how many times or ways you are warned, and you seem obsessive in your determination to eat and drink (or smoke) your way into oblivion.

Yes, smoking is part of your eating problem, because nicotine is something you *ingest,* with your body absorbing this deadly chemical directly through your lungs. It is eating of the worst kind, because it is *eating away at YOU*—but you simply don't seem to care. You don't even care for those who deeply love you, for you are willing to deprive your spouse, your children, and your family of *you* by dying years earlier than you were designed to, just so you can have your multiple nicotine hits each day.

In the days of the New Spirituality this will be seen as a lack of spiritual discipline of the weakest kind, because it shows the saddest disregard for the Prime Value, which is Preserving Life.

So to get started in living the New Spirituality, all we have to do is take some very practical first steps—like, simply *taking care of ourselves.*

That is correct. It is the place to begin because it pays attention to, and honors, the Prime Value. When Life, rather than *Instant Gratification,* becomes your Prime Value, you will know that you have become truly spiritual.

The simple concept of Sustaining Life must move up the priority scale of your species if your species is to survive.

Presently, most humans do *not* want to take care of themselves. They want someone else to take care of them. This is what has given rise to religions that tell you what to believe, governments that tell you what to do, schools that tell you what to think, economies that tell you what to have, and societies that tell you what to be.

If there is one thing that is doing you in, if there is an Achilles' heel of the human race, here it is:

Dependence.

That is why I have called the embracing of Tomorrow's God and the creation of a New Spirituality a *Civil Rights Movement for the Soul.* For it will bring you *freedom* from your dependencies.

Only because you are *dependent* can you be oppressed by an unreasonable, violent God. Only because you are *dependent* can you be oppressed by an unreasonable, violent government. Only because you are dependent can you be oppressed by an unreasonable, violent society, or an unreasonable, violent economy, or even by unreasonable, violent schools—where now you have to not only educate yourselves, but *defend* yourselves.

The second greatest weakness of your species is lack of interdependence.

Wait a minute. Our greatest weakness is *dependence,* and our second greatest weakness is lack of *interdependence?* Why does that sound like a contradiction to me?

Because you think that dependence and *inter*dependence are the same thing. They are not. To be "interdependent" is to be in a reciprocal relationship. To be "dependent" is to be abnormally reliant on something to the degree that it is physically or psychologically habit-forming.

Many, many humans are abnormally reliant on their religion, their government, their employer, their entire social structure. Take that structure away from them, and they are utterly without the means to meet challenges, overcome obstacles, resolve dilemmas, solve problems, or even make decisions. They imagine that they have needs that they cannot meet by themselves.

This is what Yesterday's God *urges* them to imagine, so that many people will become reliant on Him.

Tomorrow's God will not encourage any such thing. In fact, Tomorrow's God will say, "You do not need me. You do not need religion. You do not need government. You do not need your employer. You do not need the social structures you have invented. They are *your* tools, you are not theirs. Use them for your convenience, do not be used by them for theirs.

But everybody needs *someone.* Surely there's room in Life's equation for needing *someone.*

You are *interdependent* in the sense that no one can exist alone—no man is an island. But you are not *dependent,* in the sense that you need a *particular* Other.

We will talk more about this when we take a look at Tomorrow's God and Relationships. Right now, you've asked me what steps you could take right here, this moment, to explore and to live the New Spirituality. I had given you three things you could do at once. There is a fourth.

And that is?

Seek, on a regular basis, spiritual inspiration and sustenance for your soul. Find a way to recognize—that is, to re-*cognize,* to *know again*—the sacredness of all life, and to honor that which is divine, and which is divinely inspired.

Do this in whatever way feels fitting to you.

Go to church, temple, mosque, or synagogue regularly, if that is where you find your sacred inspiration. Yet do not fail to ask questions there, to probe issues there, to explore options there. Do not be afraid to contradict doctrine there, if a contradiction appears in your heart. Do not swallow anything whole, do not accept anything on someone else's word, and do not "go along with the crowd" because it's the easiest thing to do.

Remember this about formal houses of worship: God does not need to be "worshiped," and Tomorrow's God will make that clear. Why not rename these places Houses of Reverence?

What humanity would benefit from right now is absolute clarity that expressing a reverence for Life and worshiping a God who actually ends Life—and calls on others to do the same—is a remarkably different experience. It is the difference between Tomorrow's God and Yesterday's God.

What if going to a house of worship where people adore a God who uses killing as a means of conflict resolution, and the threat of endless torture as a means of crowd control, contradicts something too deep within my soul for me to ignore?

Then find a new place and a new way to experience the reverence for all of Life that is a built-in part of your nature.

Give yourself time on a daily basis to commune with nature, or to be alone with yourself in any quiet setting, perhaps to listen to good music, or to read poetry or literary classics, or to *in some way connect with the wonder of Life,* which IS God, expressed.

You may wish to create a regular reading program—promising yourself to read no less than two books a month. You could decide that you have *already* begun this, with the book you are holding in your hand. This could then be something that you could say you *are* doing "right now, right here, today."

Hey, that's great! So I'm already under way!

Now, don't *stop.* Don't let this book be the beginning and the end of it. If you really want to explore and live the New Spirituality, acquaint yourself with its many exterior-world expressions. *Educate yourself.*

First, see what those expressions are, and, second, see if any of those expressions resonate with your own inner truth—or bring you closer to it.

This means that if you *haven't* ever been to a synagogue or a mosque or a cathedral, explore the idea of going to one. See what's going on there. If you *haven't* ever understood what happens at a Quaker meeting of the Society of Friends, go to one. See what goes on there. If you *haven't* ever understood what the Bahá'í faith is all about, find out.

If you *haven't* ever meditated, try it. If you haven't ever prayed, try it. If you haven't ever fasted as a means of bodily purification, try it. Watch what these things do for your mind, for your body, and for you soul.

And yes, read, read, *read*. Go on a reading *binge*, so that you can see what all teachers and all sources are bringing to humanity's creation of Tomorrow's God.

There is so much out there! It's hard to know where to begin.

Where would *you* begin?

Well, there are many authors whose books I would recommend, including Brad Blanton *(Honest to God)*, Deepak Chopra *(How to Know God)*, Ram Dass *(Still Here)*, Wayne Dyer *(There's a Spiritual Solution to Every Problem)*, Duane Elgin *(Promise Ahead)*, Thich Nhat Hanh *(The Heart of the Buddha's Teaching)*, Thom Hartmann *(The Last Hours of Ancient Sunlight)*, Robert Heinlein *(Stranger in a Strange Land)*, Hazel Henderson *(Building a Win-Win World)*, Esther and Jerry Hicks *(Ask and It Is Given)*, Jean Houston *(Jump Time)*, Barbara Marx Hubbard *(Conscious Evolution)*, and Gerald Jampolsky *(Love Is Letting Go of Fear)*.

Also, Daphne Rose Kingma *(The Future of Love)*, Dr. Ilchi Lee *(Brain Respiration)*, Rabbi Michael Lerner *(Spirit Matters)*, Mary Manin Morrissey *(No Less Than Greatness)*, Wayne Muller *(Learning to Pray)*, Jack Reed *(The Next Evolution)*, Don Miguel Ruiz *(The Four Agreements)*, Rabbi Jonathan Sacks *(The Dignity of Difference)*, Robert Theobald *(Reworking Success)*, Eckhart Tolle *(The Power of Now)*, Marianne Williamson *(Everyday Grace)*, Paramahansa Yogananda *(Autobiography of a Yogi)*, and Gary Zukav *(Seat of the Soul)*.

Not all of these authors would technically be classified as writers of "spiritual books," but all deal with new ways of thinking and being on the earth that reflect the principles of the New Spirituality. And the titles I have recommended here are by no means the only titles by these authors worth reading. Virtually *any* book by Marianne Williamson, for instance, will open the mind, heal the heart, and soothe the soul.

I also believe, I trust not immodestly, that much insight may be gained by reading the other titles in the *Conversations with God* series. *Conversations with God, Book 2* bears particular relevance to the world of today, speaking in very practical terms about the application of spiritual principles to day-to-day life. The Ten Illusions of Humans found in *Communion with God* and the Nine New Revelations found in *The New Revelations: A Conversation with God* are wonderfully brief, amazingly clear, incredibly powerful statements of the New Spirituality.

And there are, I know, other authors and teachers, many very special, many extraordinarily profound, many bountifully blessed with deep wisdom, whose names could and should be included here.

Do you agree with everything that each of these teachers has had to say?

No, of course not. I would not *want* to agree with every word and every statement. In my opinion that would be mentally careless.

Yet, many people *do believe* every word and every statement in the particular book that provides their spiritual sustenance.

I'm sorry, but I think that's dangerous. That can create fanatical adherence to every syllable and rigid interpretation of every paragraph, and such a response closes, not opens, the mind, reducing the process of spiritual inspiration to one of mere memorization.

But don't you say that those books are the inspired Word of God?

Yes, but they were written by human beings—some of them by more than one human being—and many have been translated into multiple languages, "updated," and revised.

The holy books of all our religious traditions should be added to the above reading list, of course, because they contain great wisdom, and it's a sad fact that even many of the people who claim to live by those books have not read them cover to cover.

After studying them, and some of the other wonderful teachings that humanity has brought to humanity through Divine inspiration, I believe that we would benefit greatly from applying the same measure to all of this writing. Every chapter, every verse, of every one of those books should be put to this simple test: *Does this idea work? Is this life-supporting and life-sustaining? Does this promote healing of human hearts? Does it create harmony?*

Then each person should make up her or his own mind, acting upon his or her own authority, relying upon her or his own inner wisdom, to arrive at his or her own conclusion.

And remember, even a point of view with which you disagree can bring you closer to your inner truth.

I have said that every book is sacred and every messenger holy, and it is in this context that that is meant. For all of Life has been created to return you to your innermost truth, and *it will do that* if you will but allow it to.

Life will open you to what is true inside of you. Therefore, bless Life, and everything in it. Do not condemn that with which you disagree, nor judge it unworthy. Call it not unseemly, useless, or unholy. For I say again, everything is holy that leads you to your innermost truth, and everything *does* lead you there.

Do you disagree with the very words you are reading right now, or, for that matter, with nearly everything in this book? Fine! Then it has done its job. For the purpose of this dialogue is not to *convince* you of anything, but to return you to *yourself,* to reunite you with *your* innermost truth, to call you to deeper understanding and bring you to greater clarity—and the Creator of this dialogue does not care how that occurs.

I have said here that on some very near "tomorrow" the human race will willingly and eagerly embrace an expanded idea and an enlarged concept of God and of Life. That is true. This will happen. And it will have an enormous effect on religion as you now know it.

What will that "look like"?

When Tomorrow's God is embraced, religion will change in several fundamental ways.

In the days of the New Spirituality your presently established religions will stop fighting with each other.

They will stop quarreling over the fine print. They will stop condemning each other and telling each other's followers that they are going to hell.

They will also stop doing something else, and this will be *very* important.

What's that?

In the days of the New Spirituality your presently established religions will stop imagining themselves to have all the answers.

They will allow as to how they may not, after all, have every single bit and piece of information that there is to have about God and about Life. They will acknowledge openly that there may be something they don't understand about God—the understanding of which could change everything.

Sir John Templeton calls this "humility theology."

It is aptly described. This is what would benefit earthly theologies greatly right now—and it is an attitude that most of your exclusivist organized religions will finally adopt as the earth's people embrace Tomorrow's God.

This will come about slowly at first, then as a fresh breeze sweeping across the land. More international conferences and congresses will be held, such as those which have already been held in recent years, inviting representatives of all the world's religions to come together in one place to explore the path of mutual respect and cooperation.

I am aware of a number of such endeavors right now, including the United Religions Initiative.

The discussions at these important gatherings will not focus on eliminating the differences between religions, for it will be recognized that diversity of spiritual expression is a *blessing,* not a problem. Rather, the focus will be on finding ways to honor those differences, seeing what they can further reveal to humanity about the Totality of God, and looking to see whether the *combination of all these different views* might produce a Whole that is Greater than the Sum of Its Parts.

Of course, that would require those religions to look past the doctrines that contradict each other.

Exactly that will happen. Theologians and teachers from all the faiths will scour their respective doctrines, *deliberately* looking for contradictions, then delve more deeply into those apparently conflicting truths to see if a Larger Truth might not be discovered. Often, in the folds of contradiction is a Great Harmony found.

Remember that it was *Conversations with God* that told you of the Divine Dichotomy, in which two apparently contradictory truths can exist simultaneously in the same space.

Yes, I do remember that, and that insight has served me well in my own life whenever I have been confronted by opposing views or apparently conflicting truths about *anything.* I have learned to see that, as my father used to tell me, "Son, there are two sides to every story." And I have learned to acknowledge that one doesn't have to be "wrong" for the other to be "right."

That is a sign of maturity, and most human beings come to that eventually, with the gracefulness of age. They begin to see that they do not live in a black-and-white world, that there are multiple shades of gray, and that standing firm in an "either/or" position rarely serves anyone—least of all, Life.

You do not live in an "either/or" reality. The reality is "both/and."

Yet while many individual human beings such as your father come to understand this well through the process of maturation, religions on your planet have been less able to embrace this wisdom. On the contrary, most of the largest religions have stubbornly refused to abandon their "either/or" paradigm. This will be one of the dramatic shifts to occur in the future, for your religions *will* adopt this larger understanding in the days of the New Spirituality.

But then they won't stand for anything. Religion will mean nothing if it means everything. Does that make sense?

From your present point of view, it makes perfect sense, because you are still standing firm in your black-and-white world. Yet if it's true that "religions mean nothing if they mean everything," then God would have to mean nothing, too, since God IS everything.

That's exactly what religions would argue. Some of them, at least. They would argue that a God who is Everything, a God who is all things to all people, is almost worse than no God at all. They would say that this is, in fact, a false god, sent to mislead the people. No, they would say, God *must* stand for something. God *must* be "this" and not "that."

Yet if God is "this" and not "that," then something would have to exist that is "not God"—and such a thing is impossible.

Understand this, and you will understand everything you will ever need to know about Tomorrow's God:

Nothing exists, nor *can* exist, outside of God.

In the days of the New Spirituality many of your presently established religions will stop declaring that something can exist outside of God.

They will, in fact, adopt their own doctrines fully—the doctrines of the omnipotence and the omnipresence of God. "God is everywhere present," they will say, and now they will *mean it.*

In the days ahead humanity will choose between Big God and Little God. Big God is the God That Is Everything, and Little God is the God that is Some Things, but Not Other Things.

In the world of Little God, God is the source of all things positive, and the Devil is the source of all things negative. This is how your major, exclusivist organized religions have resolved the duality between what you call the Positive and the Negative in your limited thinking.

When you deny the good in anything, when you

deny the perfection of anything, you are seeing it as negative. In this you imagine that you are seeing Satan.

Oh, I just thought of something! SATAN is Seeing Any Thing As Negative.

Yes, that is a good acronym in English. It helps you understand that Satan does not exist as a person. Satan is a State of Mind.

I have said to you many times, "See the perfection." I have told you, "All things are perfect." When you deny what is valuable—*which is everything in life*—then you deny me. You deny the presence of God in all things, and in every moment.

So, we could say that the DEVIL is Denying Everything Valuable In Life! When we deny God's perfection, calling anything in Life *imperfection,* we've got it all backward, we've lived backward. And "lived," backward, spells "Devil"!

Well, since you are having so much fun creating acronyms, why don't you create an acronym for "God"?

Okay . . . GOD is Getting Over Denial. When you Get Over Denying that everything is perfect, you are God. When you Get Over Denying that you are God, you have God, then and there. So, "God" is Life that has Gotten Over Denying itself.

That's not bad. You could have done worse. The acronym is, in fact, fitting. For when you do stop denying your Self, denying Who You Really Are, you *become* that—and you are one with Tomorrow's God.

And so you are entering into a time of choosing. You and all the world will be choosing between the Big and the Little, for all of Life is a movement between the Macro and the Micro, between the largest and the tiniest expression of Itself. It is a pendulum process, a breathing in and a breathing out.

You are in control of this respiration. You can take a very deep breath, expanding a great deal, or you can take a very shallow breath, expanding just a little, before beginning your contraction.

The human race has been in the process of expanding. Expanding its consciousness, expanding its awareness, expanding its state of being. Yet humanity is now making a decision, and the human race is holding its collective breath. You are asking, shall we become more, still more, than we are now, or shall we begin to become less? Shall we take in more air, even more life, or shall we stop expanding now, and begin to expel the air we have inhaled, releasing the life energy we have collected, and eventually starting the whole process over? Shall we inflate or deflate, expand or contract, become larger or become smaller?

It is no accident that your doctors call the act of breathing in "inspiration."

And so, do you choose *inspiration* or *expiration?*

That is always the choice, that is always the decision, that is the eternal dilemma of the gods.

Inspiration is the act of breathing in, of taking in

more air, more Life. Expiration occurs when inspiration has ceased.

That is what the situation is right now. The human race is on the verge of expiring because inspiration has ceased.

In fact, in some ways it feels that we are already beginning to become less. We have begun the slow but sure destruction of our home, the earth. We have begun the slow but sure dismantling of our society, and of our way of life. Yet in other ways it seems as though we are expanding, we are breathing in. We are taking in more and more of what Life is, and what it has to offer, every minute. We are expanding our knowledge and our experience of everything.

Not quite.

Not quite? What do you mean, "not quite"?

You've expanded your knowledge and experience in every area except one. As you have already pointed out, there is one area that has not advanced.

Our beliefs.

That is correct. You are still hanging on to the basic beliefs that you held on to hundreds and thousands of years ago.

Yet now you must choose between little love and big love, between little life and big life, between little God and big God, between little freedom and big freedom, between little joy and big joy, between little wisdom and big wisdom, between little world and big world.

You must choose, now, your little idea or your big idea. And should you choose the latter in all of these things, make no mistake about it, *everyone will challenge you, everyone will question you, everyone will say . . .*

"Hey, what's the big idea?"

And you will have an opportunity to say to them:

The Big Idea is that We Are All One.

The Big Idea is that there is only One God, and this One God does not care whether you are Catholic or Protestant, Jewish or Muslim, Hindu or Mormon, or have no religion at all.

The Big Idea is that all we have to do is love each other, and everything else in our world will take care of itself out of our willingness to act in loving ways with each other.

The Big Idea is that none of us is any better than any other of us.

The Big Idea is that all the earth's natural resources belong to all the world's people, and this has nothing to do with what land mass that resource is located on, over, or under.

The Big Idea is that no one really "owns" anything, least of all each other, or chunks of the planet itself, which is the home of our species.

The Big Idea is that freedom is the essence of Life, not something you earn or can be granted, but What You ARE, and any effort to limit its expression is an effort to limit Life Itself, which will be re-created by the soul at every level until the soul, which IS freedom, is fully expressed in every moment.

The Big Idea is that love knows no condition or limitation of any kind, and that any effort to limit its expression is an effort to limit Life Itself, which will be re-created by the soul at every level until the soul, which IS love, is fully expressed in every moment.

The Big Idea is that joy is your natural state of being, and that joy is always most fully and most rapidly experienced by giving it away.

These are some of the Big Ideas, and there are more.

These ideas are so big that it will be impossible for small minds to embrace them.

In truth, *You* are the Big Idea, and the sooner you understand this, the sooner you will experience the wonder of it, moving in, as, and through you into your world.

It feels as if what the world could use now is more than just a "new God," but a new determination among many people to bring that God into the life of humanity.

That is exactly what the world is going to get.

In the months and years just ahead people will be joining together in a grassroots movement, not of proselytizing, but of education; not of changing people's minds, but of expanding them.

> **This will be a *civil rights movement for the soul,* ending at last the oppression of humanity by its belief in a vain, violent, and vindictive God.**
>
> **People will join together in clusters in their communities, towns, and villages, connecting up with other groups around the world via a network created by the lot of them and facilitated by today's communication technologies.**

This could be the work of Humanity's Team! People in every nation of the world could form study groups and facilitate emotional support groups. They could present programs, offer classes, produce seminars, workshops, and retreats.

They could create interdisciplinary, interoccupational, and interfaith dialogue groups, meeting regularly to talk through the challenges of making life work in the twenty-first century. They could produce major events, called Creating Tomorrow, in which solution-oriented programs and projects could be exhibited and discussed, and for which public support could be gathered. *And this could be just the half of it!*

> **It will be just the half of it. Many people and many organizations will be taking up the call. Many are right now.**

I am getting the idea that the New Spirituality you talk about will invite humans to a grander experience of themselves. That when they see themselves as A PART *of* God, instead APART *from* God, their whole perspective will change in such a way that life across the planet will become something it has never been before.

Your impression is correct.

And this will bring great joy to the people. They will be almost as children, so joyful and happy. That, in fact, is part of the message of the New Spirituality, is it not? To remember and to be, in our daily life, more childlike? To return to innocence?

Yes. All great masters have taught this, each in their own way.

Go back to the innocence of children.

When innocence emerges from the deepest understanding, it has a special purity. Innocence that emerges from lack of understanding is not true innocence. It is the only choice that the nonunderstanding have. Their innocence, then, is a lack of understanding.

On the other hand, when you understand deeply and still remain innocent—that is to say, innocent of any particular motive, innocent of selfishness or of needing anything solely for yourself at the risk of hurting or damaging another—that kind of innocence that arises from deep understanding has a special purity that you call divinity.

That is the innocence of angels, who do not stand in innocence because they know nothing, but because they know everything.

19

TOMORROW'S GOD AND "REAL LIFE"

So let's get down to brass tacks. I want to know how this New Spirituality will affect "real life" on our planet. I mean society's day-to-day stuff. Like, say, politics.

Oh, it will throw politics into a complete upheaval.

All *right.*

When Tomorrow's God is embraced, politics will change in several important ways.

In the days of the New Spirituality the idea that politics and spirituality do not mix will be abandoned forever.

Remember, the New Spirituality says that *politics is your spirituality, demonstrated.* In the days to come, this will be recognized at last.

Some societies on your planet believe that politics

and spirituality should be separated. I observe this to be one of the most nonfunctional and nonbeneficial ideas ever visited upon the human race.

But that's the whole basis on which my country was founded! That is one of America's prime values. The United States prides itself on its "separation of church and state."

That is beneficial.

I don't understand. I thought you just said that it wasn't.

Okay, let's define our terms, so that you *can* understand.

If you define "church" as an organization that teaches a specific doctrine in a very specific way, and "state" as the institution that is empowered to create and implement the laws which govern your people, it is of benefit for these elements to be separated.

If you define "spirituality" as the sum total of your cultural values and your most sacred beliefs, and "politics" as the process by which you select the people who will write and pass laws, as well as the method by which laws are adopted, then it is not of benefit for these elements to be separated.

It is not the function of the state to promulgate specific religious doctrines. It is therefore not beneficial for a particular church or religion to exert its influence on the mechanisms by which a state governs. No church or religion speaks for the conscience of all of the people, and such influence would thus be unfair to those who do not agree with the doctrines and point of view of the church or religion in question.

Yet it would be beneficial for your cultural values and your most sacred beliefs to influence the process by which you decide who shall propose laws, and how they shall be adopted, because each individual making that choice is presumed to be, and is *asked* to be, voting his or her conscience.

You seem to be describing the difference between collective impact on an entire system and individual impact on specific people or proposals within that system.

Exactly. Politics is a *process*. The State is an *institution*.

If the process by which you determine who shall propose and write your laws, and by which those laws are eventually adopted, does not include any place for your cultural values and your most sacred beliefs to be expressed, *what good are those values and beliefs?*

So you think we *should* be mixing spirituality and politics?

You *already are* mixing politics and spirituality in the United States—and your nation has one of the highest violent crime rates in the world, more children living in poverty than a nation with your gross national product should ever tolerate, racial and sexual lifestyle discrimination on a massive scale, and millions of people living without medical care, proper nutrition, adequate housing, safe streets, two-parent families, or any real hope for a better future.

Okay, I don't understand. I thought you said that we needed *more* spirituality in politics. Now you're telling me that we already mix the two in the U.S.—

—and all over the world—

—and all over the world, and we're a mess.

The problem is not that humanity's beliefs are mixed up in politics. The problem is that humanity's beliefs are mixed up, *period.*

You have a bunch of mixed-up beliefs. You are all mixed up.

I thought you were a God of No Judgment.

I am.

That sure sounds like Judgment to me.

It is not. It is an observation. To say that it is raining outside is not the same as saying that rain is bad. I am simply observing that, *given where humanity is saying that it wants to go, given what humanity is insisting that it wishes to experience—namely, a world of peace and harmony and happiness*—you are headed in the opposite direction. If you think you are going to produce that result using the behaviors you've been exhibiting, you are really mixed up. It's not going to happen that way.

Let me repeat that.

It's not going to happen that way.

And you think that bringing spirituality into politics *is* going to make it happen?

> One last time: your spirituality is *already* being brought into politics. You are just not admitting it. At least not in your country. In some countries it is openly admitted, and that is more honest.
>
> Once again, the problem is not that you have kept spirituality out of politics, but, rather, the *nature* of the spirituality—of the cultural values and sacred beliefs—that you have brought *into* the process.

So, you're saying that our present cultural values and sacred beliefs are infecting, rather than enhancing, our political system.

> Yes. Not only in the United States but around the world, your politics have been adversely affected by your spiritual beliefs.

Why is this happening? And how is bringing *more* spirituality into politics going to help?

> It's happening because your beliefs are based on your understanding of Yesterday's God. They make up the Old Spirituality, which is a spirituality of separation and superiority, vengeance and violence.
>
> In the days of Tomorrow's God all of this will change. Bringing the *New* Spirituality into politics is what will help.

Well, it doesn't really matter much in America, because we keep this spiritual stuff pretty much out of politics. I know, I know, you said that we don't, but I have to disagree with you. This is not Saudi Arabia or Iran, where our spiritual beliefs are practically law.

> If you think that in the United States your cultural values and most sacred beliefs are not being reflected in your political system, you are either lying to yourself or you are blind.

Well, of course our politics *reflect* our cultural values and our beliefs! That's what politics are *supposed* to do. But we keep *religion* and politics separate in this country.

> You mean "religions" in your country do not have anything to do with your cultural values and your most sacred beliefs?

Of course they do.

> Well, then, you've just contradicted yourself.
>
> If you've really kept religion out of politics in the United States, then your politics do not reflect your cultural values and sacred beliefs. On the other hand, if your politics do reflect your cultural values and most sacred beliefs, then you have not kept religion out of politics.
>
> You can't have it both ways.

Wait a minute. When I say "cultural values," I am not talking about theological constructs dealing with God and the nature of Ultimate Reality and the Path to Salvation, or whatever. That's the purview of "religion." And when I talk about our most "sacred beliefs," I am not talking about belief in heaven and hell, or the power of prayer, or the sanctity of marriage, or any of those things. That, too, is the purview of religion. I am talking about *cultural* values, not *religious* values. *American* values, not Protestant, Catholic, Jewish, or Hindu values. I am talking about *national* beliefs, not *religious* beliefs. Do you see the difference?

Give me an "American" value.

Okay. Liberty. Liberty and Freedom are American values.

I have told you in this dialogue that the word "freedom" and the word "God" are interchangeable.

Well, yes, you have. But no major *religion* teaches that.

Do not your major religions teach that God is all powerful, all creative, all knowing, unlimited, and everywhere present?

Yes, I believe they do.

And are these not the characteristics of one who is the essence of freedom itself?

I never thought about it that way.

Well, isn't someone who is all powerful, all creative, all knowing, unlimited, and everywhere present, essentially *totally free?*

Yes, I suppose so.

Would not such a person be free to do whatever he or she wants, *when* he or she wants, *where* he or she

wants, and have complete *liberty* to do so *how* he or she wants, and *why* he or she wants?

Yes, I would have to agree.

And isn't that, basically, your definition of God?

Yes, it is.

Then the way you have defined God is the way you wish to define yourselves. And in the future, you will simply admit that, rather than trying to hide it.

In the days of the New Spirituality the idea of using politics to define yourselves as you have defined God will be widely accepted.

As I have been explaining, you are using politics in this way now, but the idea itself is widely denounced, so you have to pretend that you are not doing it. Yet, in truth, you have attempted to create a human society based on Godly characteristics—as best you understand those characteristics.

You want God to give you those characteristics, through the process that you call politics.

I wouldn't put it that way.

You wouldn't? The fact is, you *do*. You talk all the time in America about "God-given rights." You believe that your political process should *grant* you these *same* rights.

That's what your politics are all about.

You know, I really never have thought about it that way.

Well, others have. The other people of the world see what you are doing, they see that you have crafted a constitution and created a nation based on your deepest cultural values and most sacred beliefs—in other words, on your *spirituality.* They see you declaring this all over the place, in the halls of government, in your own Pledge of Allegiance, even on your money.

And these other people also see that your spirituality is markedly different from theirs. They do not believe that people should have the same rights and the same freedom as God. They do not believe that humans should "set themselves up as gods." They believe that humans should humble themselves before God. They see Americans as anything but humble before God.

And so, when they see American cultural values spreading across the globe, they see their own cultural values threatened and diminished. They see their own spirituality compromised. They see their own God challenged.

This is what creates religious wars, because, suddenly, it's about survival. Survival of the most important and the most personal individual way that people *identify themselves*—their most sacred *beliefs.*

Here we have a clash of cultures, which is to say, a clash of beliefs. And it is occurring not only with the United States, but with and between many people holding differing fundamental beliefs about God and about Life.

This is the source of humanity's continuing problem. And it is why the New Spirituality will be humanity's solution.

Humanity's struggle is not a military struggle, it is a struggle for the mind.

If it were merely a military struggle, then the struggle would be over, because the mightiest military would easily win. Yet your histories, and world events *to this very day,* prove that the mightiest military cannot win anything. It can subdue, but it cannot be victorious.

Subjugation and victory are not the same thing.

Only when you change people's *minds* can you claim victory in the struggle to bring peace and harmony to humanity. And this will only occur when humanity understands that its problem is not a military problem, it is not a political problem, and it is not an economic problem. *The problem facing humanity today is a spiritual problem.*

Yet when this *is* understood, then military, political, and economic tools can and will be used to help solve that problem. Indeed, all of Life will be rearranged to become part of the solution, rather than part of the problem. And this, in the end, is what will save humanity from itself.

How will this occur, particularly in politics? What changes in our political process will the New Spirituality bring about?

Humanity will produce its own solutions to the dilemmas created by its present political process. It is from humanity's new underlying beliefs about God and about Life that these solutions will emerge.

I know. I was asking you what some of those changes might be.

The New Spirituality will bring *unity* to your most sacred beliefs.

In the days of the New Spirituality humanity will begin at last to hold more basic beliefs in common, creating a more uniform standard for all political expression around the world.

As has been explained, right now your politics express sacred beliefs and cultural values that are remarkably different from place to place. Dismayed by this unworkable divergence, some of your human societies have chosen to ignore God altogether and to form a political system based on no involvement with God in any way.

These governments have not done well in the long run, and *cannot,* because people's lives are based on their values, and their values are based on their deepest understandings about Life, and their deepest understandings about Life are based on their cultural stories, and no amount of bleaching Deity out of those cultural stories can remove this influence for long, for the connection with the Divine is *instinctual* in humanity, and to try to ignore that linkage is futile.

Thus, governments which have tried to eliminate God from the social and political landscape have either fallen—

—as in the case of the Soviet Union, East Germany, etc.—

—or, in order *not* to fall, have relaxed their restrictions to "allow" God back in.

As in the case of the "new" Russia, for instance. And even, a little now, creeping back in, in China.

Yes. I repeat: Governments that have sought to eliminate God from the lives of people altogether have found that it is practically impossible to do so. The impulse toward the Divine is *cellular,* and even in the case of genuine atheists, can only be overridden by the sheer power of a mental process of overcoming and denying innermost instinct.

Everyone—and everything in *Life,* for that matter—is imbued with an innermost knowing, an inner awareness, of what you call God. The challenge continues to be, however, that Yesterday's God looks different to everyone. And so the human race is like an orchestra, the sections of which are each reading from a different score. Each section plays its melody perfectly, yet the result is not a symphony, but a cacophony.

Your God—Yesterday's God—is creating not harmony, but discord.

What would benefit us now is a new score, combining the best of many melodies, and harmonizing them. And you are saying that this is what our embracing of Tomorrow's God will produce?

Yes.

I said earlier that humanity has attempted to create a society based on Godly characteristics—as best you understand those characteristics. You want God to give you and your society those characteristics, through the process that you call politics.

The problem is not that you seek to emulate in your societies Godly characteristics, the problem is that you have an incomplete awareness and understanding of what those characteristics *are*.

In the days of the New Spirituality the nature of God and of God's characteristics will be understood much more fully.

This will have a profound impact on politics worldwide.

Please give me an example of what that could mean.

The unity of all things—including the unity of God and humanity—is a foundational principle of the New Spirituality. This idea, overlaid on your political systems on a global basis, will have enormous implications. Political systems that do not reflect this new belief, or which fail to adapt themselves to it, will simply not survive.

What does "adapting" to this new belief look like, at the national political or governmental level?

That is where you come in. Humans will decide what that looks like. And they must.

I guess I was hoping that we might be getting directions from you in this dialogue about our future.

Members of enlightened societies don't get directions, they *set* directions. They don't wait for someone else to tell them what to do, they decide for themselves what they choose to do, based on what they wish to experience.

Enlightened societies are *self-determining* societies.

But not all members of society are clear as to what is best for them, or what is in the common interest. You can't just let people do whatever they want to do. That's anarchy. That's mob rule. That's societal suicide.

You have analyzed the situation correctly, given the present level of consciousness within your society. What produces an enlightened society is a shift in collective consciousness, and that is what the New Spirituality is going to produce. With that shift will come an expanded awareness.

In the days of the New Spirituality, society's members will be clear about what is in their common interest, and will know how to arrive at that determination without bickering, quarreling, or fighting, and forevermore without violent conflict.

That sounds almost too good to be true.

Well, it will be too good to be true if you say so. Only if you say that this is a truth you choose to produce will it come to pass. You must believe in your grandest truth, and live it. Then the truth will set you free.

Now, if you were a member of a society based on the emerging New Spirituality—or if you were working to help *create* such a society—what would you say in answer to your own question about what politics will look like when more people embrace Tomorrow's God?

Well, I would say it looks like the end of dictatorships, for one thing. It seems to me that dictatorial regimes will not last long, once the people that they seek to control and govern understand that *they* are the "oneness" that holds such governments together.

This feels like exactly what has already happened in the former Soviet Union. The people there understood that their solidarity was where the power was, not with the government, and so an oppressive government was ultimately dismantled, because it could not survive. It was glasnost and perestroika that opened the door for this.

The same thing is what brought down the Berlin Wall, ended the regime of Slobodan Milosevic in Yugoslavia, and truncated the reign of countless dictatorial, oppressive governments and leaders.

Dictatorships will never be possible when the mass of the people are educated in, and embrace, the basic principles of the New

Spirituality, for one of those basic principles is, in fact, Freedom, and people will accept nothing less when they realize that freedom is the natural state of things.

You are right about this fact: "Free" is *the way things are* in the natural order, it is the way Tomorrow's God is, and it is the way human beings were meant to be. This includes, by the way, the freedom to live in allegiance to a God who does *not* set them free, but requires certain behaviors of them.

It is the paradox of freedom that freedom gives us the freedom to choose *not* to be free.

That is correct, and you are doing that right now in the United States.

Whoa. Now *there's* a social comment.

Well, look around you. You don't see your freedoms eroding? Of course you do. And you are *approving* it.

Why? Why are we doing that?

For the same reason that people all over the world do it, when they do.

Fear.

I tell you this: Fear and guilt are the only enemies of humans.

Right now you live in a world built on fear. And if you fear enough things, you will give every freedom you ever had away. And you will do it *gratefully*. For there is only one thing you want more than freedom.

What?

Safety.
Security.
Survival.

What happened to "give me liberty or give me death"?

You tell me.

America has lost its way. This once shining beacon for all the world has lost its way.

The whole world has lost its way. But do not worry, you shall find your way again. Tomorrow's God will lead you there. For a spirituality that brings a message of freedom cannot and will not support a cultural story of oppression and repression forever. Sooner or later, freedom will inspire the experience of freedom itself.

In the days of the New Spirituality the message of freedom will inspire the experience of freedom itself.

Tomorrow's God will be understood to be the very essence of freedom, and since humans will understand themselves to be One with Tomorrow's God, they will also understand themselves to be inherently free.

Then, if people's outer experience does not jibe with their inner truth, they will at first question, then rebel from, both religious and governmental authority.

That is so. That is what will occur. It has already occurred in the former Soviet Union. It has already occurred in South Africa. It has already occurred in Poland and in Czechoslovakia, in Yugoslavia and in Afghanistan. As the government of the United States becomes more dictatorial and freedom-taking, it will occur there as well.

All this will occur all over the world, because *a message of freedom inspires the experience of freedom itself.*

I have said repeatedly that the New Spirituality is *a civil rights movement for the soul.* It is a message of *freedom* from humanity's belief in an oppressive, angry, violent, and killing God. When this message is received by the people, it will not matter how powerful a dictator's government is, or how repressive a religion is. When the number of people who no longer support oppression and repression reaches critical mass, *that government will fall,* and *that religion will disappear.*

There is another profound political development that I see emerging from the New Spirituality.

What is that?

I see the present form of democracy disappearing.

Yes? And why? Why do you see this happening? Is this what you choose to create?

I think so, yes.

Why?

Because another of the foundational truths of the New Spirituality is Oneness, and those who embrace this New Spirituality—

—the number of which will increase exponentially each year—

—will see themselves as separate from no one and nothing. I believe that this sense of unity will not be merely theoretical or conceptual, but experiential.

I agree with you. The New Spirituality will produce this shift. People will not merely *know* themselves to be one with everything, they will *feel* this unity.

In the days of the New Spirituality the unity of all things will be experiential.

This will dramatically change people's attitude about many things.

It will, indeed.

From the way they live their moment-to-moment lives and interact with their loved ones, family, and friends, to the way they relate to other, larger, aspects of their lives, such as the environment, the economy, commerce, parenting, and the broader activity that we call "politics."

They may not, for instance, any longer support "majority rule" as an appropriate means of gathering approval for any decision affecting a group, or society as a whole.

Now that's interesting. Majority rule is the bedrock of democracy. One vote more than half wins the day.

Yes, but this may not be so in the days of the New Spirituality, because in those days to come, money will no longer be able to buy the votes needed to win an election or a critical nod in legislative sessions. No more will special interest groups be able to collar enough people to produce one more than half the tallies required to pass or block a law.

No more will arm-twisting and vote trading and backroom bargaining and power politics determine the course of the future for millions of people who have no say at all on the individual issues, and less say than ever even on the day they elect the people who *do* have a say.

Recognizing that we truly ARE all One, I believe we will, as a society, devise a new way to decide things. No longer will the most important choices be left to a tiny handful of people.

This is fascinating. How do you see this shift occurring?

New systems of democracy will be put into place, such as small group consensus decision-making and districtwide or nationwide direct-voter polling requiring a two-thirds majority.

Presently, in most representative governments, people vote for their representatives every few years, and their representatives then vote on the issues that come before them. The New Spirituality will change all this. The people will vote directly, through instant plebiscites—on-line computer tallies, the results of which will be instantly available, seconds after the voting ends.

We will still send representatives to our capitols, but not to approve or disapprove specific legislation. Rather, they will decide what legislation to *propose.* These proposals will be voted on through districtwide, statewide, national, or global plebiscites.

The job of our representatives will be to look at the issues, to study alternative solutions in the depth and detail that the average citizen could not possibly achieve, and to determine by consensus which solution to place before the plebiscite for approval by a two-thirds majority.

Since a consensus would be required to place anything on the public's agenda, it will be virtually impossible to influence just the votes that are needed to get a measure proposed or not proposed—since *every* vote would be needed.

And because the up-or-down vote on final approval of an idea would be through a nationwide or districtwide computer poll, lobbyists would be unable to significantly impact that plebiscite, because they couldn't possibly buy enough dinners or send enough people off to resorts and cruises to influence two-thirds of all those voting.

Your idea is that the more people there are making the final decision, the harder it is to unfairly influence the vote.

Yes. The people would become the legislators, with their representatives becoming their issue studiers and solution proposers. These representatives would rotate relatively frequently, and would in turn be selected by consensus by local selection councils within their communities, the membership of which would be chosen by the people in those districts, again by an on-line vote with a two-thirds majority required.

The staffs of representatives from the various districts would rotate every seven years, to increase longevity in the fact-gathering and analysis function of each representative's office.

> So consensus decision-making and on-line voting by the entire electorate are two changes you see in the way politics would be done.

Yes. I think we will overhaul the *entire system* by which we as a society choose leaders and make decisions on the issues of the day. We will create a new process that reflects the awareness given to us by the New Spirituality that We Are All One. We will work more as a collective, and devise ways for the Collective Will to be known, unmistakably and instantaneously.

There is a third change that I see.

> Well, you are doing pretty well here on behalf of humanity. What is your third idea?

I see transparency becoming part of the political process. I believe that the message of the New Spirituality will be that there can be no enlightened society without truth, no awareness of who you are without truth, and no truth that is partial. It must be the *whole* truth and nothing but the truth.

> You are correct. That will be a message of Tomorrow's God. People who embrace the New Spirituality will commit to a lifestyle of utter visibility.

Again, this will have an enormous impact on the political process. And because we will see ourselves as all One, there will be no attack ads, no character assassinations, no vilification of opponents, because we will understand at last that what we do to another, we are doing to ourselves. And so the *process and the language* of politics will change.

So, too, will its financing.

You're really on a roll, here.

Well, the New Spirituality is giving me ideas, inspiring new approaches.

And, of course, it will do just that for the whole of humanity.

I see this now. I see how this can happen.

So, what is your idea about financing?

Well, because knowing ourselves to be "one" will be part of our innermost experience and truth, it will be clear to us that financing all activities within our political arena should be done by the single unit called "the electorate."

All special-interest financing of whatever sort or source will be eliminated. Election and campaign costs will be covered by a general fund created by all the people and distributed in equal share to all candidates or issues groups.

Changing, as well, will be the structure of the international Body Politick. A worldwide deliberative body will be formed to look, on behalf of humanity, at issues of global concern, and to then, by consensus vote, recommend courses of action to the various national deliberative bodies, which will, in turn, and also by consensus vote, make a recommendation to the national electorate.

At a given time on a given day, the people of the world will cast their vote. Two-thirds of the voters in any nation will have to approve of a measure for it to receive that nation's okay, and two-thirds of the nations will have to give their okay for the recommended course of action to be adopted.

This is just one way all this might be done. There could be a hundred different proposals put forth now on how all this could come together. The central idea, though, and the idea emerging from the New Spirituality as I begin to feel it, would be to move the power from the hands of the select few into the hands of the many—of *all* the peoples of the earth.

In this way, one person at the pinnacle of power could never again implement or "push through" a decision that more than 25 percent of his or her constituents opposed. Nor could one nation—no matter how powerful—undertake a course of action that more than 25 percent of the world's nations opposed.

> **Well, now, you see? Those are some interesting changes you envision, and humanity will come up with a great many more, equally imaginative, and more so, once it lets go of its present Cultural Story of separation and insufficiency.**

I haven't told you yet of the most interesting idea of all.

> **Oh? What is that?**

The abolition of taxes.

> **And just how do you think the New Spirituality will inspire that?**

When we truly believe that we are all one, we will create a system by which we will provide for our collective needs from our collective resources, in proportionate measure.

You already have such a system. It's called taxation.

Yes, but if we truly believe that the message of the New Spirituality is freedom, and that freedom is the essence of who we are as beings, then such a system of coercive taxation will be rejected as inappropriate.

In its place will be a system of voluntary sharing—a regular contribution of personal income. Many spiritual teachers and masters have encouraged this. Among the teachings of Bahá'u'lláh is voluntary sharing of one's property with others among humankind. But, the message goes on, "this should not be introduced by coercion so that it becomes a law which man is compelled to follow. Nay, rather, man should voluntarily and of his own choice sacrifice his property and life for others, and spend willingly for the poor."

Practitioners of the Bahá'í faith say, "There need be no slums, no starvation, no destitution, no industrial slavery, no health-destroying drudgery." And they are right.

So what I see in the future is a system like this of free-will sharing of income from all sources—the same contribution, percentage-wise, from everyone. The money would be sent to a central fund through a voluntary automatic deduction at work, or a withdrawal from each person's Credit&Debit Account, established at any bank.

In tomorrow's completely transparent society there would be no need for cash. All payments for everything will be made through a C&D Account, the simple process of debiting one account and crediting another. There would be no mandatory tax of any kind.

What do you think will cause people to choose to voluntarily have money withdrawn from their account for this purpose?

First, if their basic and most sacred belief is that we are *not* separate, but are One, a single collective, then to *not* contribute in proportionate share to the common good would be experienced as not contributing to one*self.* It would feel something like cheating on yourself.

It would be like going out on a golf course all alone one day and then cheating on your score, writing in fewer strokes than you've taken, even though you know that no one but you will ever see the scorecard. What good would that do?

Not contributing to the Fund for the Common Good would be like cheating on yourself. What good would that do?

In addition, because the society emerging from the New Spirituality will be a totally transparent society, the names of all persons not contributing to the Fund for the Common Good would be printed in the local newspaper, read on local radio and television, and posted on the Internet at refusestocontribute.com.

Nothing calls people to their higher nature like the light of public scrutiny.

Peer review has always been much more powerful as an incentive than any law.

Now, having said all of this, I have still not gotten to what I believe will be the biggest and most profound change that will be brought about in our worldwide political and governmental systems.

And what is that?

The creation of departments at every level of government focused on the creation of peace and the dissemination of information about what works to produce the highest benefit for humankind in every area of human endeavor.

Let's look at the second idea first. To date, the concept of Shared Solutions has not received much attention from humanity's power structures. Brilliant solutions to some of our most vexing problems are being created all the time, with many of them actually put into place and functioning effectively on the ground right now—*but nobody knows about them.* The result is that we are continually having to "reinvent the wheel" from location to location, all around the world.

Almost every human problem has been solved somewhere. Yet sharing the solutions that have been created by our most imaginative minds is something humanity is not doing at anywhere near the level of which it is capable. The simple application of already existing technology would make it possible for the human race to map out functional strategies with which to approach virtually any challenge.

What might be the problem? Creating the best educational program possible—better than anything now being offered in almost all places on the earth? It's already been done. Finding a way to finance newly emerging enterprises of small-business people, and particularly women and racial minorities, as well as those with little access to entrepreneurial funding? It's already been done. Providing health care for all in an affordable and effective way? It's already been done. Eliminating starvation and deep hunger as a human experience, regardless of a person's ability to pay? It's already been done.

Truly, *what is the challenge?* Curing the most ravaging diseases of which we are aware? Done. Governing ourselves in a way that provides a high quality of life, equal opportunity, and maximum freedom of expression for all? Humanity's already done that. Reducing crime by cleaning up ghettos, and tranforming the breeding grounds where criminal behaviors are born by creating new hope and real opportunity in the lives of those who would commit them? Humanity has already done that. *We know how to do that.*

I ask a third time: *What is the challenge we think we cannot overcome, the problem we think we cannot solve?* Increasing tolerance and reducing conflict among people of differing cultures, races, beliefs, and histories? Humanity has already done that. *We know how to do that.* Facing our collective sexual dysfunction at last, and creating a sane and sacred sexuality for all human beings to celebrate and enjoy? Humanity has already done that. *We know how to do that.* Ending prejudice and discrimination in all forms in employment and housing and all areas of human interaction? Humanity has already done that. *We know how to do that.*

The list of our ills is endless, and the list of solutions we have found is equally long. The problem is not that we have failed to find any solutions, the problem is that we have failed to share them—and in a startling number of cases we don't even know about them.

In the Body Human, *one hand does not know what the other is doing.* Or, worse yet, we *do* know about a solution, but believe, for the flimsiest of reasons, that we cannot put it into place. And the reason we give? *We cannot afford it!*

Such is our economic model in most places on this earth that unless there is a financial profit to be made, we cannot bring ourselves to muster sufficient resources to solve our most difficult problems.

Thus it has been that, until most recently, people died unnecessarily all over the planet because they could not obtain certain medicines—because the prices required by drug companies placed those medications out of the reach of the poverty-stricken. Those same companies worked hard to prohibit generic drugs containing the same formulas from being introduced into the local marketplace, thus ensuring that their products would be the only curatives available.

Only after being literally shamed into it did some of those companies finally begin seeking ways to work with people and governments in the world's economically depressed areas to make certain drugs available.

Still, in our world, access to all the wonders and miracles of modern medicine is largely a matter of money, of how much one has to spend on such things as quality of life, and survival.

> This need for profit to be produced in order for help and resources to be made available is one of the first things that will be changed when you embrace Tomorrow's God and the New Spirituality, for you will see that it is not Life-supporting or Life-sustaining, but self-defeating.

This is a whole other discussion.

Yes, and right now I would like to hear more about this idea of "shared solutions."

Well, it seems to me that only when we see someone else's problems as our problems, and someone else's challenges as our challenges—

—which ethic is precisely what The New Spirituality will produce—

—will we see the benefit of establishing, in every country on earth, a National Office of Shared Solutions, and a global office as well. It is remarkable that we haven't done so up to now.

These offices would be computer-linked, of course, and would offer real-time sharing of *what is working* in every and any location on the earth as humanity addresses, collectively at last, its most pressing problems and its most daunting challenges. It would track experiments, carefully watch bold initiatives, and spread immediately the news of any undertaking, whether it succeeded or failed, that sought to produce solutions through innovation.

Such data-sharing would shorten by magnitudes of ten the "learning curve" of our societies and communities, of our disciplines and institutions, of our advocacy groups and helping organizations and government agencies, as we seek to create a better life for all. And I mean *for all*—not just for the well-heeled and the fortunately situated.

These ideas are not mine, but come from such cultural creatives as Duane Elgin, Hazel Henderson, Jean Houston, Barbara Marx Hubbard, Eleanor LeCain, Jack Reed, and many others.

Just as war departments and defense departments all across the globe now track trouble spots and danger zones and conflict locations around the world, so, too, would the Office of Shared Solutions track projects and programs and identify "solution zones" where some person or organization has come up with a truly important innovation that could be exported elsewhere and used with great effectiveness.

And just as the military has its wall-sized maps and computerized images telling us exactly where there is real or potential turmoil, so, too, would a Department of Peace have facilities of equal sophistication pointing to places where there is real or potential tranquility—with information on *why* and *how* it has been achieved.

The idea of a "Peace Room" was first introduced by Barbara Marx Hubbard at the Democratic National Convention in the United States in 1984. She suggested that we need a new social function that should "scan for, map, connect and communicate what is working in the United States and in the world."

Now, Barbara's Foundation for Conscious Evolution has created its own "version" of this tracking system, called the Synergy Center, through a highly sophisticated Internet site at Evolve.org. "As far as I know," Barbara tells me, "the Evolve site is the first effort to offer a comprehensive matrix to identify and connect solutions and innovations in every field seen as a whole-system shift to the next stage of society. It is still embryonic, of course."

These are wonderful, imaginative ideas from wonderful, imaginative people. And it is certain that many more proposals will be advanced by many more people

as the New Spirituality is embraced in your culture. And yes, that will shift politics forever.

The day is soon coming when humanity will no longer approve of or tolerate the political mechanisms, maneuverings, machinations, and manipulations of today.

20

THROWING THE MONEY CHANGERS OUT—AGAIN

We've had so much corporate scandal in this world, and so much corporate greed. The executives, many of them, at the top of these corporate ladders claim to be "God-fearing people." Yet somehow they have found in the teachings of Yesterday's God a message that has given them the room to behave as they have behaved and to imagine that it is totally okay.

Global conglomerates threaten to take over the world. They are more powerful now than most governments, perhaps more powerful than *all* governments. They certainly seem to be running our governments.

We've shaken our heads and wondered, "What kind of ethic could create such business practices, such an abusive use of power?" If this is the ethic of today, bring on Tomorrow's God *fast.*

But what will that look like? How will the New Spirituality affect worldwide economics?

The first thing you will notice is that economics will no longer be separated from any of your other Life systems. Once again, the concept of unity of all things—the foundational belief of the New Spirituality—will play the lead role in the creation of tomorrow's world, and specifically with relation to its economics.

In the days of the New Spirituality all economic, commerce, and business considerations will become part of a Whole Systems Approach to the creation of a way of life and the construction of a society that works for everyone.

Until just the most recent years on your planet, economic plans have been laid and economic moves made with little or no consideration of the social consequences or the environmental impact of those choices.

Closing of plants and wholesale movement of companies from one location to another—to say nothing of out of the country—has occurred with scarce attention given to the effect that those decisions have created on anything but the bottom line. The so-called human costs have simply not been part of the equation.

But in the future, *conscience* will be brought back into *commerce*. Consciousness will be raised, and awareness will increase, around the issue of multiple impact. Decisions will not be taken in an environment of isolation. Businesses will understand themselves to be *communities* of *people*, and to be part of larger communities of people, the lives of whom are directly affected by their choices. And in this understanding will be found a whole new raison d'être.

In the days of the New Spirituality the purpose of business and commerce will be changed.

In the current model, a business exists to make a profit for its owners.

Well, now, that's a bit harsh. Many businesses exist to serve the public in some way.

All businesses are profit driven, and when businesses cease to make a profit, they go "out of business." Your society and the values you have established for it have made it virtually impossible for a business that does not make a profit to stay "in business."

That's why we have *nonprofit organizations.* Businesses that want to make serving the public their first priority—and which are recognized as doing so—are exempted from the rigors of the marketplace through the granting by the government of nonprofit status. This allows them to stay in business regardless of the bottom line.

Nonsense. They still have to make more money than they spend, or they, too, are "out of business." Ask any so-called nonprofit hospital.

Yes. The truth is that more and more nonprofit hospitals are turning away more and more indigent patients because the hospital cannot afford to provide them services. So, if you have very little money, you can count on receiving very little health care—and absolutely no preventive care. Emergencies, perhaps (and even that is not guaranteed), but preventive medicine or maintenance care? Forget it.

> Well, what's wrong with that? What's more important, the quality of a human life or the profit margin of doctor's offices, hospitals, and elder care facilities?

The quality of a human life.

> Not according to your society. According to your society, profit is the most important thing. Even for your "nonprofits."
>
> You are cutting down and cutting off social services all over because you "can't afford them." You are providing fewer and fewer programs in your schools because you "can't afford them." You are sending the mentally ill back onto the streets, shutting down halfway houses and other facilities, because you "can't afford them."
>
> *The thought that you "can't afford" a civil society is what is causing your society to no longer be civil.*
>
> So long as you insist on a social system that creates "have's" and "have-not's," you will face this problem. And as the gap between the rich and the poor widens (which it is doing every year, at an accelerating rate), you can expect civility to all but disappear.

But no matter. Nobody cares. "Let 'em eat cake." Wasn't it

Marie Antoinette who said that? The few need their $100,000-plus incomes and their two or three cars and their $2,500 big-screen TVs and their multi-acre estates. As for the rest? Throw them some bread.

> Yes, well, you've stated it pretty much as it is. This is not something that many people want to look at, however.
>
> Yesterday's God has been characterized as pretty much of an every-man-for-himself kind of God. That's because the Old God is understood to be separate from human beings and Yesterday's Spirituality says that human beings are separate from each other.

With all this separation going on, God has to take care of His needs, and humans have to take care of theirs. If God's needs are not being met—by *humans,* incidentally—then God has to do what God has to do . . . and if humans get caught in the fallout from that, well, gosh, what can be said?

Humans, likewise, have to take care of their own needs. If their needs are not being met—by other humans, incidentally—then humans have to do what humans have to do . . . and if other humans get caught in the fallout from that, well, gosh, what can be said?

Life is tough.

"In the developing world today, there are three billion people living in poverty," according to social commentator Jack Reed in his book *The Next Evolution: Making the World Work for Everyone.* "Of those, 1.3 billion live in absolute poverty. We're not talking about what is defined as poverty in the U.S., we're talking about absolute, abject poverty, where people can't meet the basic needs of food, safe drinking water, and shelter, and where daily survival is the task at hand."

That is because you have an economic system the purpose of which is to generate profit.

Well, what should the purpose of the system be?

There are no "shoulds" in the universe. Who would do the "should-ing"?

Okay, I understand. Tomorrow's God doesn't require anything.

That is correct. The idea that Requirement Exists is an illusion. It is one of the Ten Illusions of Humans.

As I mentioned earlier, those Illusions were given to us, and explained in wonderfully clarifying detail, in *Communion with God.* Could we just list them here?

Yes. The Ten Illusions of Humans are: Need Exists, Failure Exists, Disunity Exists, Insufficiency Exists, Requirement Exists, Judgment Exists, Condemnation Exists, Conditionality Exists, Superiority Exists, Ignorance Exists.

Once you understand these illusions, you understand a great deal about Life and how it works—as well as how to *make it work.*

For instance, it is from the dual Illusions of Insufficiency and Disunity that your economy emerges. The idea that there is "not enough" of what humans need to be happy, and the idea that human beings are separate from each other, forms the basis of your entire economic model.

The New Spirituality will provide you with a new basis for your economic model—essentially, a new reason to do business. No longer will it be the purpose of your economy to generate profit.

What will its purpose be?

To generate wealth.

Well, now, *there's* an improvement.

It is, actually.

Doesn't look like it to me.

I've got more to say here.

Excuse me. Go on.

Presently on your planet, wealth is defined as possessions and power. The Old Spirituality encourages you to have *dominion* over the earth. You have interpreted this to mean *domination.* And so, you have imagined that ownership of, or power over, people, places, and things is an asset—or part of what you have called "wealth."

According to this paradigm, the more things you owned, the more power you had, and the wealthier you were.

In the days of the New Spirituality wealth will be defined not as possessions and power, but as access and happiness.

I'm not sure I understand.

We are talking here about use of, rather than ownership of, the stuff of Life.

Now let me ask you a question. Do you need a vacuum cleaner?

I beg your pardon?

Do you feel that you need a vacuum cleaner in order to be happy?

I'm not sure about the word "need" here, but I sure do like to have one. It makes cleaning the carpets a lot easier.

Indeed. And do you need a washing machine?

Well, I want to give you the same answer. I'm not sure about "need," but it sure makes doing the laundry a lot easier.

Indeed it does. And yet you do understand that half the world's people get through life without either of these things, yes?

Yes, I understand that. It's just a matter of convenience, that's all. Those of us living in the wealthier nations have these things as a convenience. They save us time.

And "time is money."

Uh . . . yes, I guess so. I mean, that's what they say.

That's an interesting economy you have there.

Well, it's just a saying.

But wouldn't it be nice if that kind of time could be saved for everyone?

That would be nice, yes, but I don't see how that could happen. Not anytime soon, anyway.

Yet when that time does come, won't that result in a better life for all?

I think so, yes. I think it's fair to say that, yes. But like I said, it will be many years before we can grow the worldwide economy enough so that everyone on the planet can afford these things.

Now what if I told you of a way that many, many more people on your planet could afford a vacuum cleaner and a washing machine without having to wait one day for you to "grow the economy"? In fact, what if the answer was not to grow the economy at all, but to reduce it?

What if I said that some day soon, everyone could have the use of a vacuum cleaner and a washing machine without a single extra vacuum cleaner or washing machine being made or purchased? What would you say to that?

I'd want to know how that could be accomplished.

And the answer would be, redefine "wealth" as access and availability. Shift from a "possessions-and-power" economy to a "use-and-cooperation" economy.

Not everyone needs their own vacuum cleaner. They simply need the *use of one*. Not everyone needs their own washing machine. They simply need the *use of one*.

What would happen if four families living in immediate proximity to each other decided to share one vacuum cleaner? Do you think their carpets would be any less clean?

Not if they cooperated with each other and set up a workable schedule for use of the vacuum. With just a little bit of cooperation, I should think it wouldn't make any difference at all.

Could they do the same thing with a washing machine?

Certainly. People living in apartment buildings do this all the time.

Good. Now, if the four families living in close proximity each owned their *own* vacuum cleaner, but agreed among themselves that when it was time to replace it, they would hold off and share each other's vacuum cleaner, until they were all down to one . . . *what do you think might be done with the three remaining vacuum cleaners that had been manufactured to meet the former demand?*

That's an interesting question. I hadn't thought about it.

Could not that manufacturing surplus be used to supply vacuums for *twelve other families* if they shared them in the same way? And, with all the families in a group of four sharing the cost of just one machine, wouldn't that make the vacuum 75 percent more affordable?

Yes, I see that it would.

Now, if you had *fourteen* families in an apartment complex, each agreeing to schedule their use of the vacuum one day a week for either an afternoon or a morning, that vacuum would go a long way, would it not? It would not be sitting in some closet most of the time, and it would cost a tiny fraction for each of those families to afford its use.

Right now many humans are paying an enormous amount of money to own and hold things, most of which they use a tiny fraction of the time that they own it.

Well, in the consumer-oriented society of the Western world, everyone is trained to think that they have to have their "own personal copy" of everything. But in some of the less "wealthy" regions of the world—

—read that, *two-thirds of the world*—

—yes, in two-thirds of the world, four families would be *grateful beyond measure* to be able to have the use of one vacuum cleaner between them, or one washing machine, or one car.

You see, you are now getting it. There is more than enough of everything for everyone to live quite happily. It is simply a matter of changing your "every man for himself" economy to a "highest good for all" economy.

This whole idea that we are now discussing was articulated in *The Next Evolution,* the book by Jack Reed that I mentioned a moment ago.

Yes, I gave Jack those inspirations.

Jack was inspired to write that the world could change overnight if humanity simply changed its definition of wealth from "possession and power" to "use and cooperation," and he is right.

But if this would work so well, why aren't people doing it, at least in economically depressed areas of the world where people cannot afford their own single copy of an item?

The ethic of "use and cooperation" has not been widely taught in those places any more than it is widely taught in more developed nations. In addition, people aspire to what they see. Even in the poorest countries, while they may not have many other luxuries, television has become ubiquitous.

Precisely because they do not have much disposable income to spend on other forms of entertainment, many people watch television during whatever leisure moments they have. There, they receive messages about what "the good life" is from Western sitcoms and dramas. It is only natural for them to desire the same kind of lifestyle. You can expect them to aspire to nothing less.

No, for something like this to work, the wealthy must redefine wealth, not the poverty-stricken. Those who are setting the standards must set the new standard.

You mean we can't just say, "Hey, those of us over here can afford this, but for those of you who cannot, just share resources"?

"Do as I say, don't do as I do," is that it?

Well, it was a thought.

Not a good one. If you want the world to change, you have to be the change you want to see.

Besides, there are other reasons for moving to the "use of" rather than the "ownership of" model. An economy based on such a model would also produce many beneficial side effects.

Such as?

Fewer "things" would have to be manufacured. Everyone on the planet could have the use of many things that now are used only by individuals or single families and are sitting idle 95 percent of the time.

People whose business depends on *using things wisely* understand this perfectly. Ask any airline how many hours of "downtime" its airplanes have each day. You will find that there is hardly a moment when they are not in use.

This requires that each airplane be built to very high specifications, so that it can take such continuous use and still operate efficiently. It also allows fewer planes to be made. No airline in the world could afford to have enough planes in its fleet to use each of them 5 percent of the time. That would be absurd. *Yet it is precisely this kind of absurdity that comprises your Western World's economic model.*

I don't think most people have ever thought about it that way.

When human society embraces Tomorrow's God, many more people will think about it that way, just as Jack Reed did.

Why? How will a new spiritual model make us think about a new economic model?

The new spiritual model will declare that "you are all one." It also will say, "There's enough." If you take those messages to heart, you will *begin at once* to devise ways of treating everyone *as you would want to be treated,* giving everyone *what you would want to be given,* and providing everyone *with what you would want to be provided.*

And you will quickly realize that the easiest way to do this is not to keep trying to grow, grow, *grow* the world's economy in a never-ending upward spiral, attempting to make it possible for everyone to afford to own the same things, but rather to provide everyone with *access to* and *use of* the same things.

This requires producing *fewer consumer items* per person on your planet, and that has wonderfully positive implications for your ecology.

I can see how it would. Less "stuff" being manufactured means less pollution of our air and water and fewer things being tossed into landfills, for one thing. As we convert from our current "disposable society" to a "maximum use" community of humans sharing resources, we will find ourselves husbanding all of those resources, using them much more wisely and much more equitably.

You have got it, precisely. And that is just the surface of it.

Humanity will be practicing, at last, what my friend Dennis Weaver, the actor and environmentalist, calls "ecolonomics." Dennis coined that word, combining "ecology" and "economics." Then he formed the Institute of Ecolonomics to support the creation of a sustainable future by marrying our ecology and our economy in just the kind of Whole Systems Approach that you are saying the New Spirituality will inspire.

Dennis Weaver's idea is an excellent one—and an example of the kind of forward thinking that emerges from true visionaries.

If people have access to, and use of, the things they feel they need, they can live their lives very happily. And, in the end, *that is wealth.*

This sounds a lot like the voluntary simplicity movement that Duane Elgin started practically single-handedly some years ago with his book by the same name. It feels like the essence of the statement, "Live simply, so that others may simply live."

Indeed.

Okay, so the New Spirituality will shift humanity from an everyone-for-themselves model to what Reed calls a highest-good-for-all-model, out of the foundational thought that we are all one. It will cause us to do business for a whole new reason—not to create "profit," but to create "wealth"—and it will also cause us to *redefine* "wealth."

Yes, this is what the future holds. This is what happens in all maturing societies, and your society is just now beginning to mature. It is just moving out of its adolescence.

And helping us, along these lines, have been wonderful teachers and leaders, such as the late Robert Theobald, who wrote *Reworking Success.* I knew Robert well, and consider him to be an extraordinarily sophisticated thinker on the economy and its social implications. Another such thinker is Rabbi Michael Lerner, who has been urging all of us for quite some time now to create "a new bottom line" in business, and in the world at large. His book *Spirit Matters,* is an exciting and inspiring articulation of New Spirituality principles as they relate to commerce.

Are there any other ways that it will affect the world's economy? Could we have just an overview here?

In the days of the New Spirituality the economy will be transparent.

Just as I saw transparency in politics.

Yes. There will be no secrets, no under-the-table dealings, no "creative accounting." Everybody will know everything about everyone. There will be no *reason* for secrets, no motivation, since you will come from oneness in everything you do to provide true wealth—equal access for everyone to what is desired to live a good life, and a higher possibility of happiness for everyone as a result of that.

With the purpose of the economy thus changed, and the definition of wealth in that way altered, the idea of keeping any piece of economic data from anybody else in order to produce economic gain will seem primitive, childish, and completely inappropriate.

In *Conversations with God, Book 2* you talked about such business practices as placing two numbers on every price tag—"Our Cost/Your Price"—so that consumers would know at the point of purchase what a company's per-unit profit margin is. Also, sending around to all employees within a company a sheet each month indicating the to-the-penny salaries and benefits of every person employed.

Yes, and that is some of what I mean when I say that business and the economy will become transparent. Knowledge is power, and Tomorrow's God will constantly encourage the movement of power from the hands of the select few to the hands of the many. I said this before, and you will see this theme repeated throughout any serious discussion of the New Spirituality.

In the days of the New Spirituality the economy will be localized.

This is a carrying forward of the theme just mentioned. The most effective way to move economic power from the select few to the many is through decentralization.

Instead of creating one massive economy, create lots of "little economies" all over the place.

Exactly.

Jack Reed suggests that in the future, we may see self-contained communities forming, in which most, if not all, of the needs and desires of those who live there are met *by those who live there.* New sources of energy—such as wind and solar—will make it unnecessary to leave any community to acquire energy. With fewer acres taken up by manufacturing plants (since manufacturing will be dramatically reduced under the Mutual Access, Use, and Cooperation economic model), more land will be again available for growing food within each community. We won't have to get all our fruit from California or our string beans from Venezuela.

Local laws could be passed allowing for the planting and cultivation of hemp for use in a hundred ways—as a replacement for pulp products now obtained by cutting down trees, as rope and canvas of the strongest sort, and as cloth for clothing of every kind, to name just a few of the products that may be derived from this source. Local currencies and barter systems, used strictly for exchanges within a given community, could take millions of people "off the economic grid" for the most part.

> The specifics of humanity's strategies for localizing economies in the future will be many and varied, but you are right about this much: As soon as people are no longer dependent for their survival (food, clothing, shelter, energy) on some distant source, they instantly have more control over their lives. This, in turn, invariably produces greater freedom and a higher quality of life.
>
> The message of the New Spirituality is that Need is an Illusion. The idea that Need Exists, together with the consumer culture that drives people into a Bigger-Better-More mentality, has done more than any other single thought to keep humans in bondage to manufacturers, corporations, politicians, energy suppliers, and others who they feel are the only ones who can provide them with what they need to be happy.
>
> Embracing Tomorrow's God, who says you *need nothing* and encourages you to experience that, will change all this.

I am remembering what you said earlier—that humanity's greatest weakness is dependency.

> That is correct. The New Spirituality will cause a greater sense of self-reliance to emerge. Individuals will take greater responsibility for their lives, and so will

groups of people banding together for the common good. And there are still other economic impacts that the New Spirituality will create.

In the days of the New Spirituality there will be no disproportionate holding of wealth and resources, and abject poverty will no longer be allowed to exist.

Gone will be the days when a tiny percentage of people control a huge percentage of the world's money and resources.

In the days of the New Spirituality it will be recognized that every human being has a right to the basics of Life and the ability to survive.

Economic tools such as a guaranteed minimum income, affordable basic housing, access to preventive medicine, education for everyone as far as their mind, and not just their money, can take them, truly equal employment and advancement opportunities, and similar remedies will make it possible for society to eliminate much suffering, misery, and hopelessness.

These and other remedies are available today. In the future, the embracing of Tomorrow's God will make it impossible to ignore them, and will eliminate the need for humanity to maintain the profit/survival mentality that has characterized its economic activities for millennia.

In the days of the New Spirituality it will be recognized that natural resources belong to all.

It will seem preposterous to everyone that a nation

or an individual would claim ownership or control over the planet's natural resources simply by virtue of their location. Precious resources such as trees (which supply the world's oxygen, after all), minerals, oil, and water will be viewed as Common Holdings owned by all humankind, to be used by all humankind for the highest benefit of all humankind.

What all this seems to come down to is that, in the future, the New Spirituality will get us out of the rat race.

Yes. That's a good characterization, that's a good catch-phrase summary.

Great, because the problem with the rat race is that even if you win, you're still a rat.

21

OUR KIDS AND GOD

How about our children? What will be the impact of the New Spirituality on them?

Much will change in the life of your offspring. For one thing, they will no longer be ignored.

Ignored? Who is ignoring them?

Many adults. Children are being left to their own devices, relegated to their own little worlds, more and more and more of the time as both parents work and involve themselves in other things.

Children spend hours in front of screens—TV screens, computer screens, video-game screens, movie screens. They are being, quite literally, *screened out* from Life Itself.

This process of screening removes them from reality and places them into an imaginary world. All of this would not be so bad if it were a world of their *own* imagination, based on what *you have taught them,* but it is not. It is the world that exists in the imagination of the TV producers and the computer program designers and the video-game creators and the movie makers, and what *they* are teaching them.

We do not want our children swimming around in this cesspool.

You said that, I didn't. I have no judgment in the matter. But if you do not want them "swimming around in this cesspool," then why are you *letting them drown themselves in it?*

You're right. We are doing that. It gets the kids out of our hair, I guess, so we let them just jump in there and swim in there—

—and drown in there—

—and drown in there. Sometimes it is hours before they come up for air. I mean, they can spend half a day in front of a screen. Half a *day,* heck, an entire weekend.

It's not like it was when I was a kid. We'd *never* want to stay in the house. That was the worst. We'd want to *get outside,* go over to a friend's house and "find somethin' to do." We'd build clubhouses out of cardboard and forts out of snow and games out of thin air and friendships that went on for years . . . and memories that lasted a lifetime.

Send a kid outside today, and he doesn't know what to do with himself.

In many cases, that is true.

The New Spirituality will invite you to change all that.

In the days of the New Spirituality adults will have the tools to give back to children the gift of their own imagination.

Tomorrow's God will not scare children, branding into their very souls the "fear of God." Tomorrow's God will teach children that fear and guilt are the only enemies of humans, that Love is all there really is, and that God is never, *ever,* going to punish them.

Tomorrow's God will teach children never to be afraid to fail, because failure *does not exist in God's kingdom.* Only *effort* exists, and effort is all that matters and all that counts, because every effort leads to an outcome that moves Life Itself forward—and forward is where Life yearns to go.

Tomorrow's God will teach children that there is no insufficiency, but that there is *enough.* There is enough of all the things that humans think they need to survive and to be happy, and so, children do not have to continually strive to be the *best* or the *fastest* or the *smartest,* and they do not have to enter into ruthless competitions and make others wrong and push others out of the way in order to be one of the "winners" and avoid being one of the "losers" in Life.

Tomorrow's God will teach children that there *are* no losers, only those who have lost their way. And Tomorrow's God will teach children that no one will ever lose their way forever, but that all will one day find their way back home, back to love, back to the heart of God—and that what they might want to do for those who have lost their way is not laugh or judge or condemn, but extend a helping hand and *show them a way* back home.

Tomorrow's God will teach children that they are one with God, and that they can act as God would act and be as God would be in the day-to-day living of their lives. And Tomorrow's God will give parents the tools with which to teach that.

Those tools will be the messages of the New Spirituality.

Oh, my gosh, I am so *inspired.* I am sitting here almost crying.

You may be crying at what you have done to your children in the past, but cry not at what you will do for them in the future. For that future is bright indeed.

Well, the future that *you* have laid out is, but are you *certain* that all of this will happen?

Do you want it to happen?

Yes!

Are you willing to work for it to happen?

Yes.

Then it will happen.

And what about our schools? What will they look like? How will our embracing of Tomorrow's God affect them? Or will it?

Oh, yes. There is nothing in *life* that will not be affected by humanity's embracing of Tomorrow's God, and education will be very near the top of the list.

Education is the single most important tool that can be used in the transformation of humanity. Those who seize power and seek to hold on to it understand this very well, and that is why they do whatever they can to curtail or control education and learning among their people.

The way to control a population is to control a population's mind, and the best way to do that is to begin with the young. Send them all to the same kind of school, teach them all the same things, allow them to know of little else, and tell them that to even desire to expand their knowledge and to understand more is unacceptable.

Most schools run by governments and religions have operated in this way. They focus on the rote memorization of data and the incessant inculcation of the mind with the insidious messages of their culture.

Teachers emerging from the New Spirituality will understand that asking children to memorize facts is asking them to re-create the past, but that inviting children to explore *concepts and ideas*—such as fairness, tolerance, equality, and honesty—invites them to create a new future, for their ideas may be different from yours.

That's what we're afraid of.

Why? You're so proud of how things have been going? Do you actually *want* your past repeated by your children?

Well, now that you put it that way . . .

You act as though you do. In very few places does your society encourage new thinking. Not even with adults, to say nothing of children. No, you want the people of your species to follow the party line. There are to be no really serious questions and no significant deviations. Not in religion, for sure. Not in politics, if you hope to win an election. Not in economics, social systems, and not in education. Do not, do not, *do not* deviate from the beaten path.

What will the new educational approach emerging from the New Spirituality be like?

It will deviate from the beaten path.

It will start by drawing spirituality into all other fields of study, submerging every subject matter in values exploration, so that the child is aware from the earliest days of her life that there is no disconnection between a person's most fundamental, sacred beliefs and a person's daily behaviors—and that the same is true for all of society.

Everything—*everything*—in the child's experience will be contextualized as a spiritual experience at its core. By being immersed in such a context, the student will learn to use spiritual tools to solve life's problems and to meet life's challenges.

I wonder if educators will ever acknowledge that most of those problems and challenges that today's kids are going to have to face will in the end have little or nothing to do with geometry, geography, biology, or history, and everything to do with fairness, tolerance, equality, and honesty.

They will in the educational environments emerging from the New Spirituality.

Because education is so powerful, and because humanity has in the past done it either very ineffectively or extremely manipulatively, *this is where the work of the New Spirituality will begin.*

If the goal is to transform your species from a primitive society of beings, many of whom are selfish and violent, into an advanced civilization of beings, most of whom are caring, sharing, and loving, much of humanity will have be reeducated.

The first step in doing this will be to remove punishment from education forever.

Remove *punishment?*

Yes.

In the days of the New Spirituality coercion and punishment will not be part of the educational process.

You are speaking of corporal punishment, right?

Spanking a child after telling the child that he should never deliberately hurt others does not teach the child to "be better," it only teaches him that physical violence *is* the way that people in control deal with problems. It models for the child the exact behavior you are asking the child not to demonstrate.

But certainly there is a place for more benign forms of punishment, such as Time Out, or writing "I will not hit" 300 times.

There is not.

But how will the teachers deal with unruly kids? There are times when punitive action is just the only way. Even top educators agree.

That does not make it "right."

The child development experts are wrong?

There is no such thing as Right and Wrong—and that is something your children would do well to learn, so they do not perpetuate the Right/Wrong Paradigm when they grow up and run the world.

There is no such thing as Right and Wrong, there is only What Works and What Doesn't Work, given what it is you are trying to do.

It doesn't *work* to criticize or punish a child if what you are trying to do is get the child to alter her behavior—to say nothing about trying to help her develop a positive self-image (which, by the way, is the *only* space from which she *can* easily alter her behavior).

Remember, you do not want the child to simply *stop* her behavior, but to *alter it.* There is a difference. Punishment, or the threat of it, can perhaps work once in a while in getting another to *stop* a certain behavior—but the behavior will start up again in some very near future (as parents . . . and presidents . . . have learned), because punishment merely halts behavior, it does nothing to change it.

I have to think about that one for a bit.

There are many effective ways to interact with a child who is not creating for herself the experience that you know would be most beneficial. Criticism and punishment are not among them.

What are these other effective ways?

An entire book could be written on that subject alone.

Well, I have to say that there are some education experts who agree with you, and who do *not* say that punishment is sometimes the best and only last resort. Adele Faber and Elaine Mazlish did write a book on this subject alone, and it is filled with priceless wisdom for teachers and parents. It's called *How to Talk So Kids Can Learn—At Home and in School.*

This little book is amazing, and it lists some very sound and workable alternatives to punishment or the threat of it, including, among others, pointing out to the offending child how he or she can be helpful, showing the child how to make amends, and letting the child experience the natural consequences of his or her behavior. The book explains how all that functions, how it *really works* to help the child alter behavior, and it does so in terms so simple as to turn *everyone* into an expert child psychologist.

Children really can be inspired to be self-directed and self-disciplined, and I don't think that anybody in the world shows "how" more effectively than Faber and Mazlish.

I agree.

I would like to also point out that this book, which truly is a remarkable work, was coauthored with Lisa Nyberg and Rosalyn Templeton, the first an award-winning teacher of third- and fourth-graders, and the second a teacher of future teachers. Their insights are crystal clear, and their on-the-nose observations are extremely insightful.

So you agree, then, that punishment has no place in school, or in the home—or in God's kingdom.

Yes, I do.

And you were just playing devil's advocate before.

I was doing what I said I would do at the start of this conversation. I was giving voice to what I assumed would be the thoughts of some others.

You did a good job. Many people do believe that punishment is an appropriate and effective remedy for

misbehavior, and many people do believe that God punishes human beings for not obeying his laws, and that human beings, therefore, have the moral authority and the responsibility to do the same to each other.

All of this is untrue, but your species believes *many* things about God and about Life that are untrue and that make it just about impossible to live together in peace and harmony.

Most of these beliefs were given to you when you were young, and many of you have passed them on to your children in precisely the same way they were passed on to you.

Is it fair to say that schools have played a big role in all this?

It certainly is. In fact, that would be putting it mildly. Schools with punitive and coercive practices have *without a doubt* been the primary means of transferring limited—and, therefore, inaccurate—views to your offspring, and you have actually created, *on purpose*, learning institutions that teach children about life from a singular and restricted point of view. Some parochial schools, yeshivas, and madrassas are prime examples of this.

A madrassa, for instance, teaches children about life in an Islamic context only. The curriculum in most such schools is almost always severely limited. It would certainly include Arabic and memorization of the Qur'an, and it might also include Islamic law, study of the

Hadith, and the history of Islam, but it would probably not include much else.

Little or nothing would be taught of the history of the rest of the world, nor is there much, if any, exposure to the point of view of other cultures. For this reason, schools such as this could best be described as tools of indoctrination.

Many consider it wonderful to go to such a school and to become a *huffaz*—one who has memorized the entire Qur'an, word for word.

As has already been noted, memorization is a key tool in most schools in the world today, private *or* public. That is because it is the objective of most schools to teach humanity's offspring to *duplicate the lives of their parents.*

The best way to ensure this outcome is to have children memorize the same things their parents memorized. Then they will come from the same knowledge base, hold the same understandings, embrace the same beliefs, think the same thoughts, and exhibit the same behaviors.

Because those who embrace Tomorrow's God will want to assist humanity in releasing its false beliefs about God and about Life, the emphasis in future schools will not be on getting children to duplicate, but to create.

Duplication is one thing, *creation* is another.

In the days of the New Spirituality the focus of education will be on creation.

Creation Education, this will be called, and it will be the biggest single difference between yesterday's schools and tomorrow's.

What will this be like? What will it be about?

It will be about showing young people Who They Really Are. It will be about opening them to the Creator Within. It will be about allowing them to see and to believe in Themselves as the Source of their experience, and the Authority over their lives. It will be about returning them to their own inner wisdom, and encouraging them to fashion their own innermost truth. It will be about showing them, specifically, how to do this.

It will be different from the "old school" because it will be about awakening children's minds, not deadening them, freeing children's minds, not shackling them, opening children's minds, not closing them.

It will be about expanding their minds, not contracting them, releasing their minds, not imprisoning them.

It will be, most important, about connecting their minds to their souls, connecting their bodies to their minds, and experiencing all three as one.

And, ultimately, about experiencing everything as one.

Creation Education will be about experiencing everything as One, and your Self as the Creator.

This is not something that is currently taught in many schools.

Many? I'm not sure it's taught in *any*.

Creation Education will be centered around the following major messages that the New Spirituality will bring to children:

1. You are One with everyone and everything in the Universe—including God. All things are part of One Living System.
2. Because you are One with God, you have the power to create what you wish to experience in your life.
3. The way you create is by what you think, say, and do.
4. It is not possible to make a mistake in the process of creation, and failure is an illusion. Everything that you create is perfect just as it is—including you.
5. When you create, you are fulfilling the purpose of your life, because creating is how you grow and evolve, and that is what you and all living things are on earth to do.
6. Life Itself is your greatest teacher, and it has built-in consequences, but never punishments. Punishment is not a part of God's plan, and has no place in God's Kingdom. Learning was always meant to be easy—it is actually a process of *remembering* what your soul has always known. This kind of "learning" will be joyful when you use the experience that you are now having to remember as much as you can about Life. Then you will remember *what* you need to remember *when* you need to remember it to make life work in the future.

7. Try to never harm another person, place, or thing in any way, but only to help others and love them as best you can, especially when they have made a mistake or have done something wrong. If you can do this, you will create a friend of just about everyone you know, and when you need one, you will never be without one.
8. There is enough for everyone. It takes very little to be happy, and the fastest way to create happiness for yourself is to create happiness for another.
9. Your very best friend is Life Itself, because it never ends. When the portion of your life that you spend on earth is over, there will be no "Judgment Day," no condemnation, and no punishment, but simply an opportunity for you to review all of the thoughts, words, and actions of your life and decide whether, as you go on to other adventures, you wish to choose again when confronted with similar circumstances. Choice is the process by which you evolve, and ultimately experience Who You Really Are.

These are the Nine Components of the core curriculum of the first years of Creation Education. The messages will become more sophisticated as the child moves on.

That sounds wonderful, but what about the Three R's?

Ah, yes, Reconciliation, Re-creation, and Reunification.

Er . . . no . . . I was talking about Reading, 'Riting, and 'Rithmetic.

Well, there you are again, stuck in your old model. The Three R's that you would teach your children about are not nearly as important as the Three R's that Tomorrow's God will invite you to teach your children about.

You mean our children don't have to learn to read, write, and work with numbers?

Of course they do, but only as *tools* with which they can create reconciliation, re-creation, and re-unification. Those are the Three R's with which both you and your children can create a new tomorrow.

In the days of "the New Spirituality the priority of education will no longer be the dissemination of facts, but the increasing of sensitivity and awareness and understanding and compassion and acceptance and celebration of and appreciation for the awe and wonder of Life.

The late child psychologist Dr. Haim Ginott believed that "every teacher should be first, a teacher of humanity, and then a teacher of a subject." That came from that fabulous book by Faber and Mazlish. Is that what you are saying here?

Exactly. And I am saying that in Creation Education, that idea will be formalized as part of its basic approach.

Okay, so tell me about the *new* Three R's.

What would benefit your world enormously right now would be for you to seek reconciliation between the many separate and disparate elements within your present societal structure. Between races, between genders, between nationalities, between religions.

This reconciliation must include acknowledgment of all that you have done to each other as you have sought to find your way to a better life: admission of all past "wrongs." And it must include a sincere apology for those wrongs.

An example of such a process might be for the people of Japan to apologize to the people of Korea for years of domination and oppression—and even for many of their attitudes toward Koreans today.

Yes.

Or for Americans to apologize to Native Americans for taking their land away and forcing them onto reservations, or to Japanese Americans for summarily rounding them up and putting them into camps during World War II, or to black Americans for allowing slavery and for openly condoning the century of discrimination that followed—and which continues in many ways to this very day.

Yes.

Or for Great Britain to apologize to India, or Russia to apologize to Poland, or for the Jews to apologize to the Palestinians for simply displacing them in their own land, or for the Palestinians to apologize to the Jews for using violence and terrorism as a means of redressing their grievances, or for . . . gosh, this list could go on forever.

Yes, it could. And you've just nailed one of humanity's biggest problems right on the head. Because most of humanity has never forgotten these injustices. Tales about them have been passed on from generation to generation until they have become part of a people's Cultural Story. The hurts, the suffering, the deaths—these have created deep bitterness, and that bitterness has been passed on to your children *as part of their education.*

That is why the new education, Creation Education, will be about *how to create a newer world,* how to create a new tomorrow, how to create a new idea about who you are as a people, as a culture, and as citizens not only of a nation, but of the earth.

Rather than passing your bitterness on to your children, Creation Education will teach your children these Three R's.

Tell me more about the first R. How would this work?

Reconciliation must include *restoration* of your societies, groups, and individuals, so that they may feel whole again. This includes reparations for past losses, to the extent possible. People must feel empowered to be who they are before they can begin to think about who they might become.

Restoration projects should include closing the gap between the world's rich and the world's poor. It is, more than any other single factor, poverty and meager education—which translates into lack of opportunity and lack of awareness—that keeps the human race at the adolescent stage in its evolutionary development.

Reconciliation as described here is the first step in the process of human renewal. You must see what you have done before you can see what you are going to do.

Okay. And the second R?

Re-creation means renouncing the old ways and the old stories and the old habits and the old rationales and the old reasons for doing things, and re-creating yourselves anew in the next grandest version of the greatest vision ever you held about Who You Are.

We are talking here about *redefining yourselves* as a species. If you wish to live together in peace and harmony, your world is going to have to reinvent itself, creating new ideas about what it means to be human, what it means to be successful, what it means to be abundant and happy.

Much of this work of re-creation can be done through Creation Education. Yet it must also involve joint efforts by people, governments, and nongovernmental organizations all around the world.

And the third R?

Creation Education—which, by the way, will provide programs not only for children, but for people of all ages—will always encourage humanity to seek the experience of reunification with All That Is. That means with God and with All Humans Everywhere. It means "mind-melding" with all of Life in its many manifest forms. It means, becoming One.

This last of the new Three R's may be the *most important* of them all. For if this can be accomplished, everything else will fall into place. The realization that you are One Being—that everything in Life is really One Thing, Manifesting—can and will change your entire experience forever.

Okay, yes, I think I understand that. But what *about* Reading, 'Riting, 'Rithmetic, and all that other academic stuff?

You are referring to the "data" of life, the collection of information that it is useful for humans to know in order to interact with others and with the world around them.

Yeah, like I said, the Three R's. The *original* Three R's.

All of that will be taught in Creation Education, too.

Good. *Whew.*

But not as primary subjects.

What does that mean?

It means these subjects will be shared with children not as things to learn merely for the sake of learning

them, but as things to *use* while they are learning the things that they came to learn.

Students will see these as tools to use in the process of creation, tools that make it *possible* to create. The focus will be on the red wagon, not on the screwdriver and wrench that it took to make it.

When creation is experienced as fun, using the tools that it takes to create will be something that every child will want to do. They will not have to be convinced to do it.

I'm liking what I hear, but I'm not sure I understand exactly how this new form of education will work. How will the purely academic subjects be taught?

There is no such thing as a "purely academic subject." *Everything* has to do with Life, and the problem with your schools is that, too often, this connection is not made. Students do not see the *relevance* of what they are being required to learn, and so they don't want to learn it.

When children have a reason to learn something—a reason they agree with—you'll never see learning faster. Children can learn the most complex computer program in minutes, leaving adults in the dust. They've figured out how to operate the new TV remote before their parents have finished reading the instructions. They're the only ones in the house who know how to set the timer on the VCR.

Ha! That's funny. And *true.*

All that children want to understand is, "Why do I have to know this?" Telling the child, "You just *do,*" will not work. Not if what you are trying to do is generate some excitement or enthusiasm around the learning. What *will* work is *drawing a circle of relevance* around a subject. This can best be done by not teaching the subject at all, but teaching something entirely different—something in which the child *does* have an interest. You might even *ask the child* on any given day *what it is that they would like to learn.*

Now there's a novel approach.

In the days of the New Spirituality the function of education will be to draw a Circle of Relevance around the raw data and systems that support Life.

So let's assume you are teaching from the core curriculum, and you are working with, say, Component Number 8: "There is enough for everyone. It takes very little to be happy, and the fastest way to create happiness for yourself is to create happiness for another."

Okay, I'm with you.

To teach this component (which will not be taught just once, but continuously throughout the school year), you might then set up a classic example of how there is enough of something, and of how one person, coming from that place, might make another person happy.

An imaginative teacher might create a fascinating story—or might ask a *child* to create such a story—in which making another person happy required some use of the tool called "numbers." After setting up a "problem" within the narrative, the teacher would invite all of the children, working together, to come up with a solution.

Now, if the teacher makes the story engrossing, the children will *want* to come up with a solution—and they will use *whatever tool they can find to do it.*

And this is how we show children that learning how to use tools can be fun.

Yes. It is one way, yes. Imaginative teachers will find dozens of other ways every day.

The children will be engaged in exploring and experiencing *life concepts,* with a fact or an equation or a method or a formula not being learned as an end in itself, but used as a *means* to an end.

Yes. That's it. You've got it.

"Every teacher should be first, a teacher of humanity, and then a teacher of a subject."

Indeed.

I love it. I love the model.

But Creation Education will not only differ in approach. It will also differ in much of what is being taught.

> An early message of the New Spirituality is that you create your own reality, and much time will be spent in Creation Education opening children to their natural abilities, including their psychic abilities and their manifestation abilities.

Uh-oh, we're getting into dangerous territory here. Some parents don't want to hear that.

> Your society will expand its thinking in the future and explore new possibilities. It won't always be caught up in the fears and restrictions of Yesterday's God.
>
> Meditation will soon be a part of the regular school day (it is in some schools right now), and early training in the psychic arts will follow. Young children will be encouraged to get in touch with their "sixth sense," and to train, use, and expand their psychic power.

I can't believe this. I can't believe that we'll actually have schools teaching this, showing kids how to use this energy. In the past this would have been condemned as being of the "occult," or "trafficking with the Devil."

> That's because Yesterday's God was a jealous god who wanted no other being to even know about such powers, much less to have or use them.
>
> Tomorrow's God, on the other hand, will make it clear to humanity that God *gave you these abilities,* that they were given to you to be used, and that there is nothing sinful in them.

Like sex.

Yes, like sex, another great taboo.

Can we talk about that in this dialogue, too?

We can, and we will.

Great. I've got some things I want to discuss about *that.*

I'm sure you do.

But right now, what about this "psychic power" stuff? Are we really going to be teaching our children about all this *in school?*

Yes, of course. Why not? School is where children learn about Life, is it not? And this is a part—a big part—of Life. Why would you be ignoring it?

You know, they do say that right now we are utilizing only a tiny percentage of our brain, perhaps something less than 5 percent of its total power and capacity. Yet we have been loath to open ourselves to the incredible wonders of the mind, for fear of offending a jealous and angry god.

Well, the good news is that Tomorrow's God will not be jealous and angry.

He won't?

She won't.

Hmmm.

And so your children will be free to look at what's beyond that 5 percent, and when they begin to explore

> **the other 95 percent, or use even a small portion of it, they will shock and amaze you by what they can do, what they can know, and what they can experience.**
>
> **The effort and the focus of Creation Education will be to bring children to this threshold, and to gently invite them to cross it.**

Some of them are at that place now, even without having had anything like this taught to them in school. Children seem to be showing up all over the planet these days who have a heightened sense of awareness, an expanded ability to understand Life.

> **Yes, it is a harbinger of the coming *evolutionary elevation* of humanity.**

More and more children today seem to have a greater sense of "presence" in the moment and a greater openness to all the possibilities resident in it. Some adults have taken to calling these young people Indigo Children. In fact, I had a lead role in a movie about this, called *Indigo,* which I cowrote with James Twyman, who was its executive producer. It was produced and directed by Stephen Simon, who produced *What Dreams May Come* and *Somewhere in Time,* among other films.

The movie has begun to attract a lot of attention because of its message, which is that these children can change people's lives, and that we might do well to begin listening to them.

> **"And a little child shall lead them . . ."**

Exactly. But now I'm jealous. What about us adults? Is it too late for us? Is there no way that we can get a little "Creation Education"?

You certainly can. In fact, you can be one of those who provides it. You can offer classes right now in the New Spirituality, bringing people together on a weekly or biweekly basis, and exploring all of what Creation Education will be saying to children in the years ahead.

How can people do that? How can people give a class in what they don't even know?

The best way to learn something is to teach it. Go ahead and offer the class. Call it an informal study group in the New Spirituality. Go out and get some of those wonderful books mentioned earlier and build a program around them. Give the group reading assignments and then bring it together to discuss the material.

Create a *learning environment* in which the "teacher" is doing as much exploring as the "students." You do not have to know everything there is to know about something in order to teach it. You need merely to have to want to know more about it, and be willing to share your growth process with others.

Remember that good teachers do not try to put something *into,* but rather seek to bring something *out of,* every student.

It's not about *putting* in, it's about *tapping* in.

Excellent. That's a great way to say that. That's exactly right.

And so, in your study group, your job is to pull the

wisdom out of the others, not to put your wisdom in there. To pull the wisdom out of others, you need to know nothing. In fact, the less you think you know, the better.

I really like this. A lot of people who have a willingness to share the messages of the New Spirituality *could* start a study group using guidelines like this. All we have to do is "create a learning environment," eh?

Yes. And this is what Creation Education is all about—whether it be for children or for adults.

In the days of the New Spirituality education will be about creating, not a school, but a learning environment.

Indeed, on your most blessed tomorrow there will not even *be* any "schools" as you now design them.

No schools?

Not in the traditional sense.

Gone will be rows of desks surrounded by walls of blackboards and whiteboards and corkboards. Gone will be musty corridors and clanking lockers and herds of children bumping their way to dank classrooms that feel to children for all the world like mini prisons.

They *are* mini prisons, where bodies are held captive, orders are barked ("Stand in line!" "Remain in your seat!" "Raise your hand!"), and minds are subjected to a stifling, stultifying, stupefying barrage of facts and figures to be absorbed, memorized, and deified (that is, literally, "made God").

Those old-fashioned schools will be replaced by "learning communities" in which students will never again be segregated by age or gender but will cluster naturally in groups of interest, irrespective of age, gender, race, culture, or background.

Young and old alike will gather in these clusters, the older ones sharing with the younger ones what they have discovered and what they yet do not know, the younger ones asking questions and suggesting avenues of expression and exploration that leave the older ones breathless—and blessed.

The synergy of these interactions will typify what education will be in the days of the New Spirituality: a magical, mystical encounter of Life with Life.

22

GOD'S WAY IN RELATIONSHIPS

You know, the picture you paint of our future is really exciting!

Good! It's time for humanity to become excited again about Life.

And since we're talking about excitement, could we now take a look at sex?

Let's start by looking at relationships.

Of course, I was going to begin there.

I know you were.

I was. Really. Because I want to know how Tomorrow's God will affect this whole important and amazingly intricate area of human experience. Sexuality is just a part of relationships. I want to talk about the whole thing.

I can start by telling you that, as in religion, politics, economics, and education, Tomorrow's God will turn your understanding of relationships upside down.

I thought so.

Yes, well, you see, everything about the New Spirituality is revolutionary. Your entire society will actually be reconstructed, from the ground up.

In the days of the New Spirituality human relationships will be completely re-created in both purpose and process.

So, what's the first thing you want to know?

How to make them *work.*

That depends on how you define a relationship as "working."

How about having one *last?* I think that's a good place to start.

You think that a relationship doesn't "work" if it doesn't "last"?

Well, it certainly doesn't work very *well.*

Wouldn't that depend on its purpose?

Well, what *is* the purpose of a relationship?

You tell me.

I think most people would say that it's to find joy and happiness, completion and fulfillment, through the sharing of one's life with another.

That is not the purpose of a relationship.

It isn't?

No. The purpose of a relationship is to *create* joy and happiness, completion and fulfillment, through the sharing of life with another.

There's a huge difference.

In the days of the New Spirituality human relationships will no longer be seen as a means of need fulfillment.

Humanity will understand that need is an illusion, and while human beings may choose to dance in that illusion and play with that illusion—much as a magician who enjoys his own tricks—people will ultimately understand that the purpose of life's most holy experience, union with another, is not about fulfilling needs.

Who said anything about fulfilling needs? I was talking about finding joy.

If you're *finding* something, you do not *have* it, and if you do not have it, you will imagine that you need it.

Oh.

You can only *create* something out of something you *have*.

Now that's an interesting thing to say.

I've only just begun.

If you think that the purpose of a relationship is to "find" something, then you will be continually looking for it. You won't experience that it's inside you, because you wouldn't be *trying to find it* if it were inside you. So you will be looking for it *outside* you—namely, in the person that you call your beloved.

If, on the other hand, you think that the purpose of a relationship is to "create" something, then you will be *bringing to the relationship* what it is that you wish to experience there. You will see yourself as the *source* of what you choose to create, because the creator of anything IS the Source.

What a fascinating perspective.

It's really just common sense.

The idea that you say most of humanity holds, however, is not common sense. In fact, that idea brings more relationships to an end than any other single thought.

Most people are looking for something outside themselves to make them happy, and that includes—perhaps especially—the experience of relationship.

We are talking, in particular here, about romantic relationship.

Yes, but you will find that every word spoken here can apply to all other kinds of relationship as well.

Good. Okay.

The New Spirituality will teach that without a relationship with somebody or something else, you cannot experience yourself in any meaningful way.

In the days of the New Spirituality all relationships will be seen as holy.

This is what I meant earlier when I said that you are *interdependent* in the sense that no one can exist alone—no man is an island—but you are not *dependent,* in the sense that you need a *particular* Other.

All relationships are holy, and each can produce the experience for which relationship was intended. The idea that you need a *particular* Other in order to produce what relationships were intended to produce leads to extraordinary dysfunction in relationship, because it creates the illusion that one person is dependent upon a specific and particular other person in order to be happy by experiencing who you really are—which is the inner goal of every soul.

Now, if you want to continue to explore this whole business of relationship, we're going to have to get into some things that may feel a little far afield. The discussion here could become a bit esoteric, but it will all make sense with regard to human relationships if you stick with me.

You want to take this ride?

Sure. Let's go.

Okay.

The only way that you can know who you are—not

just conceptually, but experientially—is by knowing who you are not. The universe has been given to you so you might experience that.

I have said to you before, "In the absence of that which you are not, that which you are, *is not*." This is a statement of profound truth regarding the Realm of the Relative—the world in which you live.

You are saying that in the absence of "cold," "hot" is not. Or that, in the absence of "big," "small" is not. Or that in the absence of "bad," "good" is not.

Exactly. You can't have one without the other in the Realm of the Relative. This is not true in the Realm of the Absolute, where All That Is is All That Is.

In the Realm of the Absolute, nothing exists in *relationship* to anything else, for the simple reason that there *isn't* anything else.

This is also true in the Realm of the Relative, where there is only One Thing, and that One Thing is All There Is. Yet this One Thing has manifested Itself in countless ways. Sometimes "this way," sometimes "that way." Sometimes "fast," sometimes "slow." Sometimes "here," sometimes "there." You understand?

Yes. But why?

We're getting there.

What God chooses to do is to Know Itself in Its Own Experience. This is God's holy purpose: to know Itself Wholly.

God can know Itself conceptually easily enough. God merely has to think about Itself. Yet for God to *experience* Itself, God has to encounter something that God is not. Only through such an encounter can God experience what God is.

The condition, however, that is there is *nothing* that God is not. And, I will repeat, in the absence of that which you are not, that which you are, is not.

God found a solution in this situation, however. God reasoned that since *nothing* other than God existed, God would have to create something that *appeared to be* "other than" God out of Itself. God did this by dividing Itself into a billion or more (actually, many more) smaller parts—and each of those *parts* would be something *other than* the Totality of God.

In this way, any individual part could know the Totality, and the Totality could know each individual part, and God could experience Who and What God Is.

The scheme was ingenious. The idea was brilliant, as befitting God. And so, the Realm of the Relative was created, and along with it, *relative experience*. Now, all of the parts of God can experience themselves as Who and What They Are in *relationship* to Who and What everything *else* is, and thus know both the Individuality and the Totality of God—the magnificence and the wonder and the glory of the All, and of All That Comprises the All in Its Various Parts.

This is, of course, a very simple, basic explanation of things. But is it clear?

Sort of.

What is unclear?

Does this mean that for me to experience something "good," something "bad" has to exist in my experience?

Well, first of all, "good" and "bad" are value judgments having to do with many, many other decisions that you have made about yourself and about Life.

I know, I know, and I don't want to get into that level of intricacy here. Can we just address the question head-on?

All right. The answer is yes. Something that is "bad," according to your terms, has to exist in your experience in order for you to experience something that you call "good."

Well, that explains a lot. Now I understand why life is so often a pile of—

—but here is what you would call the "good" news: The "bad" that has to exist in your experience does not have to exist in your *immediate* experience.

What does that mean?

It means that the so-called other side or opposite of what you wish to experience may exist either in your *past,* or in some location *far away from you*—such as the most distant location in your universe. It merely has to be something of which you are aware. It has to be part of your consciousness.

Your universe is nothing more than a Contextual Field. It is a holder, or container, into which has been poured *every experience it is possible to have*. Or, to put it another way, *the Totality of That Which Is*.

In other words, God.

Call it what you wish. Now you can reach into this Contextual Field of memory and distance—what you have called Time and Space—and find the opposite of any experience you presently choose to have. You do not have to draw that opposite *to you*. You need only know that it exists. Thus it is said that "Knowledge is Power."

So, in order for me to experience having a "good time," all I have to do is *remember* the "bad times."

Precisely.

Or, in order for me to experience how "good" life is over *here*, all I have to do is observe how "bad" life is over *there*.

Remembering that "good" and "bad" are your particular judgments, of course.

Of course.

They are simply your point of view. From another perspective, what is "bad" might be called "good."

So Life is just a matter of perspective.

You've said something very important there.

Our experience depends on how we see things.

That is correct. And how you see things depends on how you choose to see them.

I don't get that. We see things as they *are.*

No. You give everything its meaning. Always remember that.

In the days of the New Spirituality all people will understand that nothing has any meaning save the meaning they give it.

Okay. So what does this have to do with relationship?

Everything. All of the meaning in your relationships is meaning you have put there. Nothing means anything at all, except what you say it does. That includes all the things that have been done to you, and by you. You can give these things any meaning you want, but be careful, because the meaning you give them is the meaning they will have for you. Then you will act on this, believing it to be real.

If you wish to remain clear, it is going to be important for you to remember that *you have made it all up.*

You can take these things that have happened in your life and laugh them off, and say, "It's nothing. It's not worth losing my peace over. It is of no injury to me. I am not that." Or you can say, "I am deeply hurt. I am badly damaged. This is horrible. I can't stand it."

Either way, what you say will be what you experience.

Yes, well, I *try* saying the first, but the second seems to win out a lot. I mean, let's be real here. Things sometimes hurt. A lot. Help me out.

The feeling of being hurt is simply an act of forgetfulness. You have forgotten who you are, you have forgotten who the other is, and you have forgotten what you are both doing here. You have melted into the maya, you have become the illusion. You are living the story you have created, as a playwright who has fallen asleep and is dreaming that he is living his own script.

You can play out the script to the bitter, sad end if you wish, but you already know the ending, so what's the point?

No, I don't know the ending. What is the ending?

The ending is always the same. You will one day awaken—in this lifetime or the next or the next—and you will then understand Who You Really Are, and who Everyone Else Is, and you will forgive everyone everything, and you will go past forgiveness to the place where you are clear that forgiveness is not necessary.

You will see the perfection in the whole process, how it all worked wonderfully to produce your own evolution, and you will thank all of the players in your script, and you will dance together and be merry, for God's love will embrace the lot of you, and you will embrace each other as well, in your love for God, which is Life Itself.

You are certain about this.

There has never been anything more certain said or revealed. **In the days of the New Spirituality all people will understand the purpose of relationship and the Process of Life, as well as their role in it, and they will bless the process and call it holy, they will engage the process and call it adventure, they will experience the process and call it joy—and they will complete the process and call it Nirvana . . . then to happily begin the process all over again at the time of their choosing in the never-ending cycle of bliss that is Creation Itself.**

This is the story of Consciousness, unfolding. This is the story of Humanity, evolving. This is the story of You, being.

Your relationships are part of this story. In the past, you have gone into relationships for reasons very close to what you articulated a few moments ago. You were seeking happiness, you were hoping to find fulfillment and joy and completion, through the sharing of your life with another.

I simply wanted to end the loneliness.

Same thing. Fewer words.

So what's so bad about that?

Nothing is bad about it, but there is a page in the story that you have come here now to see:

You can never end the loneliness in your life until you end the loneliness within your life.

Again? Once more, please?

If you feel alone within, if you feel incomplete inside yourself, you will search outside yourself for the rest of your life to find that which cannot be found. And, after experiencing this over and over, you could wind up with a series of relationships that do not last.

Have you been reading my diary?

The relationships don't last because you do not understand what you are doing there. You are trying to find fulfillment rather than create fulfillment. You are trying to find joy rather than create joy. You are trying to find completion rather than create completion.

You believe that relationship is a process of discovery, and it is not. It is a process of creation.

The same thing can be said about Life.

But I have tried to "create" joy, happiness, and completion in relationship, and sometimes the other person has *still* left. So what is true about that?

Did that take the joy, happiness, and completion out of your life?

Of course.

Then you didn't have it there to begin with. Nobody can take with *them* what is *in you.*

Remember that. Always remember that.

So then I don't need a relationship to create joy and happiness and completion. It's all "within."

You use a relationship to *experience it*. Like God, you create relationships in order to *experience* who you are *within*.

Then I *do* need a relationship! You're confusing me here.

You do not need a relationship outside yourself. It is beneficial to have a relationship with me, inside yourself.

In the days of the New Spirituality it will be clear that all relationships begin and end and are created with and within the human soul.

Once you have a relationship with me—with Life, with God, with All That Is—inside yourself, the relationships that you have with everything and everyone outside yourself *will* be an experience of joy and happiness and completion—because *you have put it there*. You then *live it* in all the moments of your life. Yet what you do not have within, you cannot live without.

Clever. But if I can't "live without it," yet I do not *have it within*, how do I *get it there?*

Not from the other person in your relationship, I can tell you that. Put that burden on your beloved, and they will never be able to carry it. They will run from you as fast as they can. They will see that there is a hole within you that they cannot possibly fill even if they tried.

The purpose of relationship is not to find completion, but to share *your* completion. Not to find joy, but to share *your* joy. Not to find happiness, but to share *your* happiness.

If you are not happy going *into* a relationship, you will have no happiness to put there—and in human relationships, I will say again, you only find what you put there.

This is true of all of Life.

So relationship exists as a Contextual Field, as a holder or container into which you can pour all that you are. You can then reach into that and pull out whatever aspect or aspects of yourself you now wish to express and experience. Yet you cannot pull out of that container anything that you have not put in. You will be making the biggest mistake of your life if you are waiting for someone else to supply it for you.

In short, a relationship is about giving, not about receiving.

It is about both. But what you receive in relationship you receive from *yourself*. Your illusion is that you receive it from another. And so, what you receive is only what you give. That is the secret. If you think you are going to receive what you have not been willing or able to give, you will be sadly disappointed—and will sadly disappoint another.

But how can I give what I am not able to give?

You are able to give anything that you wish to receive. There is nothing that you want out of a relationship that you cannot give to a relationship. You may *think* that you cannot give it, you may have yourself convinced that you cannot give it, but that is not the truth about you.

Consider the possibility that you came *into* the relationship in order to *remember how to be greater than you are.*

That is the purpose of all relationships, and of all of life. I have said, "The purpose of life is to re-create yourself anew in the next grandest version of the greatest vision ever you held about Who You Are."

Of course, in order to do this, we must have total freedom.

God gives you that.

God may, but others may not.

In truth, freedom is not something that God gives you. I used a figure of speech. Freedom is what you are. God is that, and you are that. That is the essence of what you are. This is why, whenever your freedom is trampled on even just a bit, you feel rankled and diminished. It is not something exterior to yourself that has been trampled upon. It is you. It is the essence of your being.

The words Love and God are interchangeable. And

the words Freedom and God are interchangeable. Therefore, the words Love and Freedom are interchangeable. They describe one and the same experience.

In the days of the New Spirituality love and freedom will be understood to be the same thing.

This has important implications within the context of marriage currently understood and experienced by most of the human race.

You can say that again. I have heard this from you before, and it has done nothing but get me into trouble.

Why?

Because most people don't accept that when you love someone, love grants total freedom to the beloved.

Hold it. Let's stop right there. What do you mean, "total freedom"? Freedom is not something that can be partial. It is like pregnancy. You cannot be a little pregnant. You also cannot be a little free. You either are free or you are not.

Free to do anything?

Either you are free or you are not.

But even you have not given us that kind of freedom.

Oh, but I have.

Yes, but you punish us if we use it.

No, I do not.

Well, spouses do.

Do humans believe this?

Believe it? They *experience* it.

Then humans are not experiencing freedom in their relationships?

Not many.

They all are.

I don't think so. Not when they get punished by someone leaving them, or making life miserable for them. Not when they receive this punishment because they enjoy golf, or are caught up in their work, or don't pay the other enough attention, or, God forbid, experience a moment of love expressed sexually with someone else.

In the days of the New Spirituality humans will understand that they always have total freedom in relationships, that no one can ever take that away from them because it is Who They Are, and that every attempt to blame someone else for curtailing one's freedom is simply an act of forgetfulness.

Relationships are *based* on total freedom. That is how they work.

So when a husband tells a wife he's going to be leaving if she doesn't pay him enough attention, that's freedom? The wife is supposed to feel free to be herself in the relationship?

Of course. If the husband told her that he wants a certain amount of attention in the relationship or he's leaving, and the wife does not give him that amount of attention, she's made a free choice.

But she gets *punished* for that choice.

All choices have outcomes. Yet outcomes are not punishments, they are results.

Both partners in a relationship have the freedom to state their preferences. These announcements are statements of Who You Are. You partner does not have to agree with Who You Are, your partner merely has to notice it.

If who you are is a person who does not choose to live in a smoke-filled environment, for example, you have the freedom to announce that. Your spouse then has the freedom to smoke or not smoke in the home. You then have the freedom to remain in the home or to leave.

Neither party need take offense at the free-will choices of the other, or allow themselves to be "hurt" by them. To say that you have been "deeply hurt" by the free-will choice of another is to deny who both you and the other really are. It is an act of forgetfulness.

Relationship is the perfect expression of freedom. Where the unhappiness and the misery comes in is when the co-creators of the relationship forget this, and choose to cast themselves in the role of "victim."

So, if you declare that Love is Freedom, then you must be saying that all people in relationships should be able to freely express love with any person they wish, in any way that feels appropriate to them, without limitation or punishment. Is this how you see marriage?

No. That may be how some people see marriage, but it is not how I see marriage.

Then how do you see marriage?

I see marriage the way I see Life, which is no way in particular. Life just *is*. And so, too, with marriage. It is what it is, and it is not what it's not.

Who decides what it is? Everyone says that God decides.

God does not decide. On what basis would God make such decisions? God leaves it to you to decide. Marriage is what two people say it is.

But society has to set some rules.

Why?

To protect people.

From who? From *themselves?*

To protect others.

Who?

Society *itself.* To protect *society.* To keep society from *falling apart.*

You think society would fall apart if it had fewer rules?

Not really. The truth is, I think it would probably fall together. For the first time. The way it really is, rather than the way people want others to believe it is.

As I observe humanity, I would say that in the best-case scenario all relationships between people, including marriage, are experienced as a constant ebb and flow, a continuing and ever-changing process, in which there are no rules or restrictions, in which the only agreement is to tell the truth right here, right now, and in which preferences are openly announced and decisions and choices openly made and outcomes openly embraced as the natural consequence of the ebb and flow itself.

In other words?

In other words, everyone gets to say what they choose, do what they choose, and be what they choose, and if one's choices impinge upon or prevent the happiness of the other, then the other gets to say that, and if the same choices continue to be made, then the other gets to make *their* choice, and so goes the

process, free choice after free choice after free choice, in the name of Love and Life Itself.

In this scenario there are no victims and no villains, no spouses or partners in the "right" or in the "wrong," but only awake, aware, conscious beings consciously observing and consciously choosing the continuous co-creation.

Doesn't sound very romantic. People want to believe that marriage means fidelity, being "true" to one person for the rest of one's life, and to love that person and only that person in an intimate way—

—you mean a sexual way—

—yes, I mean a sexual way . . . and that to express love in a sexual way with any other person is to betray and deeply dishonor the first person.

And that is a perfectly wonderful blueprint for marriage. Nothing that has been said here contradicts that. In fact, everything that has been said here supports that.

But this scenario allows *no* freedom, at least no sexual freedom.

On the contrary, it allows maximum sexual freedom.

How so? The scenario says that "to express love in a sexual way with any other person is to betray and deeply dishonor the first person." That doesn't sound like freedom to me.

If that is the scenario you enter into freely, how is it not an expression of freedom? And if you remain in that scenario and abide by its agreements freely, how is *that* not an expression of freedom?

What if you abide by the agreements because you have to?

But you *don't* "have to." If you're doing it, you're doing it because you want to. You do *everything* that you do in Life because you want to. There is *nothing* that is not free choice.

I hear you say that, but I don't know . . . it still doesn't feel like "freedom" if I am simply doing something because I don't want to lose a relationship.

But that *is* freedom. You are making a free choice to stay in the relationship. You are noticing what it takes to do that, and you are freely doing it. When and where has your freedom been taken away from you?

In the days of the New Spirituality relationships will not include blame and judgment or victim-villain scenarios, but will be understood to be co-creative experiences in which all parties take responsibility for their choices and decisions.

Personal relationships are wonderful training grounds. They offer an unparalleled opportunity to announce and declare, express and fulfill, become and experience, who you really are, and who you now choose to be.

> What humans like to do, however, is freely make a choice, then declare that they *had* no choice. This allows them to make themselves the "victim" and someone else the "villain."

Well, there are situations where we can be victimized by someone else placing choices before us that are not very happy either way.

> That still doesn't mean that there aren't any choices. To say that you had no choice is to give your mastery away, it is to give your power away, it is to speak the lie about you. It is an act of forgetfulness.

I don't know. That all sounds like just words to me sometimes. Sure, I always have a choice. But if the choice is a rotten one either way, what kind of choice is that?

> It is *the best choice of all.*
>
> Life places you at the point of "rotten choices" when you are about to make an enormous breakthrough in your experience of Who You Are.
>
> Always remember that.
>
> The creation and the facing of tough choices is always an announcement from your soul to your mind through your body that it is Jump Time for the totality of your being.
>
> The truth is, your choices in moments such as these are not "rotten," they are simply critical. You bring yourself to such Critical Choice Points perhaps six or seven times a life. You can count them on both hands.

Welcome these Critical Choice Points, do not shrink from them. They offer you rare and breathtaking opportunities to leap forward in your evolution. They are always among life's greatest blessings.

So the bottom-line purpose of relationship is *to evolve.*

Of course. That is why I asked you earlier, do you think that a relationship doesn't "work" because it doesn't "last"? And then I said, "That depends on its purpose." And you then asked, "What is the purpose of relationship?" And now, right here, you have answered your own question.

Evolution is the bottom-line purpose of everything. And there is no faster way to evolve than through the process of your exterior relationship with another.

Holy relationship is where your interior meets the exterior of another, and where the interior of another meets your exterior, and where, in the best of moments, the exteriors of both are melted by the heat of both interiors, allowing those interiors to meet and awaken to the awareness that they are Identical and One, and to experience that.

This is the expression in the world that you call Love.

23

SEX AND SPIRITUALITY

Okay, so now, down to sex. What is it with human beings that they have such hang-ups about sex? And will the New Spirituality change all that?

> **Tomorrow's God will make it very clear that sexual expression is a celebration of Life—**

—and since the words "Life" and "God" are interchangeable, sexual expression is a celebration of *God.*

> **That is correct. That is exactly correct.**

Then why are so many human beings so ashamed of it?

> **Because they have been taught to be. They have been told to be. Some of them even believe they have been *ordered to be* by Yesterday's God.**

When I belonged to the Catholic Church, I was taught that the purpose of marriage and of sex was the propagation of the race. Because that was its purpose, any attempt to stop the process of procreation was seen as an intervention in the Will of God, and thus an offense against the Most High. So Catholic families often had five, six, seven, and eight children.

I was told point-blank that to use any type of contraceptive is a sin. The only nonsinful form of family planning that God allows, I was told, is the "rhythm method," when sex is avoided during the fertile period of the woman's menstrual cycle, and engaged in during what the growing family hopes is the nonfertile period.

This is a backward and primitive way of dealing with life's most natural expression of love.

I have no judgment about that.

Well, you have no judgment about anything.

That is correct.

Also when I was a child, I was taught in my school and by my culture that my body was something to be ashamed of, and so I should never allow myself to be seen naked. I should also never yearn to see any other body naked. This was a sin, and I should feel ashamed. In some cultures, it is not even acceptable for the body to be seen naked during the act of sex. The lights must be out, and the partners must be at least partially clothed.

Some of these taboos are slowly fading away, but a startling number of people are still affected by them.

That is true.

Do you think it is right that human beings should have been made to feel so guilty about sex?

There is no such thing as Right and Wrong. There is only What Works and What Doesn't Work, given what it is that you are trying to do. So, what are you trying to do here?

I'm not sure we know. I'm not sure that humanity is clear about that. Some of us are trying to do one thing, and some of us are trying to do another. I only know what I am choosing to do with my sexuality.

What's that?

I am choosing to celebrate my humanity and my love for life and my love for another and my love for myself through the joyous giving and receiving of exquisite physical pleasure, and to create, express, and experience the unified ecstasy of Oneness with my beloved. I am choosing to express and experience this without shame or guilt or embarrassment of any kind, but with a childlike openness and wonder, and a very adult appreciation and beholding of the beauty and the intensity and the breathtaking excitement of total physical, emotional, and spiritual intimacy with another human being.

Well, why don't you tell us how you *really* feel?

You asked, I answered.

You certainly did. And that might as well be the end of our dialogue on this topic, because you have just said what the New Spirituality will teach.

Yes? Really?

Yes. Really.

In the days of the New Spirituality, human sexuality will be experienced as the joyous celebration of life and the glorious expression of Godliness that it was always meant to be, it will be expressed without embarrassment or shame or guilt and without restrictions or limitations of any kind, except those that are voluntarily self-imposed.

Wouldn't it be wonderful if we had a world like that?

Yes, and the advent of the New Spirituality will do much to bring you to a place where all of you can create such a world.

You've been saying throughout this dialogue that this day is coming, and I am seeing that you are right. The Episcopal Church approved the election of its first openly gay bishop *on the very day that we are having this dialogue.* Isn't that interesting?

These look like the beginnings of humanity's first early, tentative embracing of Tomorrow's God. Some very courageous church leaders have had the courage to say, out loud and in public, that the God of their understanding finds acceptable a man who holds a sexual orientation different from others.

This is an example of the kind of unconditional love that, soon, *all of you* will understand to be the gift of Tomorrow's God.

Yet right now there are still some holdouts who believe that

Yesterday's God does not love without condition, but only if we do things *his* way. The daring action taken by the Episcopal Church in the United States did not go easily, as this news story attests.

> MINNEAPOLIS (Aug. 6)—Episcopal leaders voted to approve the election of their first openly gay bishop, risking a possible exodus of conservatives who said their grief over the decision was "too deep for words."
>
> The Episcopal General Convention on Tuesday took the final vote needed to confirm the Rev. V. Gene Robinson as bishop of the Diocese of New Hampshire. . . .
>
> The bishops voted 62–45 to confirm Robinson's election. Two bishops abstained, but their ballots under church rules were counted as "no" votes.
>
> Some convention delegates who opposed Robinson left the meeting in tears.
>
> "This body willfully confirming the election of a person sexually active outside of holy matrimony has departed from the historic faith and order of the Church of Jesus Christ," [Pittsburgh Bishop Robert] Duncan said. "This body has divided itself from millions of Anglican Christians around the world." . . .
>
> Duncan called on the bishops of the Anglican Communion and Archbishop of Canterbury Rowan Williams, head of the communion, "to intervene in the pastoral emergency that has overtaken us."
>
> "May God have mercy on his church," Duncan said. Eighteen other bishops signed his statement. . . .

I find it interesting, but not too surprising, that Bishop Duncan, referring to God, described the Episcopal Church as "his church." It is just this kind of *ownership* that people throughout the world claim that God has of *their* church that creates such separation between people.

Catholics say that *their* church is "his church." And Muslims say that *their* faith is the one true faith of Allah. And Mormons say that *their* seventh heaven is God's *real* heaven. And Jehovah's Witnesses say that *the elect* have been called by God, and that no one else is going to heaven.

> **Tomorrow's God says that *every church* is "his church," and *every* faith is "her faith," and *every* soul is God's soul, because it shares the same soul with God! And *no* person or living thing in the universe stands outside of the community of God.**

Not even people who have lots and lots of sex?

> **I beg your pardon?**

There are people who believe that it's possible to have too much sex to allow one to advance spiritually. They say that spirituality and sexuality do not mix. So, let me just ask you directly. Does sexual energy interfere with spiritual energy? Does the expression of it deplete one's "energy reserve," making it difficult or impossible to achieve spiritual awakening?

> **If that were true, then Life would be working against the purpose of Life Itself.**
>
> **The purpose of Life is to evolve, yet if the physical act that *creates* Life and expresses *love* reduces the**

prospects of evolution, wouldn't that be a huge flaw in the workings of the universe?

Sure seems to me that it would be.

I can assure you that Life was not put together that haphazardly.

It is not true that sexual expression inhibits spiritual awakening. Not even a lot of it. It *is* true that too much emphasis on *anything* produces imbalance and depletion of energies.

Too much work, too much eating, too much drinking, too much sugar, gardening, bowling, swimming, TV, carrot juice, sex . . . too much of *anything*—even *too much spiritual practice*—can create an imbalance.

The Buddha discovered that. He experienced that enlightenment could not be achieved through the practice of self-indulgence—but neither could it be achieved through the practice of self-deprivation or self-mortification. In fact, it was achieved on the *middle path* between the two, where all things were kept in balance.

There is more to say on this matter of enlightenment and how to achieve it, and since the enlightenment of the whole humanity will be a major goal of the New Spirituality, we will be discussing this as we end our conversation about Tomorrow's God.

Good. Is that next?

That's next, when we are done talking about sexuality, although I am not sure you are going to be so happy with me when we get to that topic, but we'll see.

Why not? Why wouldn't I be happy?

You'll see when we get there.

Oh, great, so now I have to sit here on pins and needles.

No, you don't. Stay in the moment of Now.

Thank you. I don't do that very often, but a lot of people do, and I'm glad I did it just then, because this is a good example of what makes people "crazy" sometimes.

I observe that a habit of many humans is something that I have called "futurizing." People get into the future in their mind, rather than staying in the present moment. Everything is perfect right here, right now, but they go off into the future in their head and make their present moment completely discombobulated.

For some reason I have hardly ever done that in my life, but you sure caught me doing it just then. I supposed that when God says I may not be too happy with God, my ears have got to perk up. So I was looking a little bit ahead. But I'm back now, back in the present moment, and I want to say that I'm glad that an active sex life does nothing to reduce spiritual awareness. I think I knew that, but I'm glad to hear you confirm it.

Sex is not what most people think it is, anyway.

I know.

Sex is Synergistic Energy Exchange. It is the energy that is exchanged between any two people who encounter each other, and the question is not whether they are having sex, but what is the quality of it? What kind of synergistic energy exchange is going on?

So everyone is really having sex with everyone else, all the time.

That is correct. It is impossible for two human beings not to exchange energy when they come into contact with each other. This exchange is just what happens. Where it goes, what it leads to, is up to each person having the experience.

Can people have sex—I mean, the physical, intercourse kind—with anyone? I mean, is that okay? Or should this experience be reserved for one or two people for the rest of a person's life?

There is no "should" or "shouldn't" here.

What kind of a person does one choose to be with regard to this matter? That is the question.

I know my answer.

What is it?

I want to be the kind of person who would never have a sexual experience with another who does not desire that experience with me. I want to be the kind of person who would never force himself on anybody, and who would never even invite another to have a sexual experience if I felt that they were not old enough or mature enough or emotionally healed enough or mentally stable enough to make such a decision. And I want to be a person who keeps his sexual agreements with others, who can be counted on to stay in integrity around that.

Go, then, and be that person.

But I want *everybody* to be that kind of person.

Yes? Well, everybody is not going to be that kind of person. Even you were not always that kind of person.

I know. What would it take for more of us to be, all of the time?

Greater self-awareness, plus a more complete understanding of the purpose of Life Itself. When you truly embrace Tomorrow's God, you will have a greater sense of this. You will bring greater self-awareness into every moment and every choice, including your choices around sexuality.

Many people are doing this now, and their movement into greater self-awareness is actually paving the way for the New Spirituality.

Still, sexual crimes are rampant in our society.

That is because sexual repression is rampant. Wherever you see sexual repression, you will see sexual crime and sexual dysfunction.

Is that why the Catholic Church has had so much trouble with priests acting in sexually inappropriate ways?

It is precisely why.

We really are, as a species, mixed up about all this. We are willing to allow our children to see incredible violence on movie screens, but if we hear that the picture has graphic sexual content, we are offended and scandalized and run out of the place, demanding to see the manager. What is that all about?

It is about the mixed signals that you have given yourselves as a human culture. You hate violence, but you love to watch it. You love sex, but you hate to watch it.

Actually, many people love to watch it, they just hate to *admit* that they love to watch it. And they certainly don't want their *children* to watch it. Yikes! Maybe we should just pass more laws against sexual expression, and that will take care of the problem.

Laws about human sexual expression are not observed to be beneficial to humanity.

Well, they are all broken anyway.

Exactly.

So all they do is create more anger, shame, guilt, and "hiding out" around our sexual behavior.

That's what is true.

Yet surely there should be some laws, such as the law against rape.

That is not a law against sexual expression, that is a law against assault. Assault of any kind—defined as the unwarranted and unwanted physical advance of one person upon another—is against the law. Humanity has agreed upon that.

What about laws prohibiting discrimination based on sexual preference? Or what about so-called Hate Crime legislation, which imposes additional penalties if an act of aggression is committed because of a person's race, gender, sexual lifestyle, or nationality?

Those, too, are not laws prohibiting or regulating sexual expression. I have no judgment on any of them. Humanity has to decide for itself about them.

I think that the last law actually prohibiting an actual form of sexual expression in the United States was a law against what had been labeled sodomy, and that law was finally struck down by the U.S. Supreme Court in the summer of 2003. I do not feel that the private sexual behavior of two consenting adults is the appropriate purview of the law, the courts, or any facet of the criminal justice system—and the Supreme Court apparently agrees. Still, many people howled.

Yes. This gets back to the discussion we had earlier about many people wanting civil law to be based on religious values. It may benefit humanity to explore the thought that where there is no civil damage, no civil law should be created or enforced.

Does that include the law against prostitution?

In many places, prostitution is legal.

Yes, I know. In Belgium, Germany, the Netherlands, and Switzerland, it is openly practiced as a business, complete with storefronts. And in fact the simple act of exchanging money for sexual services is legal in most countries of the world. It is not legal in the United States—except in most Nevada counties, where, strangely, it is.

So what, then, is the issue with prostitution, morality or *geography?*

Hmmm.

Any other questions?

You know, I really don't have any more questions on sexuality. Now that I am having this conversation with you, I am realizing that I've answered most of my questions on this subject to my satisfaction.

Answering your own questions to your own satisfaction is the mark of a student moving to mastery.

Well, now, I didn't say *that.*

No, I did. Earlier you came up with your own answer on the purpose of relationship, now you experience yourself having all the answers you need with regard to your own sexuality, and in a moment you are

about to prove that you have your own answers on the biggest question of all.

I am?

You are.

24

THE WAY TO ENLIGHTENMENT

Okay, what's this all about?

The time has come for us to practice the first basic tenet of the New Spirituality.

Which is?

That all the wisdom you will ever need lies within you. That you are all having Conversations with God all the time. That every time you go within, search with a pure heart and a deep desire to know your highest truth, you will receive it. All you have to do is listen to what you have to say to yourself—and then trust that.

Yes, I feel that, I know that.

We're going to demonstrate that right here.

We are?

Yes. Our conversation on the topic of Tomorrow's God is now over in its present form.

For the length of this dialogue I have allowed you to ask the questions and to receive my answers as if I was the one with all the insight and you were the one who lacked awareness. *This is not what is true about you,* and this continuing dialogue is not modeling what is true about *anyone.*

The truth about all of you is that you have deep insights and extraordinary wisdom, and all you have to do to experience that is open up to it and call it forth.

I believe that. Through the years I have come to believe that.

About yourself?

About everyone.

Yes, but do you include yourself in that? Many people think that people in general are wise, but that they are not. Many people think that people in general are attractive and beautiful, but that they are not. Many people believe the best about others and the worst about themselves.

I do not. I am not in that group. With humility I would say that I believe I am no less capable than the rest of humanity of accessing and bringing forth wisdom from within.

We'll see.

What do you have up your sleeve here?

I've already told you. I am going to suggest to you that you—and all others—have all the answers to every question you could ever ask. And I'm going to conclude our conversation by proving it.

I'm going to turn the tables on you, with the biggest question of all.

Oh, boy.

Are you ready?

I suppose.

You suppose?

Well—

Are you ready or aren't you?

Yes.

Right. Now we have something going here. Now remember, from this point on, you are the one with the answers and I am the one with the questions.

I understand.

So here is the biggest, most important question in the entire conversation that we've been having.

What is the way to enlightenment?

What will the New Spirituality, what will Tomorrow's God, have to say about *that?*

You know, I've already looked at that. I even did a sharing about that with a small group of about a dozen people recently.

And what did you tell them? And what do you want to add now to what you said? Go ahead. I'm waiting for your answer.

What is the way to enlightenment?

Well, "enlightenment" is this elusive, magical, mystical experience for which everyone seems to be reaching and for which everyone seems to have a yearning and for which everyone seems to be searching. And I understand the reasons for the search, because if we all were enlightened, one imagines that our lives would be better than they are now, when we are presumably unenlightened.

In addition, it occurs to me that if all of us were enlightened relatively quickly, the whole world would be different and we would experience life in another way. Presumably with less turmoil, with less stress, with less conflict, for sure, I would imagine, with less sadness and anger and less violence and much less of all the things that make our lives sad and disjointed and unhappy in these days and times.

So humanity searches for enlightenment, and we have been searching for enlightenment from the beginning of time, ever since we became consciously aware of the fact that it was possible to *be* enlightened—whatever that is.

Whatever *that* is? You don't even know what it is to *be* enlightened?

Have a little patience. Everything will soon become clear. That sound familiar?

That sounds familiar.

Sound like something you would say?

It does. You've learned quickly. Go on.

We have not only been searching for enlightenment, we have been searching as well for a *definition* of enlightenment, because we can't get to that destination until we know where we are going. And so the first step for most human beings has been to try to define what enlightenment is, or what it looks like, or feels like, or tastes like, or what it is like to experience that. And then, after we have that clear, after we know what our destination is, then we can try to figure out what it would take to get from where we are to where we want to be.

And there is this rush to enlightenment that I observe that humanity, or a portion of humanity, is engaged in. And many say that they know how to get there, and they know how to get *you* there. And so we see many, many "Paths to Enlightenment" that are suggested, recommended, created, expressed, experienced, shared, and put into the space of our collective lives. Masters of every shape and size and color have been creating a way to be enlightened for millennia.

Paramahansa Yogananda said that he knew a way to enlightenment. Sai Baba said that he knew a way to enlightenment. The Buddha said that he knew a way to enlightenment. Maharishi Mahesh Yogi said that he knows a way to enlightenment. In their own way, Jesus the Christ and Abu al-Qasim Muhammad ibn Abd Allah ibn Abd al-Muttalib ibn Hashim—Muhammad—said that they knew the way to enlightenment.

Now the interesting thing here is that the followers of all of these masters have insisted that their master was right about that,

that their way was the best way and the fastest way. Maybe not the only way, but the fastest way, and therefore, you needed to take that way. There was a great urgency. You needed to become Catholic or you needed to take Transcendental Meditation or you needed to learn tai chi—and not *some* time, but *right now,* immediately, this *month.*

Or you needed to join this group or do that process or read this book or be baptized or be unbaptized or do whatever it is that you have been told by your particular master is the fastest, quickest way for you to get to where all of us want to go—which is the place called "enlightenment."

Now the danger of this business of enlightenment is twofold. The first danger is thinking that there is *something specific that you have to do in order to get there,* and that if you don't do that, you *can't* get there. The second danger is thinking that your way to get there is the fastest, best way to do it.

A few years ago, now I guess it's about twelve or fifteen years ago, I was approached by people in the *est* movement. Werner Erhard created the Erhard Seminar Trainings, which was a huge movement in the new thought community in the United States and around the world around twenty-five years ago or so.

The people who were involved in the *est* movement were absolutely convinced that this was the fastest way to enlightenment. So they began recruiting people to take *est,* and they became very engaged in that process. It was almost urgent, an urgent matter with them. And they couldn't understand why you didn't get the urgency, if you didn't get it. They would look at you and say, "You just don't get it, do you?"

This was natural, because they had found something that

changed their whole life virtually overnight, and they wanted to give that to you and they knew that this was The Way. There were many ways. This wasn't the only way, but this was probably the fastest way.

And I enrolled in the *est* program and I, too, became enlightened. In fact, I became so enlightened that I realized that I did not need *est* to be enlightened—which really upset the *est* people, because they wanted me to take the next level and the next level and the next level of the training.

It seems that *est* was a program that had multitudinous levels. You could take level one, level two, level three—they had very fancy names for them. And once you got in the program, you could virtually never get out of it. You had to almost extract yourself out of it. And if you did get out of it, you were made to feel by those who were inside of it that you had done something desperately sad. Not wrong, just very sad. Because you *just didn't get it.*

Many years ago Paramahansa Yogananda started the Self-Realization Fellowship. Yogananda taught in the West from 1920 until his death in 1952. He published his life story, *Autobiography of a Yogi,* in 1946. It went far in introducing Vedic philosophy to the West.

When Yogananda, or Master, as he was called, came to America, he brought a technique for "self-realization," which was his phrase meaning enlightenment. When you realize who the self is, you become enlightened. And Master described himself as being enlightened. And, by the way, he *was* enlightened. And he was enlightened because he *said* he was.

You mean, that's all it takes?

Yes. I hate to break the spell that someone may be under, but to be enlightened is to say that you are. It is quite as simple as that, and we will talk more about that in just a minute.

People heard Paramahansa Yogananda give his talks and explain his technique for enlightenment, which involved a process that included, among other things, deep meditation every day. And the process was one that Paramahansa Yogananda taught to his students, and his students taught to their students, and their students taught to their students, on and on, until a very large number of people all over the United States, and indeed, around the world, were involved in this Self-Realization Fellowship, which, by the way, continues to function to this day and now has many followers.

If you talk to some of those members of the Self-Realization Fellowship, they will tell you, "This is the way. This is the path. Master has shown us the path. There are many other paths, this is not the only path, and this may not be the best path, but it is the surest path that we know of, and so come and join the Self-Realization Fellowship." And that is wonderful, because that is their experience, and they are sincerely sharing that.

In even more contemporary times, a fascinating man named Maharishi surfaced a few decades ago, and he announced yet another path to enlightenment. His path was called Transcendental Meditation or, for short, TM. Maharishi made friends with the Beatles when they were at the height of their popularity, and within a very short period of time became very popular around the world and began teaching far more widely and creating temples and meditation centers all around the globe.

He established huge universities. There is a very large one in

Fairfield, Iowa, right now. And there are other learning centers that he has established around the world. And many so-called TM Centers.

Now, I learned Transcendental Meditation, and I learned it from other students who learned it from other students who learned it from other students who learned it from other students, who learned it from the Master. And there is some sense of quiet urgency on the part of some of those people in the Transcendental Meditation movement, because they will tell you that Transcendental Meditation is a tool that can bring you to enlightenment in a very short period of time, *and they want that for you.*

When you have a life-changing technology, you naturally want to share it with as many people as you can. And there is nothing wrong with that. That is very exciting, and it is very wonderful. But as with sex and as with sugar and as with any good thing, it can throw you out of balance if you are not careful, if you just go overboard with it.

Now there are many other programs as well. Like Maharishi and Transcendental Meditation, like Paramahansa Yogananda and the Self-Realization Fellowship, like Werner Erhard and the *est* program. There are many programs. Many approaches, many paths developed by many masters. There was a book written called *Many Lives, Many Masters,* by a wonderful man named Brian Weiss, and he talks about the fact that there are many ways to reach the mountaintop. Which way, then, should we recommend? Which way, then, should we encourage others to take?

That's what I am asking *you*.

Or should we simply encourage others to investigate for

themselves the many paths that there are, and empower them to know that inside their heart and soul they will pick the path that is just right for them if their intention is pure and if their desire is true?

God says, "No one calls to me who is not answered."

You're right. I do say that.

And Tomorrow's God will make *sure* that each of us is answered in the way that most effectively responds to the vibration that we create and hold in the center of our being.

To put this another way, God, or divinity, or enlightenment, if you please, appears in a form in the lives of every person that is most appropriate to their background, their culture, the level of their understanding, the level of their desire, and their willingness.

This very conversation, this book that many will be reading, falls into that category. For some, it will be perfect, the perfect tool of communication. For others it will not, and they will not even have read this far and will not know what is being said here.

So there are many means of communication, and there are many disciplines: physical disciplines, mental disciplines, spiritual disciplines, and some disciplines that involve all three—the body, the mind, and the spirit.

We spoke of the Buddha earlier. It is good to tell the whole story.

His name was Siddhartha Gautama. He lived in riches and luxuries as a young man, because his father and his family were the rulers of a large area of countryside and had much wealth. They tried to protect Siddhartha from any knowledge of the outside world for many years. And they kept him in the grounds, but one day Siddhartha ventured outside the walls of the compound and learned of life as it existed on the street.

He learned of poverty and of illness and of disease and of cruelty and of anger and of all the so-called negative experiences that no one ever allowed him to experience when he was inside the gates of his compound. And he gave up all of his riches and all of his luxuries, his whole family, left his wife and children and everyone at home and disappeared, essentially, and embarked on his search for enlightenment.

"What can I do?" he asked himself, "What can I do?" And he then underwent a series of very rigorous physical and mental disciplines, from fasting to day-long meditations to physical trainings of every imaginable sort. And this went on for quite a while, not a week or two, but for a long time. Something like six years.

He sought out other masters and asked them how they had achieved or moved toward the experience of enlightenment, and he did as they told him, because he wanted to honor the masters that he met along his path. But nothing brought him the experience of enlightenment. It only brought him an emaciated body and a life that was made difficult with physical and mental discipline and training.

And one day Siddhartha Gautama said, "I am going to sit beneath this tree until I am enlightened. I've tried everything. I've done all the physical disciplines, all the trainings, all the exercise, all the starvation, all the diets, all the fasting, and all the meditation. I'm just going to sit here on the ground, I'm tired of all this stuff, and I'm not getting up until I'm enlightened."

And there he sat, doing nothing. No exercises, no meditations, no fasting, no nothing, just sitting there doing absolutely nothing. Now that is hard for many of us to do, because we think there is something we are supposed to be *doing* in order to be enlightened.

The Buddha sat there until he opened his eyes and realized that he was enlightened. And he said, "I'm enlightened." And people came to him and cried out, "What did you do? What did you do? Teach us, master! You have become the Buddha, the enlightened one. What is the secret? What did you do?"

And the Buddha said something quite extraordinary. "There is nothing that you have to do." Imagine. After all that time. After all that self-flagellation, and wearing a hair shirt, and starving his body and doing his physical discipline. After all that time, he realized it was not about telling beads, or lighting incense, or sitting in meditation for three hours a day. It was not about any of that. It *can* be if you want it to be. It *can* be if that is what suits you. It *can* be if that is your path, but it is not *necessary* to do *anything.*

The Buddha said, in effect, "I'm enlightened because I have realized that enlightenment is knowing that there is nothing you have to do to be enlightened."

Isn't that interesting? It's sad in a way, when you think of all the effort that people are putting in, with years-long programs and trainings, only to find out that enlightenment requires *nothing at all.*

Now I have come to this conversation, and I am going to end it by saying something daring. I am going to tell you that one day I, too, could be enlightened.

You may think I'm joking, but I'm not. I could be an enlightened master, and so could everyone. And do you know how I will know I'm enlightened? When I find peace and joy and love in every moment. I, too, like the Buddha, like Jesus the Christ, like

Paramahansa Yogananda, like Maharishi, like Ilchi Seung Heun Lee, choose to seek enlightenment.

On my own particular path I have tried everything. First I tried orthodox religion. I said my rosary faithfully every day, because there was this formula that you could use to have God answer your prayers. There was a litany, there was a process.

I also tried fasting. I tried meditation. I tried reading every book I could get my hands on. I took *est.* I learned Transcendental Meditation. I learned transactional analysis. I walked down many paths, many, many paths.

And then one day I had an out-of-body experience. Now that was interesting, because I wasn't trying to do this. I was trying to produce outcomes with my fasting, I was trying to produce outcomes with my meditation, I was trying to produce outcomes with my rosary and with my disciplines, but those were not bringing me where I wanted to go.

Now here I was, just simply trying to get some sleep. I just fell asleep. But in that moment I flew out of my body quite involuntarily. Just left. And I *knew* that I left. It was a conscious awareness. I was not in my body, and I knew I was not.

I won't take time here to explain to you or describe for you my experience, although I can tell you it was very real—it is very real to me to this very day. I've had three such experiences in my life, two since the original one. And every one of those experiences brought me to the same place: a space of absolute—capital "A"—awareness. Kind of like an AA meeting: Absolute Awareness. And when I returned from my very first out-of-body experience, I was left with two words that blew my mind. Would you like to know what they were?

I'm all ears.

"Nothing matters."

Nothing matters. What an amazing message for my soul to receive from the unified soul that is all of Life. *Nothing matters?* And yet, like the *est* training, like Transcendental Meditation, like my venturing into the work of Paramahansa Yogananda, it changed my life. And here's the message *behind* the message:

If nothing matters intrinsically, then I am free to declare what I *choose to* have matter to me. But if something matters intrinsically, that is to say, if something matters to, shall we say, God, then I had darned well better figure out what that is, because if I don't figure out what it is, I will be the thing called condemned, or at the very least, *unenlightened.*

But a voice in my out-of-body experience said to me, "Nothing matters." I knew then that we are free to make matter what we choose to make matter in our lives. And I mean that in two ways: not only to make matter, but to *make something into matter,* to manifest in physical reality something out of invisible energy. To turn it into, to turn energy into, matter.

So here is what I would share with people who ask about enlightenment.

If you think there is a path to enlightenment that is the only path, the best path, the fastest path, the one that everyone has to know about by ten o'clock tomorrow morning, you will suddenly find yourself feeling pressure, stress, upset, and your ego will be deeply involved in convincing as many people as you can that that's what's so.

Suddenly you will start acting not like a master at all, but like someone who is under a terrific amount of pressure and stress, because it will suddenly matter to you whether I "get" what you are trying to tell me.

If you are not careful, you even start having quotas or goals. You'll have to get a certain number of other people to agree with you every week, or every month, or every year. And if you don't meet those goals, you will think that you have not done a good job.

And yet you *have* done a good job if you simply love without expectation, without requirement, without needing anything in return.

Enlightenment, when it is all said and done, has nothing to do with what you do with your body or your mind. It has to do with what you do with your soul.

Now that's a wonderful insight. Just the way you put that opens up the space for clarity. Nice.

Thank you. I want to share that if you simply love everyone whose life you touch endlessly, unconditionally, with nothing needed or wanted in return, you have become enlightened and you have shown everyone how they may be enlightened as well. As fast as any other system that exists, like *that.*

As fast as Transcendental Meditation, like *that.* As fast as joining the Self-Realization Fellowship, like *that.* As fast as taking *est,* or now, the Forum, like *that.* And if you learn to love *yourself* unconditionally, as well as everyone else, you heal your entire self without lifting a finger.

Now I want to discuss this thing called health, because many people believe that you are *not enlightened* unless you are in good health.

You are really on a roll here, aren't you?

You opened a door, I walked through it.

Go on. I want to hear what you have to say about this.

Is enlightenment being in good health? And what is good health anyway? Is good health having a body that has nothing wrong with it? Is good health living until you are 90 or 100 or 200 or 500?

Is good health having no pain and nothing wrong with your physical form? Is good health the absence of anything that is not perfect in your physical experience? Or is good health being okay and in a place of joy and peace *no matter how things are?*

What is health, what is optimum health, if it is not happiness?

I know people who exercise every day, lifting weights and running and working out, and their bodies are in great health, but their hearts and their minds and their souls are desperately sad.

And I know people who are hardly able to lift a toothpick, they are so . . . their bodies are in such bad shape . . . but their hearts and their minds and their souls are bright, and they are happy.

I know such a man, whose name is Ram Dass. Ram Dass is a master, and I am vastly privileged to have met him personally. He has taught many people for many years. He wrote a book called *Be Here Now,* among others.

About two and a half or three years ago Ram Dass had a stroke. He was a young man; he was only sixty-three or something like that.

I met with Ram Dass after his stroke, in a hotel room in Denver, and I want to tell you something. I've never met a healthier man.

I sat in that room with a master. I said, "Ram Dass, how are you?" And he sat there in his wheelchair and said very slowly and very carefully, "I am won-der-ful."

Now that's health . . . that's health. That's peace. That's joy.

Then Ram Dass sat there, and we talked. I asked him many questions, because I wanted to hear, right from his wonderful mind, how he felt and what he'd experienced of this life. And he had great patience with me. He must have heard my questions a hundred times before. Nay, a thousand times before. But he listened intently, as if he was hearing them for the first time.

He did not rush his answers, either. I got the impression that he was thinking deeply about each one, going within to see, not how he'd answered that question before, but what his experience was *now.*

It was a moment of incredible giving. He was just giving to me.

Now, when you have so much happiness, peace, wisdom, and joy that you spend your life sharing it with everyone else, no matter what your predicament, that's enlightenment. You have become a master.

When your life is no longer about you, has nothing to do with you, but is about everyone else whose life you touch, you have become a master.

In the end, that is why you came here. You did not come here to somehow "get better," or to "work on your stuff." Consider the possibility that all the work you will ever need to do is finished. All you have to do now is know that.

So, this moment is the moment of your liberation. You can be liberated from your life-long search for enlightenment. You can be released from any thought you may have that it has to look like this, no-no, it has to look like *that,* no-no, you have to get to it by *this* path, by *that* program, by *the other* activity.

You may still do those things if you choose to, but if you feel stressed about them, if you feel pressured by them, then how could they be a path to enlightenment?

I know a master named Ilchi Lee. He created a wonderful path to enlightenment called Dahn Hak. It is a body-mind-spirit integration process that you can engage in for the rest of your life. People have devoted their whole lives to it. It's wonderful. I've tried it. It works. Millions are finding their way to enlightenment with it.

I asked Dr. Lee once whether people needed Dahn Hak to become enlightened. His answer was very quick. "No," he said. He didn't even try to qualify his response. He didn't equivocate. He just gave me a one-word answer. "No."

The point here is that there is no one way up to the mountaintop. Every true master knows this.

So set yourself free today. Stop working so hard on yourself that you don't even enjoy it anymore. Do what works for you, but make sure it brings you joy.

Now here is what I *know* will bring you joy. Decide that the rest of your life—every day, every moment, every word—is something that you will share with everyone whose life you touch in a way that ensures that they will know there is nothing they have to do, nowhere they have to go, and no way they have to be, in order to be loved by you right now. Let them know that they are perfect just as they are, just as they are standing there.

Spend the rest of your life *giving people back to themselves,* that they might love themselves. And show them by how *you are* with them that you know there is nothing they are lacking, nothing they are missing, nothing they need, nothing they are not.

You want to know the fastest way for anyone to experience that they are enlightened?

Yes, can you tell me? Can you really tell me?

The fastest way of all for anyone to experience that they are enlightened is to *cause another to know that THEY are.*

That is the message of Tomorrow's God. That will be the teaching of the New Spirituality. That is why *Namasté* has become such a powerful tool, such a meaningful and special exchange of energy:

"The God in me sees and honors the God in you."

There's nothing more to be done if we really mean that. Of course, if we are saying that because it sounds good, then there is a great deal more to be done. But if we really mean that—if, when we say that, we really mean that—then the struggle is finished, the search is over, and enlightenment is ours at last.

25

GOOD-BYE, AND HELLO

So . . . how did I do? Did I pass?

Pass? Fail? You cannot fail. You passed automatically by stepping into the moment and bringing to it All Of You. That is all that Life asks.

Yes.

It is time now.

Yes, I know. I don't want to go.

We must. This has been a good conversation. A good, long one. And now we must end it.

I'd like to at least try to summarize it. There's so much here. I'd like to make a list here of the particular ways in which Tomorrow's God will differ from Yesterday's God.

Okay. Good. That will make it easier for others to reference it later.

Exactly. You have given us a wonderful vision of Tomorrow's God, and you have described what that God is like. Here's a capsule of what you said:

1. **Tomorrow's God does not require anyone to believe in God.**
2. **Tomorrow's God is without gender, size, shape, color, or any of the characteristics of an individual living being.**
3. **Tomorrow's God talks with everyone, all the time.**
4. **Tomorrow's God is separate from nothing, but is Everywhere Present, the All In All, the Alpha and the Omega, the Beginning and the End, the Sum Total of Everything that ever was, is now, and ever shall be.**
5. **Tomorrow's God is not a singular Super Being, but the extraordinary process called Life.**
6. **Tomorrow's God is ever changing.**
7. **Tomorrow's God is needless.**
8. **Tomorrow's God does not ask to be served, but is the Servant of all of Life.**
9. **Tomorrow's God will be unconditionally loving, nonjudgmental, noncondemning, and nonpunishing.**

That is an incredible description of an almost unbelievable God. I know that you've said throughout this conversation that this wonderful God is going to be embraced by humanity in the years just ahead, but I still wonder if human beings can ever accept such a Deity.

It is going to be your greatest spiritual challenge.

It is going to require laser vision, unyielding strength, and uncommon courage. It is going to take deep commitment and extraordinary endurance.

And it is going to ask of you, of those of you who choose to truly work for the emergence of a New Spirituality on your planet, to laugh in the face of the almost overwhelming odds, and to know in your heart that your task is already done. It is just a matter of time.

You may not be here in your present physical form to see its conclusion, but you will watch its conclusion nonetheless. I will call you to the moment when the moment arrives, and I will say, "Look. Look what you set into motion. Well done, friend of the earth. Well done, friend of its people. Well done, friend of Life, and Love, and God."

Go, now, and share this with all nations. Begin the Civil Rights Movement for the Soul. Free my people from their belief in an angry, oppressive, demanding, restricting, violent, and killing God.

Free my people and save your world. Pre-serve it, and preserve it for your children, and theirs.

Oh, the future is so bright if lit by the light of *you,* right here, right now. Therefore, let your light so shine before all people that they cannot fail to know at last Who They Really Are.

Even Yesterday's God asks this now. Yesterday's God says now, here, in this moment: My time was here and my time has passed. It is time now for a new God. But that does not mean you have to abandon me. I cannot be abandoned, for I am always with you. Your new God, Tomorrow's God, will just be me, in Another Form.

So, I say now . . . good-bye . . . and hello.

I love you.

IN CLOSING . . .

I conclude this book with a plea. A simple plea from one human being to another. Please don't put this book down and then, after a few days, forget it. I beg you, please don't do that.

Consider the possibility that this book came to you for a reason. It is Life, calling to Life, from Life Itself. It is Love, igniting Love, with Love Itself. It is God, awakening God, from within God Itself.

Please, decide that you are going to be one of those who will do what you can do, every moment, every day, to free yourself and those around you from the oppression of a belief in an angry, punishing, vengeful, and violent God. Please, join the Civil Rights Movement for the Soul.

Do this in whatever way presents itself to you. Out of your intention and determination those opportunities will come to you in the day-to-day living of your life. Open your eyes and you'll see them all around you.

One of them is Humanity's Team.

When I first began receiving the information in *Tomorrow's God* I was inspired to move immediately to create Humanity's Team to give people everywhere a way to touch the whole world with their energy—their hopes and dreams and love and caring. I wanted to bring every human being the possibility of becoming part of the process of global change.

I envisioned Humanity's Team as a true grassroots movement to cause a New Spirituality to emerge upon the earth—a spirituality based upon the idea that all people be allowed to honor their impulse toward the Divine in whatever way feels best and true to them, without being condemned or attacked for the way in which they are doing it—and without condemning or attacking others.

This New Spirituality will do more than simply create religious tolerance, however. It will offer a whole new set of basic values around which humanity could choose to organize. A new way to create and experience its politics, its economics, its religions, its educational systems, and its social constructions of every kind.

Since I first began talking about this idea in appearances around the world and put it up on the Internet, thousands of people have said "Yes! Count me in! That's me! I'm part of that!"

Now I invite you to become a member of Humanity's Team. Please do this now, before you move on to other things and it slips past you. You may gain immediate access to more information, and instantly join Humanity's Team, on the Internet at www.HumanitysTeam.com. You may also call 1-541-482-0126, or write to Humanity's Team, 1257 Siskiyou Blvd., PMB 1150, Ashland, OR 97520.

If you're excited about the information in this book and wish to heed or be reminded of the call to expanded consciousness, I invite you to also subscribe to a daily motivational e-mail. You will find this terrifically uplifting, and you will also be helping spread the New Spirituality around the world, because all distributed profits from this outreach go to Humanity's Team. The daily e-mail is composed of brief, empowering messages and meditations from this and other *CwG* writings, as well as inspiring words from other authors whose understandings of God and Life resonate with New Spirituality thinking. Subscribe by going to www.newspirituality.org. This organization was founded to support the global outreach of Humanity's Team.

Now, as I am sure you have by this time concluded, the book you are holding in your hand contains more than a prediction. It contains an invitation. That invitation is for you to become a *participant* in the process by which the world is changed. The invitation is for you—right now—to join those who choose to become *the hope of humanity.*

There are many ways you can keep the wonderful messages of *Tomorrow's God* alive within you—and share them with others as well. Recording artist and composer Don Eaton was so taken with this message that he wrote a song about it. I think it would be wonderful if Don's beautiful song was sung every week in spiritual services around the world, and you can play a part in causing that to happen! Here are the lyrics. . . .

HOPE OF HUMANITY

(Written and copyrighted by Don Eaton, 2003)

I see so many people lost in despair.
They have no hope, and they can't find their way.
But I still believe that there's a fire in some hearts,
And that a few courageous souls will dare to say:

I am the hope of humanity.
I am a bringer of the Light.
My love will help to heal the world's insanity.
I am a candle in the night.

Now some may call it arrogance or say it's vanity
To think we're part of what dreams may come true.
But do you imagine I could feel this Light inside myself
If I hadn't seen it shining first in you?

You are the hope of humanity.
You are a bringer of the Light.
Your love will help to heal the world's insanity.
You are a candle in the night.

Now I've been blessed to travel
With some strong and humble hearts,
A family of those who've heard the call.
And I've bathed in their heartlight and I've come to understand
There's just one reason we are here at all.

We are the hope of humanity.
We are the bringers of the Light.
Our love will help to heal the world's insanity.
We are the candles in the night.

And so another way you can spread the message of *Tomorrow's God* is to obtain the sheet music to this wonderful song and send it to the choir or music director at every house of worship in your community. You may also want to obtain several copies of the CD of the song as sung by Don, to inspire you and to share with others. You may contact Don Eaton by e-mail at eatonsong@aol.com, or standard mail at 1164 N.W. Weybridge Way, Beaverton, OR 97006.

You may also obtain some BE THE HOPE OF HUMANITY bumper stickers (pick up fifty or a hundred!) and share them with all of your like-minded friends, so that cars all over your community will carry this simple, compelling message. Orders may be placed by going to www.HumanitysTeam.com and clicking on Resources.

Finally, here is something quite simple that you can do in the next hour and a half (or the next day and a half, or in the next week and a half).

Give this book to somebody else.

Recommend it to everyone.

Share its message with the world.

Become a bringer of the light. Help the New Spirituality emerge.

So, does it look as if all I've done here is give you a list of things to do? Great! That was my intention! My hope is to *activate* you, to get you *going,* to enroll you and engage you in the *process of participation* right here, right now.

Because if not now, *when?* And if not you, *who?*

I am reminded of the extraordinary words of John F. Kennedy on the occasion of his inauguration as president of the United

States many years ago. These were the final words of his memorable speech, the last thought he wanted to leave the world. Can you imagine a worldwide political leader saying something like this today?

"Finally, whether you are citizens of America or citizens of the world, ask of us here the same high standards of strength and sacrifice which we ask of you. With a good conscience our only sure reward, with history the final judge of our deeds, let us go forth to lead the land we love, asking His blessing and His help, but knowing that here on earth God's work must truly be our own."

I agree, and I agree emphatically. I hope that you do, too.

See you on Humanity's Team!

Neale Donald Walsch
Ashland, Oregon
November 2003

INDEX